THE
ROMAN INVASIONS
OF BRITAIN

THE
ROMAN INVASIONS
OF BRITAIN

Gerald Grainge

TEMPUS

First published 2005

Tempus Publishing Ltd
The Mill, Brimscombe Port
Stroud, Gloucestershire GL5 2QG
www.tempus-publishing.com

British Library Cataloguing in Publication Data.
A catalogue record for this book is available from the British Library.

ISBN 0 7524 3338 5

Typesetting and origination by Tempus Publishing.
Printed and bound in Great Britain.

CONTENTS

FOREWORD

The Roman invasions of Britain in the first century BC and the first and third centuries AD have long been the subject of scholarly debate, the documentary evidence for them being incomplete and enigmatic, and the direct archaeological evidence negligible. These invasions were clearly amphibious operations; yet the constraints imposed on sea passages by the elements, especially wind and tide, have seldom been fully taken into account in these deliberations.

Dr Gerald Grainge is an accomplished seafarer with extensive experience of boat handling and navigation in the Channel and the Dover Strait, and he has brought a seaman's eye to the study of these invasions. He is well versed in the challenges that the sea can impose on decision making, and is very much aware of the restrictions imposed on any would-be invader of Britain by the wind and the weather, by the tidal regime, and by the capabilities of ships and crew. As a linguist he knows the difficulties inherent in the interpretation of documentary sources and, as a student of the past with a doctorate in maritime archaeology, he is also familiar with the problems of establishing former sea levels and coastlines.

In this study Dr Grainge first presents the environmental context of early cross-Channel passages and evaluates the evidence for the types of warship and troopship used by the Roman invaders. He then expounds his interpretation of the sources for the four invasions in the light of the maritime constraints and the deduced performance of the ships in the Roman fleets. I myself find his arguments convincing but, whether convinced or not, the reader will find the analysis and exposition of the maritime aspects of these invasions clear, comprehensive and enlightening.

This volume is destined to become essential reading for students of the Roman Empire, especially those wishing to understand Rome's use of the northern seas. A firm foundation of maritime determinants having been established by Dr Grainge, the way is now clear for an informed and re-invigorated debate on the Roman invasions of Britain.

Seán McGrail
Centre for Maritime Archaeology
University of Southampton

ACKNOWLEDGEMENTS

This book has its origin in research that I undertook at Southampton University in the late 1990s into the maritime aspects of the Claudian invasion. I was fortunate enough to be invited to make a contribution to a conference organised by the Sussex Archaeological Society at which the debate about the location of the landing place in Britain of the Roman legions in AD 43 was renewed. I am grateful to the Society's chief executive, John Manley, for that invitation and to my supervisor at Southampton University, Professor Seán McGrail, for suggesting my name to him.

My thanks also go to Peter Kemmis Betty of Tempus Publishing, who invited me to take my research further with this book. After reading the first draft of my typescript, he offered valuable advice which has made this a rather better book than it would have otherwise been. I should also like to express my appreciation to other members of the staff at Tempus for their help with numerous matters of technical and other detail and for their care in editing it.

Many of the maps and line drawings in this book have been redrawn professionally by Peter Atkinson of Canterbury Archaeological Trust. Peter is a meticulous draughtsman and I appreciate the conscientious work he has done with them. I am grateful to the director of the Trust, Paul Bennett, for allowing him to undertake this work.

Six people, three of them specialists in their fields and three of them lay readers, have read the book in draft. I was concerned, not only that academic errors should be picked up, but also that the book should not be incomprehensible for the general reader. The specialists were Ernest Black (Roman history), Seán McGrail (maritime archaeology) and John Manley (archaeology). The lay readers were Sarah Grainge (my daughter-in-law), Revd Richard Lea and Trisha Wells. I thank all of them for the valuable suggestions they offered for the improvement of the text. They will understand that any errors or infelicities that remain are my responsibility, as are the interpretations I offer of events of two millennia ago.

Thanks are due to a number of people and organisations for permission to use copyright photographs and other material. Acknowledgements are given in the captions. I should like in particular to record my thanks to John

Iveson, Curator of Dover Museum who kindly allowed me to take photographs of models in his Museum (*colour plates 19, 20* and *21*). I am also grateful to Ken Elks for supplying high quality images of coins in his private collection (*colour plates 7* and *9*) and to Brian Peeps, archivist of the Humber Keel and Sloop Preservation Society, for his help in providing the photograph of the Humber keel (*colour plate 17*).

Without my wife Christine's continuing encouragement, I doubt that I could have completed this book. She has patiently read numerous drafts, offered valuable comments on them and has always been unfailing in the support she has offered in so many ways.

War is a desperate business and the moment of disembarkation on an enemy shore especially so. It is all too easy to forget this in the dispassionate study of the sometimes jejune detail of the ancient sources and of the archaeological record. At two points, however, we do perceive the human reality behind the story of the Roman invasions. One is the account in Dio Cassius's *Roman History* of the mutiny of Claudius's legionaries, unwilling to embark for the invasion of Britain in AD 43. The other is Julius Caesar's graphic account of the landing of his legionaries under fire somewhere on the east coast of Kent. Lionel Cottrell compared this to the experiences of the men who landed in Normandy in 1944. In this sixtieth anniversary year of that invasion, I wish to dedicate this book to all who in our age have had to take part in air- or sea-borne landings in the cause of freedom. As a child of the war, I understand only too well how much we owe to their courage and sacrifice.

Gerald Grainge
Finglesham
2004

1

INTRODUCING CAESAR, CLAUDIUS AND CONSTANTIUS

On four occasions during the Roman period the Romans put an invasion army ashore on the coast of Britain. In 54 BC Julius Caesar followed up his lightly armed reconnaissance raid of the previous year with a full-scale invasion involving five heavily-equipped legions and 2,000 cavalry. He returned to Gaul with his legions at the end of the season. As he left, he took hostages and imposed tribute. Given the scale of this second operation, however, one may well wonder whether the campaign objective was not to reduce at least part of southern and eastern Britain to the status of a Roman province. Archaeology and numismatics certainly point to the increasing influence of Roman culture, trade and politics in southern Britain in the hundred years following Caesar's incursions.

Even allowing for this, the formal establishment of the Roman province of *Britannia* would wait another century until the reign of the Emperor Claudius. In AD 43 he put a senator by the name of Aulus Plautius in charge of the invasion of Britain. It is generally agreed that the force consisted of four legions and associated auxiliary cavalry and infantry units and may have numbered as many as 40,000 men. This would make it larger than Caesar's invasion force of 54 BC and in all probability it was the largest army ever to invade Britain; it exceeded by far the numbers involved, for example, in the invasions of William of Normandy and William of Orange, as well as the attempted invasion of the Spanish Armada.

Plautius engaged and defeated the British in a number of battles and skirmishes, including an important two-day engagement at the crossing of a river, which the sources do not name. Advancing to the Thames, he waited to be joined by the emperor. Crossing from Boulogne, Claudius arrived with extensive equipment and elephants. Taking over command of the troops from Plautius, he marched on Colchester where he received the submission of a number of British tribes. He then handed command back to Plautius, instructing him to pacify the remaining districts, and went home to Rome. His had been a whirlwind visit, lasting only 16 days, but with profound significance for the history of the island. Britain would remain part of the Roman Empire for another four centuries.

The last occasion on which the Romans invaded Britain was in AD 296. The invasion was led by Constantius Chlorus, father of Constantine the Great, and his praetorian prefect, Asclepiodotus. Ten years earlier Carausius, a Menapian officer who had been put in charge of the coastal defences in the Channel against Frankish and Saxon raiders, had responded to reports that the emperor had ordered his execution by setting himself up as pseudo-emperor of Britain. Initially Carausius also controlled part of northern Gaul, including Boulogne. However, the capture of this important naval base by Constantius compromised Carausius's control of the Channel. It was also about this time that Carausius was assassinated by one of his associates, Allectus, who now took his place as pseudo-emperor. The invasion of AD 296 deposed Allectus and successfully reintegrated Britain into the Roman Empire.

The quality of the sources documenting these invasions varies. Caesar's expeditions are the most fully recorded, largely in his *Gallic War*, written with a view to publicising to the electorate in Rome his achievements during his nine-year governorship of Gaul. Although they are detailed and specific, it is always important when reading Caesar's diaries to bear in mind that what he reports, and more significantly does not report, is influenced by his own political agenda. Caesar cultivated relationships with many leading Romans, including the orator Marcus Tullius Cicero whose brother Quintus served on Caesar's staff in Gaul and Britain. Cicero's correspondence with his brother, with Caesar and with others offers some interesting insights into Caesar's expeditions and, in particular, makes it possible to construct chronologies for them (*colour plate 1*).

The Claudian invasion is less well documented; the principal source, Dio Cassius's *Roman History*, written in Greek some two centuries after the event is, to put it mildly, garbled and confused. In particular, it does not identify the Roman landing site or sites. Unfortunately, what might have been the prime documentary source for the invasion, Tacitus's *Annals*, is not extant for the period. There is considerable archaeological evidence for early Roman military activity in Britain in the invasion period, both in East Kent and in the south-central counties. While this evidence is cited in the many interpretations of the events of the invasion, it is hardly conclusive. Archaeological evidence in this case, as in many others, does not always lend itself to precise indications about specific historical events and, in particular, to the precise dating required to identify military sites which were established in AD 43.

As for the invasion of 296, the documentary record can only be described as slight, but what there is appears relatively straightforward. The source material includes coins, contemporary panegyrics and accounts by two mid-fourth-century historians, Aurelius Victor and Eutropius. Although the historians give only the barest outline of the events leading up to the invasion and nothing at all of the way the invasion was planned and conducted, when we read their accounts alongside the panegyrics, we do get a consistent, albeit brief, account of the invasion and of the events which preceded it. Our understanding of the invasion is significantly enhanced by considering it in the context of a system of defence thought by some to have been put in place in the third century to protect the British Channel coasts, possibly from the raids of Frankish and Saxon pirates. This is known today collectively as the forts of the Saxon Shore, from a late Roman official document setting out the order of battle throughout the empire.

Each of the invasions merits study in its own right; considered together, we can develop insights into the strategic factors which would have influenced the way in which the Romans planned and conducted a sea-borne invasion. For example, in the case of Constantius, we know that his invasion fleet finally sailed in two divisions, one under Asclepiodotus from the Seine, the other under Constantius himself from Boulogne. Asclepiodotus landed somewhere on the Solent, but where Constantius landed is not at all clear from the documentary evidence, though there are grounds for a strong suspicion that his fleet rounded the North Foreland to sail up the Thames to London. However, a premature invasion attempt seven years earlier launched, it would seem, from the Rhine, had failed. The reasons both for the initial failure and for the later success of what was essentially a pincer movement can be found in the existence of the Saxon Shore forts and perhaps in an assessment of the way in which they were intended to function as a strategic integrated defence system. Yet the strategic considerations which would have influenced Caesar's two expeditions or the Claudian invasion must have been quite different.

Paradoxically Caesar's very detailed account of his expeditions to Britain is less than specific on those details which would identify his port of departure and his landing place. He says that he launched his first raid from the 'territory of the Morini', without naming the actual place of departure. For his second expedition he names the embarkation harbour as the *Portus Itius* and it is a reasonably plausible inference that it was also here that he had embarked for his raid the year before. However, except in the context of Caesar's raids, the *Portus Itius* is unknown, although both Strabo and the geographer, Claudius Ptolemy, mention an Itian promontory. In similar fashion Caesar does not identify his landing site in Britain in either year by name. Perhaps at that stage it did not have a name. This lack of clarity led historians of the nineteenth century and earlier to advance a wide range of theories about the actual route of his crossings. It was not until 1907 that the definitive analysis by T. Rice Holmes established the modern consensus that on both occasions Caesar embarked at

Boulogne and landed somewhere in East Kent, on the open coast somewhere in the neighbourhood of Walmer/Deal. Even so, there are a number of continuing puzzles. It was on this coast that his fleet suffered major storm damage in both years. It is generally agreed that the topography of Dover, with its great cliffs overlooking the natural haven of the Dour estuary, meant that no commander in his right mind would have contemplated an invasion landing here. It is odd that Caesar did not use the great natural harbour of the Wantsum in the neighbourhood of Richborough in East Kent (*3* and *colour plate 2*). In Roman and early medieval times this channel divided the Isle of Thanet from mainland Kent; Richborough at its eastern end would play a significant, if varied, role throughout the Roman period. One might understand that Caesar did not land in the Wantsum in 55 BC when his intelligence about the available harbours was severely limited, but it is hard to account for his not doing so the following year, when one would have thought that his intelligence ought to have been better. However, there are hints in Caesar's accounts that during his stay in 55 BC he had little opportunity for extensive reconnaissance and that he may well, pace all the pundits, have intended in that first year to land at Dover (*colour plate 3*).

It is the Claudian invasion that has in recent years been the subject of passionate, not to say partisan, controversy. For much of the twentieth century it was the accepted view that the bridgehead of at least a significant part of the Roman invasion force was at Richborough. On this view the Roman line of advance to the Thames would have been through Kent along the North Downs with Dio's unnamed river, the crossing of which was secured in a major battle with the Britons, identified as the Medway. In 1989, John Hind published a paper challenging this orthodoxy. His hypothesis was that the invasion fleet had landed at or near Fishbourne, in Chichester Harbour. Hind takes as his starting point the statement by Dio Cassius that Claudius was persuaded to undertake the invasion by a British client king, Verica, who had recently been exiled from his kingdom. It is, therefore, a fair assumption that the Romans' campaign objective would have been his restoration. Since Verica's kingdom was that of the British Atrebates with their capital in the Chichester region, that would be best achieved by a landing nearby in what would have been friendly territory. A landing in the Solent area, rather than in East Kent, also offers, so Hind believes, a more plausible context for the strange episode of the Dobunni, a British tribe settled in the Gloucestershire region. According to Dio Cassius, a section of this tribe submitted to Aulus Plautius soon after the landing of the Roman task force and before the crossing of the unnamed river. Hind's argument is that it is scarcely credible that the Romans could have been operating in the far west, if they had not yet crossed the Medway, and when their next objective was the crossing of the Thames and the taking of Colchester. If, however, the invasion force had landed in the Solent and was on its way to the Thames crossing, a 'flying column' could have been detached to receive this capitulation. Even so one may well question the strategic role of such a flying column, still despatched far to the west of any probable line of march to a Thames crossing.

Significant as it was, Hind's paper had little impact on academic thinking for a decade or so. Then Barry Cunliffe published a revision of his earlier book on the excavations of the Roman Palace at Fishbourne, in which he expressed his growing support for the hypothesis of a landing in the 'harbours of the Solent with the Fishbourne/Chichester region as the focus'.[1] This was rapidly followed by two conferences. The first in 1999 was run by the Sussex Archaeological Society and was chaired by Cunliffe as President of the Society. In his summing up he urged those present to keep an open mind. A 'return match' was organised by the Kent Archaeological Society in 2001. This was concluded with a vote among the audience to decide the question whether the invasion landing was at Richborough or in the Solent; unsurprisingly the vote was overwhelmingly in favour of Richborough.[2]

More recently John Manley, who is chief executive of the Sussex Archaeological Society, has published a through-going reassessment of the evidence for the Claudian invasion. In this he recognised his own bias and pointed out that few of us can write with total objectivity. My bias is that of a maritime archaeologist and a yachtsman with many years' experience sailing in the English Channel and southern North Sea. I believe that an understanding of ancient seafaring can help to interpret the evidence for specific events in the past and, in this case, the Roman invasions of Britain.

When I was invited to make a brief contribution to the conference of the Sussex Archaeological Society my immediate (and no doubt biased) reaction was that a passage down-Channel from Boulogne to the Solent by an invasion fleet transporting up to 40,000 men, together with cavalry horses and pack animals, possibly even elephants, could only have been a highly un-seamanlike venture. It would have involved an open-sea leg of more than twice the length of the passage to East Kent, it would have been against the prevailing winds, it would have involved extended cross-Channel supply lines and the probability of failing to reach the invasion destination would have been much greater. In a classic study of cross-Channel seamanship in the late first millennium BC, Seán McGrail developed a method of assessing the reliability of various cross-Channel routes which were being exploited at that period. He assigned a percentage 'relative reliability factor' to each of the routes. A route from Boulogne to the Solent did not figure among those he had identified, but the passage from Boulogne to Walmer was given a factor of 98 per cent, while that from the Seine to the Solent was assessed at 71 per cent. If nothing else, this suggested that a passage from Boulogne to the Solent would present a substantially more difficult undertaking.[3]

In characterising a putative invasion passage by a Roman invasion fleet from Boulogne to the Solent as un-seamanlike, I am not claiming that there is some absolute black and white standard of seamanship and I may indeed be applying the bias of late twentieth/early twenty-first century criteria to the first century AD. Seamanship encompasses many skills and areas of experience – so many that it is perhaps difficult to define it as a quality. Clearly it includes techniques of ship-handling, especially in difficult or adverse conditions, and an intimate knowledge of the waters in which one sails. An important element is the ability to make reliable judgements about one's own experience and ability, the strengths of one's crew and of the performance capability and seaworthiness of one's ship. The limitations of ships available to the Romans must have been a significant factor in their planning. These are examined in Chapters 3 and 4.

Manley warns against easy assumptions that the Romans thought like us. What is clear is that the Romans had a very special, even religious, awe of 'Oceanus', the personification of the English Channel and the southern North Sea. They would have seen any cross-Channel adventure as a challenge to the gods. That of course would add enormously to the prestige of any half-successful cross-Channel adventure – Caesar was awarded a 20-day thanksgiving by the Senate after his first raid in recognition of his victory over Oceanus. But the mythology did not exaggerate the challenge offered by the reality. The next chapter looks at both.

2

THE ENGLISH CHANNEL IN
MYTH AND REALITY

Oceanus

As they waited to embark for their invasion passage to Britain in AD 43, Aulus Plautius's legionaries rebelled at the thought of 'carrying on a campaign outside the limits of the known world'. Unable himself to bring the soldiers to their duty, Plautius called on the freedman Narcissus, a senior member of Claudius's staff. When Narcissus addressed the troops, he was greeted with the cry '*Io Saturnalia!*'. The *Saturnalia* was the Roman midwinter festival when slaves changed places with their masters; the jibe, roughly equivalent to 'Happy Christmas', amounted to a recognition by the legionaries that, however senior, Narcissus was no more than a former slave. The stark contrast with his present authority appealed to the legionaries' grim sense of humour and shamed them into obedience.

This episode is significant for a number of reasons, not least because it may perhaps be taken as evidence of the almost religious awe with which the Romans contemplated the crossing of any significant barrier, and especially the English Channel. It may have an echo in a curious incident a few years earlier. In AD 40 Claudius's predecessor the mad Emperor Gaius, better known by his nickname of Caligula, was in northern Gaul when Adminius, son of Cunobelinus – king of the British tribe of the Catuvellauni – fled to Gaul, banished by his father. He was received by Gaius, who was said to have claimed that the whole island had surrendered to him and who appears to have contemplated the possibility of invasion. In the event, he is reported to have done no more than line up his legions in order of battle on the beach facing the Channel and then ordered them to collect up sea shells, as booty from Oceanus. A lasting memorial of the affair was the Roman lighthouse at Boulogne, erected by Caligula to commemorate his 'victory'. This, known to the French as the *Tour d'Ordre*, survived until 1644, when it collapsed with the section of cliff on which it was standing. Rather than a memorial to a victory, however, it may have been intended as a preparation for an invasion.

While the account no doubt accurately reflects Caligula's mental instability, scholars have also seen in it evidence of a serious mutiny and

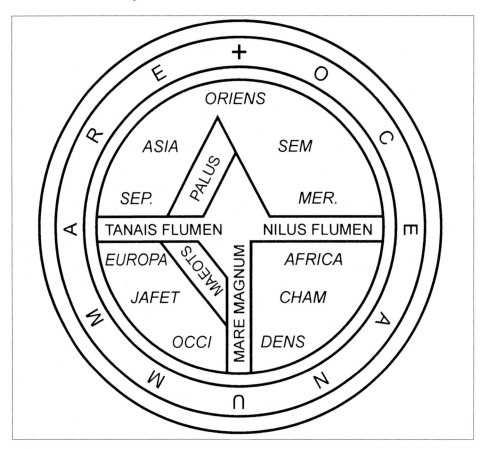

1 The map of the world according to the seventh-century bishop, Isidore of Seville. In the form of a T-O map, with East at the top, it shows the three known continents of Europe, Africa and Asia surrounded by the ocean (*Oceanum Mare*). The Mediterranean (*Mare Magnum*) forms the down stroke of the T, while the rivers Don (*Tanais*) and Nile form the crossbar. The *Maeotis Palus* is the Sea of Azov

compared it with that which confronted Plautius three years later. Peddie suggests that Caligula's order was either an expression of rage or 'a gesture of contempt' for the legionaries' behaviour. Frere and Salway see in the incident evidence that Caligula's troops were ill-disciplined, but from the accounts of the Claudian invasion three years later, there appears to be no reason to believe that Plautius's legions were normally ill-disciplined, even though they too initially refused to embark. The context being the same, an imminent embarkation for Britain, one may well see in both incidents a special dread of crossing the English Channel.[1]

For the Romans the English Channel marked a boundary of special religious significance. It was part of the great River Oceanus which encircled the whole of the known world. This idea can be traced back to the Greek geographer Hecataeus who, *c.*500 BC, described the earth as a circle around which flowed a wide river. It was refined in a map produced *c.*225 BC by Eratosthenes based on observations by Pytheas, a Greek from Marseilles, who had voyaged extensively along the coasts of north-west Europe towards the end of the fourth century BC. The concept developed into the so-called T-O map (*1*), which was adopted by early Christian writers, such as the seventh-century Isidore, Bishop of Seville, and found its ultimate expression in the late thirteenth century in the great Mappa Mundi of Hereford Cathedral.

In Roman and Greek thought rivers were more than geographical barriers. They were invested with divine personalities and to venture to cross them or to sail on them was an undertaking of religious significance demanding the performance of proper rituals to appease the god. A striking case is the River Styx, marking the final boundary between life and Hades and across whose waters the gaunt ferryman Charon conveyed the souls of the dead. In life the limit to the known world was Oceanus. In mythology he was the son of the Sky and the Earth, husband of Tethys (a sea goddess) and father of all the river gods and nymphs. Marking the ultimate boundary, he offered the ultimate challenge to the conqueror – and the ultimate glory of conquest.[2]

Writing to his younger brother Quintus, who served as a legate on Caesar's staff in Gaul, Cicero was appalled at the prospect of his brother's crossing to Britain in 54 BC. In one letter he gave vent to his relief at Quintus's safe arrival in Britain: 'I dreaded Oceanus, I dreaded the coast of that island'. In another letter written the same year, probably before the expedition left for Britain, Cicero expresses to his friend Atticus at least one of the reasons for his concern: 'It is notorious that the approaches to the island are ramparted with astonishing masses of cliff'.

Dio Cassius recounts that, during their crossing nearly a century later, Aulus Plautius's legionaries were much disheartened by being driven off course, whether by wind or tide or both. However, their spirits were raised when 'a flash of light rising in the east shot across to the west, the direction in which they were sailing'. This episode has been used to buttress the argument that the Claudian invasion landed in the Solent area on the grounds that the Solent is westwards from Boulogne. Leaving aside the observation that mariners, if not soldiers, would have been much more likely to have their spirits raised by a change of wind to blow in 'the direction in which they were sailing', rather than by a meteor shooting in any direction, Dio's readers undoubtedly took this as the description of an omen presaging a favourable outcome to the crossing of Oceanus.

The religious qualms felt by the legionaries at the prospect of venturing out on Oceanus would have been confirmed by disasters which had afflicted

Roman fleets in the English Channel and southern North Sea. The wrecking of many of the ships in Caesar's fleets off East Kent in storms in both 55 BC and 54 BC may have become distant memories by AD 43. The storm in AD 15 which struck Germanicus's naval expedition into Germany as it returned from the River Ems to the Rhine was more recent and arguably more far more disastrous. Caesar's fleets were at anchor and, although the damage to them undoubtedly seriously curtailed the scope of his expeditions, it would appear that no lives were lost, certainly not among the soldiery. He felt able later to claim that no ship carrying soldiers had been lost in either year. Germanicus had concluded that by moving his troops by sea and inland waterway, he would avoid the extended logistics and difficult terrain that an overland campaign into Germany would have entailed. After a largely successful campaign against the German tribes, the Romans withdrew for the winter. Some legions returned by land, but the greater part went by ship down the Ems into the North Sea. It was during this passage that a storm struck that scattered the fleet. It is apparent from Tacitus's account of the campaign that ships sank, while others were driven ashore onto the Frisian Islands, where men died from starvation. Some ships were driven to Britain, whence their people were returned by local kings. The catastrophe was such that Germanicus contemplated suicide. Tacitus expressly links the ferocity of this storm to the greater storminess of Oceanus compared with other seas.

Of course, one might well say that Cicero was merely giving voice to a wholly rational concern for his brother in a venture into territory previously unvisited by Roman legions, an anxiety that any modern person would understand and which requires no basis in religion to explain it. One might also claim that the legionaries of Plautius's expedition were simply motivated by a reasonable anxiety at the prospect of the unknown, exacerbated by the real memory of past disasters. Elsewhere, however, in his treatise *Germania*, Tacitus refers to another expedition, that of Germanicus's father Drusus in 12 BC, also into the southern North Sea, in terms which make explicit the religious significance of venturing into the domain of Oceanus:

> In that quarter we have essayed Oceanus himself, and rumour has published the existence of pillars of Hercules beyond our range: whether it be that Hercules visited those shores, or because we have agreed to enter all marvels everywhere to his credit. Nor did Drusus Germanicus lack audacity, but Oceanus vetoed inquiry alike touching himself and touching Hercules; and next the attempt to inquire was abandoned, and it was voted more religious and more reverent to believe in the works of Deity than to comprehend them.

David Braund quotes a fragment of verse by a member of Germanicus's army. Albinovanus Pedo, it seems, returned with the fleet and survived the storm to describe the experience in verse. A cavalry commander named Pedo mentioned by Tacitus earlier in Germanicus's campaign may well be the same man. Pedo appears to have been well known in literary circles as a poet and raconteur and as the author of an epic poem on Theseus, now lost and justly so, if the evidence of this surviving fragment is any guide. In fact this fragment has survived only because it is quoted by Seneca the Elder in the context of a rhetorical debate on the theme of whether Alexander the Great had sailed on Oceanus (in his case the Indian Ocean):

> Latin orators have not excelled in describing Oceanus; for their descriptions are either puffed up or punctilious. None of them has been able to speak with as much inspiration as Pedo, who sailing with Germanicus said:
>
> 'The sun and the day have long since been left behind them. Now, banished from the known world, they dare to go through forbidden shadows to the ends of reality and to the farthest shores of the earth. With their ships caught up in the storm, they see Oceanus rise up, that one, who is said to carry enormous monsters beneath his sluggish waves, fierce whales and sharks on all sides. The very noise increases their fear. Now vessels go aground on the mud, while the fleet is forsaken by the tempestuous wind. And now, unhappy lot, they believe themselves to be abandoned through helpless fate to be ripped apart by the beasts of the sea. Straining determinedly to see through the murk, someone is up aloft on the high prow. Seeing nothing in a world hidden from his view, these words pour out from his choking breast:
>
> "Where are we going? The daylight itself has fled and nature finally shuts down the abandoned world in everlasting darkness. Are we heading for peoples living out there under another pole, for another world untouched by war? The gods call us back and forbid our mortal eyes to know the end of things. Why do we violate strange seas and sacred waters with our oars and disturb the peaceful dwelling of the gods?"'[3]

In spite of his extravagant style, unexpected in view of Seneca's implied praise that he was not 'puffed up' like other Latin writers describing Oceanus, one can discern in Pedo's verse elements which reflect the reality of a violent storm at sea. Spray and rain can dramatically reduce visibility, the noise of wind and sea can be overwhelming and in a sudden calm, possibly the calm in the eye of the storm, sailing ships can wallow helplessly in the continuing swell.

Courtney sees in Oceanus rising up an allusion to the unfamiliar range of Atlantic tides, while the ships going aground on the mud he takes as a reference to the shallows of the Frisian Islands. In spite of these glimpses of reality, Pedo makes it clear that the fleet had ventured into regions forbidden by the gods.

In reality of course, gods or no gods, the Channel in the Roman period would have represented a formidable barrier to an invasion fleet. Quite apart from consulting the oracles before sailing, fleet commanders and their pilots needed to understand its tidal regime, its pattern of wind and weather and to be familiar with local hazards and havens. Indeed Vegetius, a late fourth-century writer of a Roman military treatise, emphasised that such was the duty of 'sailors and pilots'. Even today these factors must always be considered when putting out to sea. Of course only the most extreme conditions would prevent the sailing of a modern power-driven ship, such as a cross-Channel ferry. Nevertheless its passage must still be planned in the light of prevailing conditions. For the modern small-craft sailor, prevailing conditions can be critical; they will certainly influence the timing of his passage and may well lead to it being cancelled or deferred.[4] The mariner today enjoys services, such as weather forecasts, seamarks, buoys and lightships and, if the worst comes to the worst, has the support of the Coast Guard and of Search and Rescue services. For seafarers of the Roman period and for many centuries thereafter, the difference was stark. Not only was the mariner thrown back onto his own resources in deciding to set sail, but once out at sea, his ship was far less handy than modern sailing ships and he was much more reliant on finding favourable winds.

Sea level and coastline changes

The coastlines of north-west Europe, in particular the English Channel and the southern North Sea, are the creatures of the ending of the last Ice Age, some 10,000 years ago. Three related processes have been at work. First, with the melting of the ice sheets over much of the northern hemisphere, there has been a dramatic rise in sea level, the so-called Flandrian Marine Transgression, in the order of some 30m or more. Second, the removal of the weight of the ice from the land surface of northern Britain has provoked a pattern of land uplift in the north-west and subsidence in the south-east. In effect the British Isles have been see-sawing about a pivot line running from North Wales to North Yorkshire. These processes taken together have produced a change in the relative sea level (RSL). As far as south-east Britain and the neighbouring shores of Europe are concerned, this has meant a rise in RSL which continues today.

There was a further, but rather less significant marine transgression at the end of the Roman period, the Romano-British (or Dunkirkian)

Transgression. It has been suggested that one factor in the settlement of Britain by people from the maritime regions of northern Germany at this time may have been such a marine transgression which made their former homes uninhabitable. This is a hypothesis which finds some support in a comparison of sea levels and habitation levels on dwelling mounds (*Terpen*) between the Ems and the Elbe.[5]

Abel Briquet, whose study of the evolution of the northern coast of France is now over 70 years old, proposed a rise of some 5m since the Romano-British Transgression. He based this on the identification of a layer of peat underlying Romano-British alluvial deposits. Peat does not form in sea water. Since the bottom of the layer of peat is 5m below today's Mean High Water Springs (MHWS), this level must have been above MHWS when the peat began to form (*2*). Recent literature has been more tentative. Devoy suggests, for example, that current evidence points to an RSL 2,000 years ago in the order of 0.5-1.0m below today's levels for MHWS.[6]

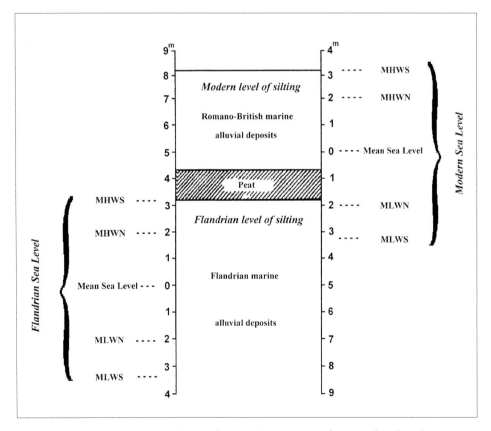

2 Relation of sea level to the silting surface and the position of peat in the Flemish maritime plain. *Adapted from Briquet, 1930, 356, with the permission of the Librairie Armand Colin*

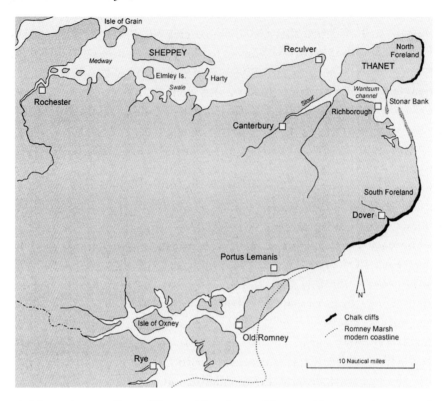

3 The ancient coastlines of Kent and East Sussex. The actual lines must be accepted as conjectural; in the case of Romney Marsh the sketch shows the three havens which evolved successively from the Roman period onwards: Hythe (*Portus Lemanis*), which was open in the Roman period, Old Romney and Rye

The third process which has been at work in the evolution of the coastlines of the English Channel and the southern North Sea is that of tidal currents, weather and erosion. A marine transgression, such as the Flandrian, initially creates a highly irregular, indented coastline as the sea invades river valleys, creeks and low-lying coastal plains to flood up to the lowest contours of rising ground. It is this that created the host of natural havens and inshore channels around the coasts of north-west Europe, which continued to be important into the Middle Ages (*3*). However, such natural havens are not stable. Once formed, the processes of silting, erosion and longshore drift tend to eliminate them by creating even, straightened shorelines. Many of these natural havens have been lost, left either far inland or represented by shadows of their former selves, for example Rye, Pevensey Bay, Sandwich and the Wantsum Channel; others, such as Dover, owe their continued existence to their economic importance and to continuing massive expenditure on dredging and artificial harbour works.

The visual evidence that the sea once created substantial natural havens over large areas of the coastal regions of lowland Britain is striking. In England the Somerset Levels seen from the Mendips; the Pevensey Levels inland of the present Pevensey Bay; Romney Marsh seen from the tower of Rye Church, all present the dramatic feature of absolutely flat stretches of marshland close to the high-water mark and often intersected by rectilinear drainage ditches. This typical feature of extensive stretches of geometrically flat land lying at a level closely corresponding to that of high tide, whether through the Kent Marshes bordering the Thames, the Medway and the Swale, or marking the former Wantsum channel dividing Thanet from mainland Kent, is the first evidence that these areas once lay beneath the sea.

The same characteristic of flat terrain coinciding with the level of high tide presents itself on the northern shores of continental Europe, in the maritime plains of Picardy and Flanders. A rail passenger going from Calais to St Omer, some 30 km inland from the coast, cannot fail to notice that the whole journey is across totally flat terrain with many rectilinear drainage ditches, which continue to be operational (4). A journey by car around the Somme estuary presents the same characteristic landscape, in which one can discern obsolete sea walls now many miles inland.

Tidal regime

In 55 BC the storm that damaged Caesar's fleet off East Kent was associated with an unusually high tide. It is a mistake to assume on the basis of this that the Romans were ignorant of Channel tides. What Caesar describes is a spring

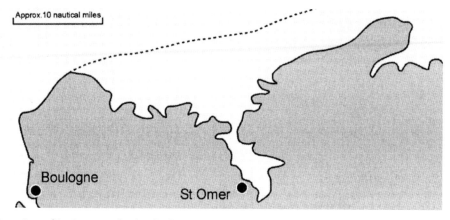

4 Location of St Omer at the head of a shallow bay. The sites of modern towns such as Calais and Dunkirk would have been under water. The firm line shows the conjectural position of the ancient coastline; the broken line that of the present-day coastline

high tide, possibly a storm surge. The only lack of knowledge that he admits to is that his men did not know that the highest or spring tides are associated with the full moon. In fact, in his account the year before of the naval campaign against the Veneti of Atlantic Gaul, Caesar gave a good description of the cycle of the ebb and flow of the tide among the promontories of Brittany and of its significance for the defence of the strongholds of the Veneti. In his description of his first passage to Britain, Caesar demonstrates that he was aware of the significance of tidal streams, recording that the fleet had the tide in its favour as it moved on from its anchorage off the South Foreland.

Tides result from the gravitational attraction of the moon and the sun as the earth rotates on its axis beneath them. Apart from the familiar twice-daily rise and fall of the level of the sea, they manifest themselves in the tidal currents which vary continually with the state of the tide. For the seafarer, as we shall see, both are important. There is also the fortnightly cycle in the amplitude or range of the tide. Spring tides, when high water is at its highest (and low water at its lowest), occur when the gravitational attraction of the moon and the sun is combined, at new and full moon, as Caesar noted, or rather in practice a day or two later. Neap tides – those with the least range – alternate with springs. There is also a seasonal cycle. At the spring and autumn equinoxes, when the sun and moon will be aligned with the celestial equator, spring tides will have the greatest range.

The tides in the eastern Channel and, in particular, the Dover Strait have a special significance for pilotage. Broadly speaking, in the eastern Channel the tidal streams flow alternately east and west, changing direction every 6¼ hours (5). In the Dover Strait, on the other hand, the streams run alternately north–east and south–west, again changing direction every 6¼ hours (6). The rate (or speed of the stream) depends not only on the state of the tide (how long it has been running), but also on how close it is to neaps or springs, the fastest rates occurring at springs. On the tidal charts (5 and 6) the rate is shown against the arrows in tenths of a knot, the first being the rate at neaps and the second at springs. Modern methods of tidal prediction can be highly accurate. If we could apply them to assess tidal conditions two millennia ago, it would help in understanding the constraints of Roman cross-Channel passage-making. Gerry Keys outlines the process of forecasting the tides:

> Although it is a relatively simple matter to calculate the astronomical tide-raising forces, the response of the water to these forces is extremely difficult to predict since the configuration of land masses and the depths of the oceans and seas all play a part. Modern prediction techniques are based on harmonic methods, relying on analyses of tidal observations which

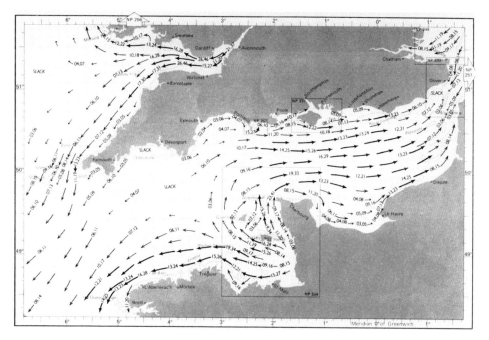

5a Tidal streams in the English Channel at 2 hours before High Water Dover

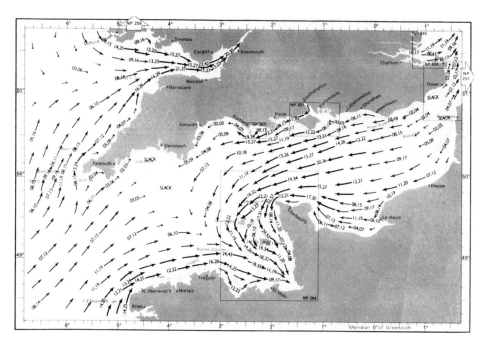

5b Tidal streams in the English Channel at 4 hours afer High Water Dover. *Reproduced from Admiralty Tidal Stream Atlas by permission of the Controller of Her Majesty's Stationery Office and the UK Hydrographic Office* (www.ukho.gov.uk)

enable the relationship between the response of the water at any place and the variation in the astronomical forces to be identified.[7]

In other words, tidal prediction depends heavily on pragmatic observations of how the water actually responds at specific locations under the influence of the 'configuration of land masses'. In the Roman period, as we have noted, the configuration of the coastline of the English Channel was certainly different; the sea level was perhaps a metre lower and along both sides of the Channel there were a number of coastal inlets and natural harbours which have since silted up. Can we really have any certainty that the pattern of tidal streams depicted in the tidal charts (*5* and *6*) would have been valid when Caesar and Plautius contemplated their crossings of Oceanus? Many have doubted it. A number of nineteenth-century scholars argued that the changes in the coastline must have altered the tidal pattern. Among the arguments advanced by Edwin Guest were that Thanet was an island; that Romney Marsh was covered by high tide; and that Dungeness did not exist. George Dowker, who considered that, as a geologist with an extensive knowledge of East Kent, he could offer special insights into the interpretation of Caesar's narrative of his British expeditions, drew attention to the great changes which he said must have occurred:

> Would no effect be produced in the tides if the water ran in at Sandwich and out at Reculver, as we know it did in Saxon times? Would no effect be felt by the tides if the Goodwins were now an island? Would no effect be created if the whole of Romney Marsh were under water?[8]

Professor Montagu Burrows, a distinguished historian and former naval officer, claimed that the width of the Dover Strait must now be 'at least two miles wider than it was some 2,000 years ago, and therefore the point of meeting of the North and South tide-streams cannot possibly be exactly the same'. He did not, however, advance any evidence to support his claim. On the other hand Sir George Airy, Astronomer Royal, formerly Lucasian Professor of Mathematics at Cambridge and an amateur historian, expressed the view that 'the course of the tides from Beachy Head to Dover will depend on the great tides of the Atlantic and the North Sea, and will not be sensibly affected by any petty changes at the east end of Kent'.[9] He was supported in this view by Sir George Darwin:

> In my opinion, Airy is absolutely right and Burrows and the others wrong. A channel from Sandwich to Reculver could not have made any sensible

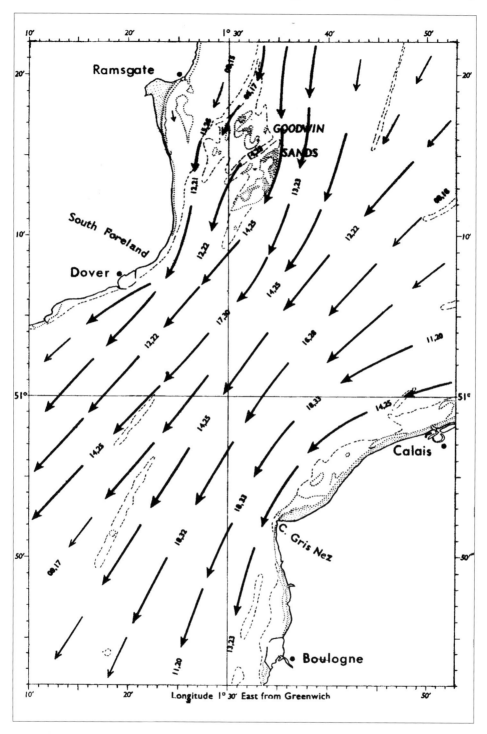

6a Tidal streams in the Dover Strait at 5 hours before High Water Dover. *Reproduced from Admiralty Tidal Stream Atlas by permission of the Controller of Her Majesty's Stationery Office and the UK Hydrographic Office* (www.ukho.gov.uk)

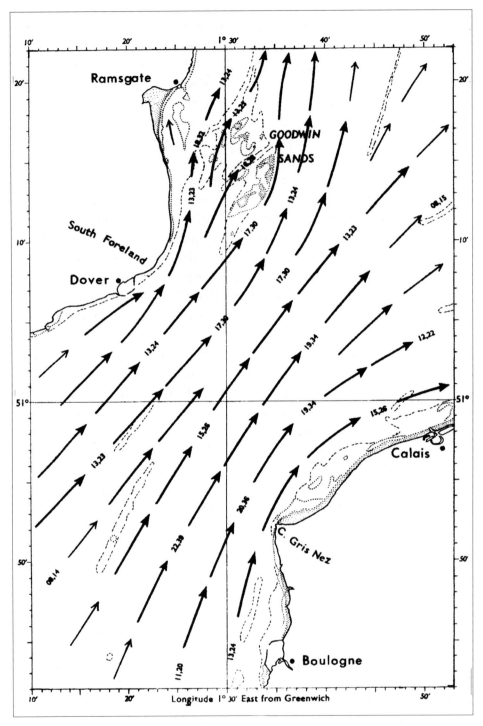

6*b* With 6*a* this shows tidal streams in the Dover Strait at 5 hours before and 1 hour after High Water Dover respectively. *Reproduced from Admiralty Tidal Stream Atlas by permission of the Controller of Her Majesty's Stationery Office and the UK Hydrographic Office* (www.ukho.gov.uk)

change, and so also it would be impossible to detect the difference if Goodwin Sands were an island. All the phenomena now observed must have occurred at the same times within, say, a minute, and with an intensity measurably identical in the days of Caesar. Even if you were in a position to indicate exactly the nature of the changes in the channel since that time, it would be impossible to compute the nature of the *excessively minute* changes in the currents.[10]

Like Airy, Darwin, the second son of Charles, was an eminent astronomer and made a special study of the frictional effects of tidal action on the Sun–Earth–Moon system. In 1882 he proposed a system of tidal constituents which gained widespread acceptance. Thus it would seem that the dispute set astronomers against other scholars. The bitterness of the dispute can be assessed by the way in which Guest echoes Airy's language when he asserts that the coastal changes he catalogues 'are no "petty changes", no *"petites modifications de la côte"*, but changes of enormous magnitude, such as are without parallel elsewhere on the British coast...'.[11]

Of course there can be no doubting the authority of astronomers in calculating celestial events many centuries ago in very precise terms. But tidal prediction is not simply a matter of predicting celestial events. It is a question of assessing the influence of those events on bodies of water whose movements are constrained by the 'configuration of land masses' cited by Keys. Moreover, it cannot be refuted that the changes in the coastline over the last two millennia must have produced at least local variations in the pattern of tidal streams. For example, tidal currents would in the past have flowed through the channel between Thanet and mainland Kent where none now flow, given that the channel no longer exists. The question is whether such local variations in the tidal regime would have been large enough to have any significant impact of the general pattern of the tides in the main body of the English Channel and Dover Strait. Airy was quite right to point out that that pattern is just part of the overall pattern of the tidal streams in the waters around the British Isles. A modern geologist, Devoy, noting that the present tidal range was apparently established *c.*2500 BC in the central coastal areas of the Netherlands, tentatively concludes that 'it is feasible that the modern tidal regime had similarly begun to operate in southeast England at a comparable date'. For our purposes it seems reasonable to accept that two millennia ago the oscillation of the tidal streams through the Dover Strait and eastern Channel every 6¼ hours under the influence of Airy's 'great tides of the Atlantic and the North Sea' would have been broadly similar to that observed today.[12]

But it must be stressed that we are not looking for the precision of modern prediction methods. Even if we assume a timing of tidal phenomena to the exact minute, as for the sake of convenience we may, the chronology offered by ancient documents, for example Caesar's accounts of his crossings, does not permit such precision. Romans divided the day into 12 hours from sunrise to sunset and the night into four watches and it was by reference to such broad divisions of time that Caesar described the timing of his crossings. In fact it is an error to suppose that in an age of non-instrumental navigation the precision of modern tidal predictions was either possible or necessary. All that one needs to know is how many hours after high (or low) water at a particular haven the tidal streams start to run in one's favour. Alternatively the onset of a favourable stream may be expressed in relation to the azimuth (or bearing) of the moon. In her seminal study of ancient navigation, *The Haven-Finding Art*, Eva Taylor quotes *The English Rutter* on tides: 'a south Moon maketh high water within Wight' and 'all the havens be full at a west-south-west Moon between the Start and the Lizard'. It is in terms as simple as this that the lore of vernacular seamanship could express and memorise the change in tidal streams off particular havens.[13]

'Working the tides' would have been important for seafarers in ancient times, as it is for today's small craft sailors. This means timing one's passage so as to exploit favourable tidal streams to the full. In some cases it is possible to carry a favourable tide for the whole passage. For example, a ship leaving Boulogne just as the tide starts to run north-east will have the advantage of a favourable tide from 2½ hours before High Water Dover off Boulogne until 4 hours after High Water Dover off Ramsgate – a total of 6½ hours, quite sufficient to complete the passage if an average of 5 knots through the water can be maintained (6). Caesar and other Roman invaders of Britain using this route would have sought to exploit these favourable streams.

In other cases the length of the passage will be such that at some time during the passage the tide will turn, perhaps several times. In the English Channel two specific cases can be identified. First there are cross-Channel passages, evidence for whose use in the late first millennium BC has been investigated by Seán McGrail (7). He identifies from archaeological and other evidence five cross-Channel routes in use immediately before the opening of the Roman period. These routes seem to be remarkably persistent over time. In the twentieth century Riley gave passage notes for yachtsmen for 14 cross-Channel passages in the area surveyed by McGrail. Of these all but three may be seen as variants of McGrail's five routes. The three exceptions are Newhaven to Dieppe, Dungeness (from places further east) to Dieppe, and Newhaven (from places further west) to Boulogne. It is also to be noted that, with one or two exceptions, McGrail's five routes are those of the main modern ferry crossings, again with Newhaven–Dieppe a notable addition. Given this persistence, we may reasonably suppose that in the period immediately following McGrail's survey, i.e. at the moment of the Roman invasions of Caesar and Claudius, his five routes were the normal routes of communication between Britain and the continent. They would be the cross-Channel routes of which the local seafarers of the day had personal experience.[14]

We have already noted that in tidal terms McGrail's route eight, Boulogne to East Kent, is a special case, being controlled by the north–east/south–west going tidal streams through the Dover Strait and being short enough to be completed, given adequate boat speed, within a single tide. So too is his route nine, Bruges to East Kent, being controlled by the coastwise ebb and flow along the Flemish coast.

The other cross-Channel routes, basically south–north, are subject to tidal streams bearing alternately on one beam or the other. This brings no special benefit in terms of speeding the vessel towards her destination, but it does not set her back on her track. What it does is to cause her to follow an elongated S-shaped track over the ground as the tidal streams run alternately east and west (for a worked example for the Norman invasion passage from the Somme to Pevensey, see 8).[15]

Let us now turn to the other category of passage which will involve one or more turns of the tide. These are the coastal passages, whose length is such that they cannot be completed in one tide. McGrail catalogues four such passages of between 95 and 250 nautical miles (7). Unlike the open water cross-Channel passages, these extended coastal passages will of necessity involve stemming foul tidal streams at some point and this might involve anchoring to await the turn of the tide. We should not assume that anchoring an invasion fleet was not a feasible option; in 55 BC Caesar anchored off the South Foreland to wait out the tide and William of Normandy is also recorded as having anchored his fleet during the invasion passage of 1066, apparently to avoid arriving off Pevensey in the dark.

There are two points to draw out from all this. The first is that in choosing a route for a cross-Channel invasion passage, the Roman naval staff would have borne in mind the extent to which it would have been influenced by the tides. All other things being equal, there would be a significant advantage in using the short crossing of the Dover Strait. If the military context demanded a landing elsewhere, say on the Solent, as we know was the case in AD 296, then the advantage would be with a south–north crossing of the Channel from an embarkation harbour, say on the Seine, or maybe even further west, than from Boulogne. It is perhaps significant that McGrail did not

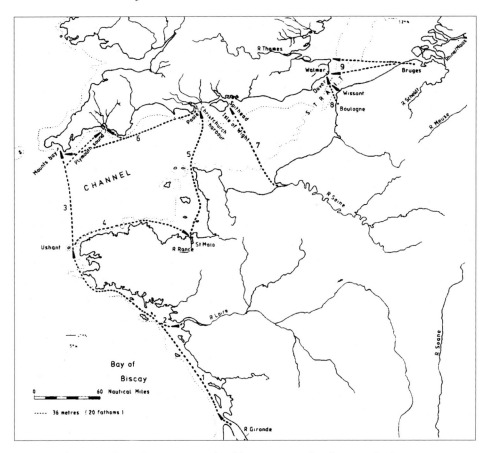

7 McGrail's nine Channel routes. *Reproduced by permission of Professor McGrail*

find evidence for a cross-Channel route from the vicinity of Boulogne to the Solent. The second point is that in his *Gallic War* Caesar gives us sufficient detail to allow us to reconstruct the tidal pattern during at least some of his passages. This gives important indications in the identification of the *Portus Itius* as his embarkation harbour and East Kent as the site of his landing in Britain.

Wind and weather

A generation thoroughly aware of the reality of climate change and convinced of the dangers of global warming may very well question how sure we can be about the climate in north-west Europe in the Roman period. Superficially the question may seem similar to the debate about the confidence we may have in describing the tidal regime in the Channel two millennia ago, but there is the crucial difference that the tides are powered by astronomical phenomena that can be precisely calculated; there can be no such precision in recon-structing past climates. There is indeed considerable evidence that over the last 2,000 years there have been significant variations in the climate of the British Isles and northern Europe. Perhaps the most well-known is that of the 'Little Ice Age' of the sixteenth and seventeenth centuries. In the late twentieth and the beginning of the twenty-first century, winters in southern England and the nearby regions of the continent are rarely severe; snow is uncommon and ice on bodies of open water does not often form. In stark contrast are paintings, such as that of the frozen Thames in 1676 by Abraham Hondius in the Museum of London or Brueghel the Elder's *Hunters in the snow*.

Wind direction is important for the seafarer. In their study of wind data from the Netherlands, Lindgrén and Neumann found evidence of some variation in the wind direction frequencies recorded in the first half of the eighteenth century (1700-1750), compared with the late nineteenth and early twentieth centuries (1888-1937). They note in particular that in the earlier period there was a greater preponderance of winds from the south-west and south-east and fewer from the south. However, they also note that other evidence for London based on diaries indicates that there is virtually no difference between the wind direction data for 1667-1700 and those for 1901-1930.[16]

Hubert Lamb was the founder and first director of the respected Climatic Research Unit of the University of East Anglia. In a number of books and papers he charted the evidence for variations in climate over the millennia and sought to identify the influence of such change on history. He identifies the period 800 to 400 BC as one of 'unmatched wetness in the west' of Britain with 'an unequalled predominance of westerly winds'. Around 500 BC the climate became wetter in eastern areas of England as well and winds became less predominantly from the west. By the beginning of the first millennium AD until around AD 400 there was a continuing recovery of warmth and dryness in Europe generally. The olive could be cultivated farther north in Italy than had been the case in previous centuries and the beech, which around 300 BC grew in Rome, was by Pliny's time regarded as a mountain tree. There is evidence of the spread of vine cultivation northwards from the Alps in the late Roman period. In general he concluded: 'There were evidently considerable similarities to the climate of our own times, except for the continuance of a somewhat moister regime in north Africa and the Near East'.[17]

We can find in Caesar's account of his expeditions to Britain some details of the weather he experienced. For his first crossing he says that the weather was fair and the wind favourable. Four days later his cavalry fleet left Gaul 'with a gentle breeze', but was struck by a storm and driven back to the continent. According to Caesar, the same storm was associated with a full moon and an

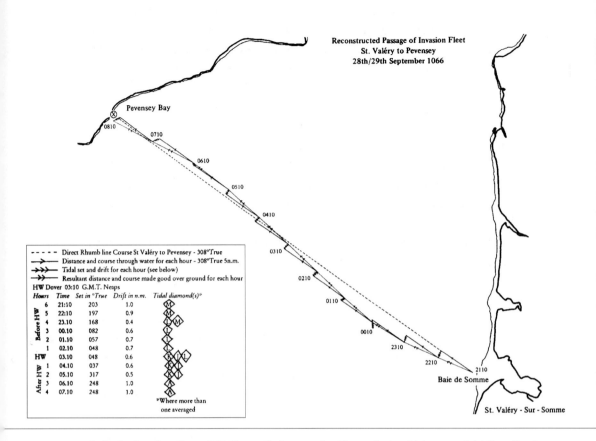

**Reconstructed Passage of Invasion Fleet
St. Valéry to Pevensey
28th/29th September 1066**

Pevensey Bay

0810
0710
0610
0510
0410
0310
0210
0110
0010
2310
2210
2110
Baie de Somme
St. Valéry - Sur - Somme

- - - - Direct Rhumb line Course St Valéry to Pevensey - 308°True
→— Distance and course through water for each hour - 308°True 5n.m.
→›› Tidal set and drift for each hour (see below)
→» Resultant distance and course made good over ground for each hour

HW Dover 03:10 G.M.T. Neaps

Hours		Time	Set in °True	Drift in n.m.	Tidal diamond(s)*
Before HW	6	21:10	203	1.0	
	5	22:10	197	0.9	
	4	23.10	168	0.4	
	3	00.10	082	0.6	
	2	01.10	057	0.7	
	1	02.10	048	0.7	
HW		03.10	048	0.6	
After HW	1	04.10	037	0.6	
	2	05.10	317	0.5	
	3	06.10	248	1.0	
	4	07.10	248	1.0	

*Where more than
one averaged

8 As the invasion fleet of 1066 travelled across the Channel, the tidal stream initially offset its
ground track to port and then to starboard and again to port during the 11-hour passage.
The assumed speed through the water is 5 knots

unusually high tide that caused considerable damage to the main body of his
fleet hauled ashore and at anchor off East Kent. The initial gentle breeze was
probably from the south-west and the best explanation of the storm is that the
wind blew from the north or north-west. The traditional understanding, in
fact Caesar's own, is that the unexpected high tide was a spring tide which
Caesar's people did not know would be associated with a full moon; however,
a storm force wind from the north-west or north, together with an associated
deep depression passing to the north would also be consistent with surge tide
conditions in the southern North Sea. For his return Caesar took advantage of
a spell of fair weather close to the equinox.

Caesar's most explicit statement about the weather occurs in his account
of the departure of his fleet the following year. The departure was delayed for
25 days by a 'north-west' wind which, he says, was 'prevalent for a great part

of every season in these localities'. The Romans counted two wind directions between each cardinal point, rather than one as we normally would (*9*). The wind direction stated by Caesar (in Latin *Corus*) is the more westerly of the two between West and North, in fact W⅓N, rather than W½N. Given the way in which the wind direction would have fluctuated, the likelihood is that Caesar was delayed by a spell of westerlies and north-westerlies. When the fleet weighed, it was with a 'gentle south-west wind'; again the term used by Caesar (in Latin *Africus*) indicates a wind closer to west than to south, i.e. W⅓S. The wind failed around midnight and it was only by rowing that the fleet reached Britain. Shortly after landing another storm blew up, in which the fleet was again damaged. Finally Caesar returned to Gaul just before the equinox in 'a complete calm'.

Lamb expresses the view that the persistent west to north-west winds which delayed the expedition of 54 BC were 'certainly nothing that would be unusual today'. In fact that comment could be valid for the general picture that Caesar gives of prevalent winds from the westerly sector, with the occasional gale and also the occasional flat calm. Of course there is no way in which we can derive meaningful statistics from his account and we could not go so far as to claim that modern meteorological data would exactly replicate wind direction frequencies of the Roman period. But we may tentatively assume that the overall picture that such data offer would be broadly in line with that which the Romans knew.

With that qualification we can be reasonably confident that the weather patterns which would have affected Roman naval operations in the Channel, both those of Caesar and of his two successors, would have been those which are characteristic of the Atlantic low, which so dominates our weather today. These patterns are modified from time to time by the effect of anticyclones or high-pressure systems. In broad terms we have prevailing winds from the westerly quadrant, created by depressions originating in the North Atlantic and travelling in an easterly/north-easterly direction across north-west Europe, giving way from time to time to winds from other directions generated by anticyclones (regions of high pressure). Depressions are low pressure systems with winds circulating (in the northern hemisphere) anticlockwise; in this they are to be contrasted with anticyclones, the wind circulation of which (again in the northern hemisphere) is clockwise (*10*).

The prevailing winds created by depressions are reasonably predictable and, as the depression moves east, there is a characteristic and marked windshift as each front passes over the observer. The usual pattern is that, as the new depression approaches from the west, it will be heralded by winds from the south or south-west, even on occasion from the south-east; as the warm front passes over, the wind will veer quite sharply to the south-west or west, and again to the west or north-west, as the cold front passes over. The wind will then return to the south-west, south or south-east, as the next depression approaches. This regular sequence of windshifts has significant implications for ancient seafarers making the longer cross-Channel passages under sail; if you leave Gaul for Britain with a favourable, south-westerly wind, it is probable that the wind will veer to west and even north-west during your passage and that you will be, as a seaman might say 'headed'. The passage of a depression is marked by a characteristic weather sequence, which is of considerable significance for single-observer weather forecasting and which is well known to mariners (*colour plates 4, 5* and *6*).

However, before the advent of photography, seamen did not have the benefit of such sequential series of photographs of the changing weather pattern of a passing depression. Like so much else in the mariner's craft, this weather lore was in former times passed down from generation to generation, often in the form of easily remembered jingles. For example:

> Backing winds and mares' tails
> Make tall ships carry low sails.

is an accurate and concise description of the weather associated with an approaching depression. The wind sequence of a depression coming up behind one which has just passed over is concisely recorded in the jingle:

> When the wind shifts against the sun
> Trust it not for back it will run.

The weather associated with anticyclones is much more stable. Anticyclones tend to move slowly or to remain stationary for some days. In summer they are associated with fine settled dry weather, sometimes with thin hazy cloud with winds often from directions other than the west; at other times of the year the sky may be uniformly overcast, sometimes with light drizzle, and in winter and early spring the winds from the north or east can be bitterly cold, sometimes associated with clear blue skies. Because pressure gradients tend to be slacker, winds are usually not very strong; indeed in the centre of an anticyclone, there is often a large area of calm. However, on the outskirts of the system, where it may interact with a depression, winds may be strong. For example, an anticyclone to the south of a depression will combine with it to produce a strong westerly airflow between them.

Single-observer forecasting was all that was available until the advent in the modern age of instantaneous communication; no doubt it would have been

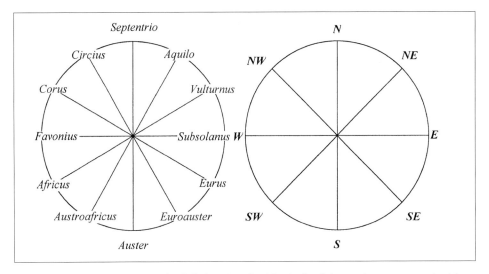

9 The Roman wind-rose on the left showing the 12 winds of the ancients compared with a compass rose showing the eight modern cardinal and half-cardinal points. The latter ultimately developed into a system of 32 points each of 11.25° and even of 64 half points, which continued until well into the twentieth century, when it was superseded by a card divided into 360°

exploited to the full by Roman naval commanders. Riley suggests that only three factors are of significance in single-observer forecasting:

  1. Observation of pressure changes with a barometer
  2. Direction and strength of the wind
  3. Cloud formation and movement[18]

Before the age of instrumentation, only the second and third were available to mariners. The limitations of single-observer forecasting need to be borne in mind. First, the weather lore we have just described is restricted in its validity: the weather sequences described are those which are experienced in that part of north-west European waters which normally lie to the south of the track of the centres of passing Atlantic lows; the weather sequence associated with a depression whose centre passes south of the observer is quite different. This would not have been a problem for Roman naval operations in the Channel as the centres of depressions usually track well to the north of the English Channel and southern North Sea.

The second limitation is that of timescale. Riley suggests that no forecast the mariner makes on his own can be valid for more than 5 or 6 hours. This may be unduly pessimistic except in a rapidly changing meteorological

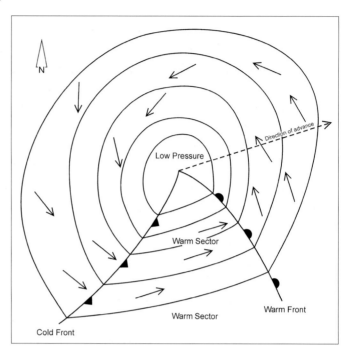

Low Pressure

Direction of advance

Warm Sector

Warm Sector

Warm Front

Cold Front

10 Schematic model of an Atlantic depression showing the anti-clockwise circulation of winds and the cold and warm fronts; note the sharp bend in each isobar as it crosses each front; this causes a distinct wind shift which is a clear indication to the observer on the surface that a front is passing overhead

scenario; Eric Hiscock points out that the cirrus cloud (*colour plate 4*) portending an approaching depression may be seen in the western sky when it is as much as 300 miles away and may give 12 or even 24 hours' notice of an approaching depression. But what the single observer cannot see is the second and third depression forming out in the Atlantic. Linked with this is the uncertainty for the single observer of the potential longevity of an anticyclone. In 1879 Captain Andrew Shewan spent 12 days beating up-Channel in his clipper *Norman Court* in the teeth of a strong easterly wind generated by an anticyclone; he was informed by a fleet of Salcombe fishermen that the easterly had been blowing for six weeks. On the other hand, although its stability will usually mean that one can count on at least a few days of settled weather, an anticyclone can decay in as little as 24 hours.[19]

The third limitation is reliability. Modern authorities emphasise the importance of using single-observer forecasting only as an adjunct to official meteorological services. What single-observer forecasting does in the modern context is to enable the mariner to add what might be termed local colour. Official marine forecasts parcel out weather predictions in terms of formal sea areas of thousands of square miles and inevitably there is a measure of local variation and to appreciate this, the mariner can use his own local observations. Of course it is very probable that, in an age when seafarers had only their own observations to rely on, their sensitivity to minute distinctions in weather patterns was much greater than ours. Nevertheless, any forecast they made was inevitably local. They would not be able to state what the present weather was a hundred miles away, let alone forecast what it would be two or three days later.

I suggested earlier that we might tentatively assume that the overall picture offered by modern meteorological data would broadly be in line with the sort of conditions which the Romans encountered in the English Channel. Such data for the Dover Strait and the eastern Channel are published in the *Channel Pilot* and *Dover Strait Pilot*. The data is given for individual meteorological stations. If we take six as relevant to Roman naval operations in the eastern Channel[20] and focus on the data for the months April to September as representative of the Roman sailing season, the following picture emerges:

1 That the winds are predominantly from the westerly sector, mainly from the south-west, is confirmed by the data from all the stations. Aggregation of the data shows that nearly a quarter (23 per cent) of winds are from the south-west and as much as 48 per cent from the westerly sector generally (*11*).
2 Winds from the easterly sector (north-east, east and south-east) constitute in aggregate only a quarter of the total (26 per cent), although there is a marked increased frequency in winds from the north to north-east between February and May. This is particularly marked at Dover and Boulogne, with the implication that, as the season progressed, the probability of a fair wind for a passage down Channel would decrease.
3 There is a marked funnelling effect created by the Dover Strait which increases the frequency and strength of south-west and north-east winds in the Strait.
4 Wind speeds generally average Force 4 (11 to 16 knots). Clearly the average covers a wide variation, but the average number of days per month with gales (Force 8 or above – 34 knots plus) at all the stations is one or fewer.
5 The mobility of the depressions coming in from the Atlantic means that the region often experiences marked variations in wind speed and direction. Certainly we can detect such rapid variations in the weather in Caesar's account.[21]

In a context in which the success of an invasion crossing depends on having a favourable wind, this weather pattern gives clear advantages to the short crossing of the Dover Strait. Should the military – or diplomatic – context demand a landing further west than East Kent then, as Asclepiodotus did in 296, the fleet would leave Gaul from a harbour further west than Boulogne.

Conclusion

We may be sure the myth of Oceanus would have heightened the apprehension felt by the legionaries, whether of Caesar, Claudius or Constantius, as they contemplated the crossing of the English Channel. By that token the triumph of the invader was the greater. We have already noted that after his first raid the Senate voted Caesar a 20-day thanksgiving, the longest that had ever been granted, for what had been trumpeted as a victory over Oceanus himself. In similar vein the inscription on Claudius's triumphal arch in Rome proclaimed his achievement in being 'the first to bring barbarian tribes beyond Oceanus under Roman rule'.

In some ways the reality justified the myth. Crossing the Channel did present a formidable challenge, particularly with an invasion army, which was not to be underestimated. It would have been a venture fraught with risks and difficulties. Quite apart from the usual logistical and tactical matters which need to be resolved for any military operation, transporting an invasion army across the Channel would have demanded special consideration of factors such as the uncertainty of the weather, the probability of favourable winds, the tidal streams and the availability of suitable harbours and landing beaches. In our interpretation of the ancient accounts of our invasions we need to remember that one way or another each of the invaders would have had to face up to these issues. However, before considering the invasions in detail, let us look at the sort of ships which the Romans would have used.

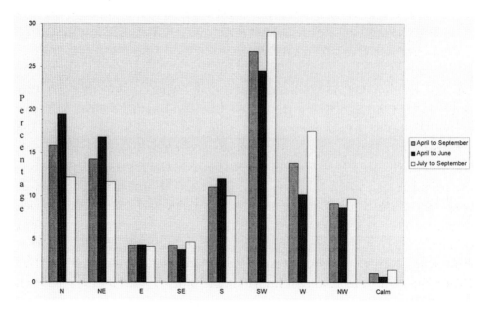

11 Wind direction frequencies (aggregated) for stations in the eastern Channel; the marked preponderance of winds from the west, south-west and north-west is clearly apparent

3

THE ANCIENT WARSHIP

Naves longae: *the Mediterranean tradition*

When Caesar's first expedition fleet approached its beachhead in Britain in 55 BC, the Britons, dashing forward with their cavalry and charioteers, hurling missiles, sought to prevent the Romans from disembarking. Caesar tells us what happened next:

> When Caesar remarked this, he commanded the ships of war (which were less familiar in appearance to the natives, and could move more freely at need) to remove a little from the transports, to row at speed, and to bring up on the exposed flank of the enemy; and thence to drive and clear them off with slings, arrows, and artillery. This movement proved of great service to our troops; for the natives, frightened by the shape of the ships, the motion of the oars, and the unfamiliar type of the artillery, came to a halt, and retired, but only for a little space.

We first encounter Caesar's *naves longae* (long ships or warships) the year before in his campaign against the Veneti, a tribe inhabiting the Atlantic coast of Gaul. Trouble had started in the autumn of 57 BC. The legions had retired to their winter quarters, the Seventh under Publius Crassus in western Gaul. Lacking sufficient corn for his legion's needs, Crassus sent envoys among the neighbouring tribes to requisition supplies. The response of the Veneti was to detain the two envoys sent to them, apparently in the hope of recovering their hostages from the Romans. Matters quickly escalated among the maritime tribes all along the coast of western and northern Gaul, including the Morini, from whose territory Caesar would embark for Britain in 55 and 54 BC. Caesar had a full-scale revolt on his hands. He ordered warships to be built on the Loire and crews to be recruited (the oarsmen from Provence), and joined Crassus from his headquarters in Illyricum as soon as the season allowed. There is a hint in Caesar's account that he also summoned a fleet of warships from the Mediterranean under Decimus Brutus. This hint is made explicit by the historian Dio Cassius, writing some 250 years later.

According to Caesar, Brutus was placed in command of the 'fleet, and of the Gallic ships already ordered to assemble'; if the 'Gallic ships' are the warships that had been built on the Loire, then it may reasonably be taken that the 'fleet' already existed and had been summoned from the Mediterranean. Caesar describes the arrival of the ships which were 'detained by foul weather, and because the difficulty of navigation on a vast and open sea, with strong tides and few – nay, scarcely any – harbours, was extreme'. This adds credibility to an image of a Mediterranean fleet struggling northwards from the Gibraltar Strait along the inhospitable Atlantic coast. Dio, clearly relying on sources other than Caesar's own commentary, not only reports the delayed arrival from the Mediterranean of Brutus with his 'swift ships', but also reports that the vessels built on the Loire were of a kind which Caesar thought to be suited to the tides of the Ocean. Even so, Caesar is quite specific in describing the ships built on the Loire as *naves longae*.

The campaign against the Veneti was to be a naval operation. The position of their strongholds, generally at the end of promontories, was such as to make a successful assault from the land difficult and pointless, since Veneti evacuated their people by sea once it was clear that the stronghold would fall. The strength of the Veneti lay in their ships and in their skill as seafarers. Caesar remarked on the large number of ships available to them and reported that they used these ships for passages to Britain. According to him, the Veneti excelled all the other Celtic tribes in seafaring and their ships were especially suited to the difficult conditions of Atlantic Gaul.

Caesar acknowledged that, while his ships were faster under oars, in all other respects the Venetic ships were superior. In particular, the rams of the Roman warships were ineffective against the Venetic ships because of their stout construction. The height of the freeboard of the Venetic ships was such as to make it difficult for the Romans to use grapnels; at the same time it gave the Veneti the advantage in hurling missiles – even the use of towers on the Roman ships did not neutralise this advantage. However, in the decisive naval battle the Romans employed the unlikely, but effective, expedient of sickles attached to long poles. With these they managed to disable several of the Venetic ships by cutting their halyards. When the rest of the fleet turned downwind to flee, it was becalmed in the dying wind and the remaining Venetic ships were picked off by the Romans one by one. Dio's more detailed account of the engagement emphasises the manoeuvrability of the Roman fleet, but it is perhaps not to be taken too literally, for it directly contradicts Caesar's on several points. According to Dio, Brutus was able to ram the Venetic fleet, using the standard tactics of breaking through the enemy line and encircling it; Venetic ships were boarded and defeated in hand–to–hand combat; others were set on fire; the Veneti did not have missiles. All in all, one might suppose that Dio is painting a conventionalised picture of a naval engagement, drawing on stock elements. Such a view is perhaps confirmed by Strabo's brief account. He states that Caesar defeated the Veneti in a naval battle, 'making no use of ramming (for the beams were thick), but when the Veneti bore upon him with the wind, the Romans hauled down their sails by means of pole-hooks'.

Caesar's descriptions of his warships make clear their Mediterranean provenance. They were armed with a ram and, at least in battle, relied on oars for propulsion. Compared with local ships they had deep V-shaped lower hulls and had a significant advantage in speed and manoeuvrability. As we have noted, for the landing in Britain in 55 BC they were fitted with catapults and slingsmen and archers operated from their decks. Whilst in the campaign against the Veneti, the Roman warships were used to engage the enemy at sea, in the expeditions to Britain they appear to have served two functions. First, as we have seen in the passage quoted, they were deployed to provide supporting fire to the legionaries as they disembarked. Secondly, they were allocated to the general staff and senior officers. We may surmise that the greater manoeuvrability of the warships enabled these men to move more easily around the fleet to exercise control.

Caesar's warships were in a direct evolutionary line from new types of warship which began to appear in the Mediterranean with the introduction of the ram in the early first millennium BC. Originally manned with a single file of oarsmen along each side of the hull, the earliest warships were designated by the total number of oars deployed: thus *triacontor* (30-oared ship) and *pentecontor* (50-oared ship). With the use of the ram as an offensive weapon, increases in the number of oarsmen brought an advantage in terms of the weight of the attack. The problem for shipbuilders was how to fit more rowers into the hull without creating an over-long and dangerously weak structure. Such would be the result, if the extra oarsmen were added to the single file on each side. The solution adopted was to introduce more than one file of oarsmen on each side of the hull and ships began to be designated by the number of files on each side, rather than by the number of rowers: thus bireme, trireme, quinquereme and so on. Although for the bireme and the trireme the designation was also equivalent to the number of tiers of oars on each side, this is not true for the higher ratings. In fact three is considered to be the practical limit for the number of tiers of oars on either side. At higher ratings there were more than one rower to an oar, at least in some of the files. Thus the four (quadrireme) might have two tiers of double-manned oars on each side, the five (quinquireme) three tiers with two of them double-manned and the six three – all double-manned. Although at least one leviathan with 40 files on each side is recorded as having been built in the late third century BC for Ptolemy IV, it would appear that ten was the upper limit for effective naval operations, none of a higher rating being recorded in active service. As far as the Romans were concerned, the six was the upper limit, being considered an appropriate craft to serve as the flag ship of the fleet commander. At the Battle of Massalia in the Civil War in 49 BC Brutus was to lead Caesar's fleet in a six and it may well be that the flagship of the fleet he brought from the Mediterranean to Western Gaul seven years earlier was also a six.[1]

The evidence of the Roman historian Livy suggests that the Romans drew a distinction between larger and smaller ships (*naves maioris formae, minoris formae*). According to John Morrison, this distinction falls between fours and threes and provides a clue as to the rating of the warships involved in Caesar's invasions of Britain. In seeking intelligence about the harbours on the British coast, Caesar expresses concern that merchants acquainted with the coast of south-east Britain could tell him nothing about harbours suitable for 'a number of larger ships' (*maiorum navium multitudinem*). Morrison sees this as a direct reference to Livy's classification, suggesting that the warships built on the Loire fell within the category of less powerful ships, while those brought by Brutus from the Mediterranean would have included some fours and fives.[2]

Another clue to the probability that the invasion fleet of 55 BC included larger warships such as these is provided by the presence at the landing of longboats (*scaphae*) and scout vessels (*navigia speculatoria*). As the legionaries disembark in face of stiff opposition, Caesar orders these smaller craft to be manned with soldiers and to move forward to bring support to such units as are especially hard pressed. We have from Vegetius, who wrote a treatise on military science in the early fifth century AD, the statement that *scafae exploratoriae* – with 20 oars on each side – were attached to the larger warships. It is to be recognised that with 40 oars these were substantial craft, perhaps in excess of 25m long, indeed comparable in terms of size with the ships used by the Anglo-Saxons for their voyages from northern Germany and Denmark in the Migration Period or with the Scandinavian long ships of the late first millennium AD. Clearly if *scaphae* were as big as this, it is highly unlikely that they could have been carried on board their parent craft. Morrison considers that they would have been towed or would have proceeded in company under their own (oar) power.[3]

An important constituent of Roman fleets was the liburnian. The Liburnians, who inhabited the Balkan coast of the Adriatic, had a special notoriety for piracy, operating in fast, handy craft. Whether the Romans copied the design of these ships or not, they adopted the name liburnian for a particular class of smaller warship, noted for its speed, equipped with a ram and well protected from missile attack; Lucan in his epic on the Civil War includes them in Brutus's fleet at the Battle of Massalia in 49 BC, describing them as having two files of rowers on each side. Depictions of warships on Trajan's Column which can be identified as liburnians confirm that they saw active service on the Danube in the Dacian Wars of AD 101-2 and 105-6 (*12*). Again, since they were part of Brutus's fleet at the Battle of Massalia, they may well have been among the warships available to Caesar for his British operations in the previous decade. The liburnian was so ubiquitous that ultimately the term came to be used of any warship, of whatever class.[4]

Naves longae: *methods of construction*

The method of construction in the Mediterranean tradition was to build the shell of the hull first and to insert the frames into the completed hull. Such shell-first methods of construction, which were widely used in ancient times, depend on some method of securing each plank to its neighbour, since there was no framework to which it could be fastened: in many traditions stitching with some form of natural twine was used; in the clinker-built tradition of Scandinavia and its neighbours the planks were overlapped and secured to each other with iron rivets. The special characteristic of the Mediterranean shipbuilding tradition was the use of locked mortice–and–tenon joints to secure each plank to its neighbour (*13*). A series of narrowly spaced slots (mortices) was cut in the edge of each plank. Into each mortice was inserted a tenon (a rectangular tongue of wood) and the next plank was offered up so that the mortices in its lower edge matched up to the tenons already in place in the previous plank. Once the two planks had been tightened up, the joints were locked by a wooden peg driven through a hole in each end of each tenon. The result was a strongly built carvel hull which would be waterproof without caulking. It was, however, a method which was expensive in time and required craftsmen trained in the technique; if the warships which Caesar ordered to built on the Loire were indeed constructed in this way, the shipwrights would have had to be recruited from Mediterranean shipyards.

Although mortice-and-tenon joints appear very early, for example in the Cheops ship[5] of *c*.2600 BC, there is also considerable evidence in the Mediterranean of the use of stitching to join hull planks edge to edge. The Cheops ship in fact uses stitching for its hull fastenings, supplemented with mortice-and-tenon joints which in the case of the hull are not locked. However, the mortice-and-tenon joints used in the superstructure of this ship are locked. On the other hand, to use locked mortice-and-tenon joints in the

12 Depiction of liburnians on Trajan's Column. *Reproduced with permission from Lepper, F. and Frere, S., 1988,* Trajan's Column, *Sutton Publishing (Plate XXVI, Scene xxxiv-xxxv)*

hull planks would mean boring holes through the outside of the planks and increase the possibility of leaking. The holes in the planking for the stitching do not interfere with the watertight integrity of the hull, since they are cut in the form of V-shaped slots which do not penetrate the exterior of the hull planking. The stitching is required because unlocked mortice-and-tenon joints would not be adequate to hold the planking together.

McGrail records that there are no clear examples of Mediterranean ships which depend on stitching alone to fasten the hull planking; stitching is associated either with treenails or mortice-and-tenon fastenings. Examining 14 wrecks which offer adequate evidence for the purpose, he outlines a hypothesis for the evolution of fastenings in Mediterranean shipbuilding from the third millennium BC through to *c*.300 BC. In the initial phase, as exemplified by the Cheops ship, hulls would have been constructed with sewn planking; dowels or treenails might have been used between the planks; the frames would have been lashed to the hull. Some time in the second millennium BC locked mortice-and-tenon joints would have appeared, but with stitching retained for critical or difficult parts of the hull. This development would have started first in the Levant, but would have spread to the eastern and central Mediterranean by the first millennium BC. By the late first millennium BC the practice of building hulls with locked mortice-and-tenon fastenings joining the edge-to-edge planking and with metal fastenings (instead of lashing) securing the frames to the hull would have been wide spread throughout the Mediterranean.[6]

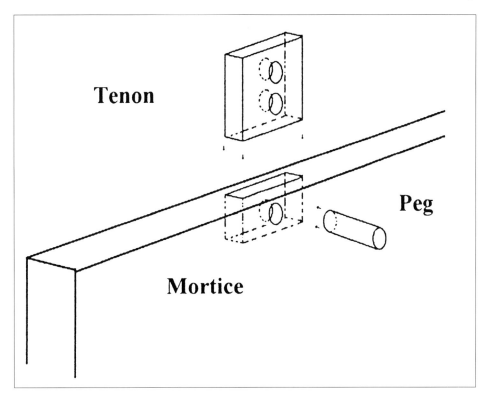

13 A locked mortice-and-tenon joint; once the tenons have been inserted into the mortices, the mortices of the next plank can be offered up. The peg finally driven in will lock up the joint

This evolution would have been driven by the inherent structural advantages of using locked mortice-and-tenon joints. These afford greater resistance than stitching, with or without dowels or treenails, to the shear forces[7] which occur, not only during launching and beaching, but also when at sea as the hull flexes in response to the waves. McGrail reports research by Coates that suggests that warships, having as they did long narrow hulls, could not have exceeded a displacement of 10 tons, if the hull was fastened only with stitching. This might have equated to the archaic *triacontor*. The demands for warships with structural integrity at higher ratings, particularly with the introduction of the ram as a naval weapon, would have led the way in the development of mortice-and-tenon building methods.

If this structural point is valid, it has an important implication for our understanding of the warships which Caesar had built on the Loire. It is possible, even probable, that they were smaller and less powerful than those which made up the fleet which Brutus is said to have brought from the Mediterranean. They may, as Dio suggests, have been especially adapted to local tidal conditions. This may conceivably imply that their structural strength enabled their hulls to stand up to the forces imposed on them by the Atlantic swell. But Caesar still calls them *naves longae*, not, for example, *scaphae* or *navigia speculatoria*. It is inconceivable that Caesar would have done so, if they were not equipped to do what warships were intended to do – engage in ramming attacks. From that it must follow that they can only have been built with the methods already perfected by Mediterranean shipwrights and known to be effective for the construction of warships.

Naves longae: *presence in north-west European waters*

The accounts of Caesar's invasions of Britain are not the only evidence of the presence of Mediterranean-style warships in north-west European waters in the Roman period. The presence of liburnians in the Roman fleet stationed on the west coast of Scotland in AD 83 is confirmed by an account by Tacitus of the mutiny that summer of an auxiliary cohort from a Germanic tribe, the Usipi. Murdering their centurions, they hijacked three liburnians, which they sailed round the north of Scotland, across the North Sea to arrive in a much weakened state on the Frisian coast, where they were treated as pirates. Such reports are supplemented by a few depictions on coins and other media, the find contexts of which suggest that they represent Roman warships as used in north-west European waters. A common feature of many of these depictions, like those from the Mediterranean, is that they show the warships being rowed. Whilst this might well be a conventional way of depicting a warship, it nevertheless is likely that this conventional image was underpinned by the reality that oars, particularly in battle, were the main means of propulsion of warships and that sail was secondary.

Perhaps the most dramatic, and certainly relevant to any account of the Roman invasions of Britain, is a magnificent gold medallion found at Arras, struck in Trier to commemorate the arrival of Constantius Chlorus in London after the defeat in AD 296 of the pseudo-*Augustus*, Allectus, the successor to Carausius. Bearing the inscription *REDDITOR LUCIS AETERNAE* (restorer of the eternal light), it shows Constantius on horseback receiving the homage of a kneeling figure representing London. Below the figure of Constantius is a depiction of a warship (*colour plate* 7). The bow is armed with a ram and above the bow is a feature which appears to be a figurehead; the stern is adorned with an *aplustre*, a curved decorated feature characteristic of Graeco-Roman ships. The vessel is being rowed and four over-sized oarsmen are depicted; such exaggeration of the scale of human figures in ancient iconography is quite normal, though it does present problems of interpretation. In the same way the number of people depicted is not to be taken at face value. There are eight oars shown on the visible, starboard, side organised in two tiers. The upper tier of oars seems to be pivoted through a cross-braced open-work gunwale, similar to those visible on the representations of warships on Trajan's column in Rome (*12*). The image shows no indication that the ship could be rigged for sailing. We may, however, suppose that the mast has been lowered and possibly left ashore with the sails and rigging. This would have been normal when a fleet was cleared for action. All in all, there appear to be significant similarities with the warships depicted on Trajan's Column and we can reasonably conclude that the warship depicted on the Arras Medallion is a liburnian.

Coins of both Carausius and of Allectus also depict warships (*colour plates 8* and *9*). Both display decorative features at the stem and stern and certainly in the case of the coin of Allectus it is possible to discern a ram. Both vessels are being rowed and again in the case of the representation on the coin of Allectus one can see something akin to the cross-braced openwork at the top of the hull, which figures on the Arras Medallion and on the warships on Trajan's Column. On the rather less well defined image on the denarius of Carausius, it is possible to discern the heads of four oarsmen and five pairs of oars, which may well represent two levels of oars. This may lead one to wonder whether this is yet again an image of the ubiquitous liburnian, although the top of the hull shows no detail corresponding to the openwork of the images of the liburnians on Trajan's Column. There is less certainty about the rating of the warship on Allectus's quinarius. It shows a single tier of oars, which emerge, like the lower tier of oars in the liburnians of Trajan's Column, from beneath the openwork panel. On that basis it is no liburnian.

The County Hall ship

There is one wreck displaying Mediterranean construction techniques found in Britain. This is the County Hall ship, discovered in 1910, when the County Hall on the south bank of the Thames in London was being built as the headquarters of the former London County Council. A dendrochronological study places the construction of this vessel some time after AD 285 using timber felled in south-east England. The associated evidence of four coins, the latest of which is a coin of Allectus, means that the loss of the ship must have occurred after his accession in AD 293. Peter Marsden puts the loss of the ship at soon after AD 300. When it was originally reported it was hailed as one of Allectus's warships, destroyed by Constantius's fleet as it attempted to escape from London in AD 296. Although this may be possible, the surviving evidence scarcely justifies so bold a claim.[8]

Although the use in the construction of this ship of mortice-and-tenon plank fastenings makes it clear that the shipwright was trained in Mediterranean methods, much about the vessel remains uncertain. Marsden's reconstruction of the hull cross-section gives a decked hull which appears to rule out the possibility that this was an oared ship. There is, he considers, some slight evidence for the location of the mast step – a gap in the frames – which coincides with the mid point of his chosen reconstruction of the length of the ship. It is this matter of the overall length of the ship which is the most uncertain aspect of his reconstruction. While sufficient of the side planking and timbers have survived to allow a reasonably confident estimate of the overall beam at just over 5m with a depth of 1.55m, neither end of the original ship survives. Assuming that the ship was symmetrical fore and aft, and that the widest part of the surviving hull was amidships, the overall length would have been 26m. Marsden rejects this as creating a ratio of the beam to the length at the turn of the bilge of 1:8.5, which he considers excessive. He opts for what he sees as a more reasonable length of 19.1m, which can incorporate into a reconstruction of the hull as a whole all the known features of the ship. However, this gives the plan view of the hull a distinctly pear-shaped look, with the maximum beam approximately two-thirds from one end.

In addition to the absence of evidence for fittings for rowing, there is another aspect of the reconstructed hull which, in my view, bears on the interpretation of the County Hall ship as a warship. It is that the plan view of the reconstructed hull does not feature the straight sides which might be expected to be characteristic of oared warships. A case in point is John Coates's reconstruction of a light 50-oared liburnian of the first and second centuries AD. This at 18m on the waterline might be broadly comparable in size to the County Hall ship, although the beam of the County Hall ship is somewhat greater. However, there is an exception to this tendency to straight sides in oared warships. It is those craft whose oarcrew, rather than consisting of so many whole files of rowers, includes on each side half a file stationed towards the middle of the ship. Such a category of ship is the *hemiolia* with one and a half files of oarsmen each side. Coates's reconstruction of a 50-oared *hemiolia* would be 21m on the waterline and would display, in plan view, much the same curved sides as would the County Hall ship reconstructed to a length overall of 26m. The ratio of the beam on the waterline to the waterline length of Coates's reconstruction of the *hemiolia* is 1:7.0. Given that the beam on the waterline would normally be greater than the beam at the turn of the bilge, this is sufficiently close to the beam-to-length ratio at the turn of the bilge of 1:8.5 to suggest that Marsden's rejection of it is questionable.[9]

Could the County Hall ship have been an oared warship? Marsden's reconstruction of the wreck as a decked ship turns on the evidence for thwarts running from beam to beam and for stanchions to support them. He rejects the interpretation of these thwarts as rowing benches on the grounds of their height above the lowest frames (1.3m). One might question the grounds for this conclusion and suggest that a height of 1.3m between the bottom of the hold and the underside of the deck is remarkably low.

As it is, it is impossible to be confident about any interpretation of the function of the County Hall ship. Marsden points out that, among Mediterranean wrecks of freighters of this period, none are really comparable, whether in terms of her elongated plan view, her framing pattern or her use of stringers with mortice holes. This and the fact that the other Mediterranean-style ships found north of the Alps were all associated with forts leads him to doubt the possibility that she was a cargo ship. He settles for the possibility that she may have had some form of official function, maybe linked to the restoration of imperial rule after AD 296. However, for him, and for us, the ship remains an enigma. The possibility that we are looking at a Mediterranean-style warship built in Britain cannot be entirely ruled out.

A new design of warship?

What is striking about the two coins of Carausius and Allectus is that, unlike the image on the Arras Medallion and indeed many other ancient images of warships, both show them rigged with a single centrally stepped mast, but without sail or yard. The inference may perhaps be that the mast cannot be lowered on these vessels.

Marsden sees the coins of Carausius and of Allectus as marking a clear break from earlier depictions of warships, largely from Mediterranean contexts, dating to the first and second centuries and even the early third century AD. These typically show an *artemon*, a bowsprit-like feature from which a square foresail could have been rigged, but do not show a main mast. Marsden considers that they offer a rather 'sleeker' profile than the rounded images of the later depictions. He offers two possible explanations for this change in the representation of warships, which he dates to the course of the third century: a decline in artistic standards; or a significant change in warship design. These two explanations are of course not mutually exclusive and C.E. Dove in a study of the coins of Carausius and Allectus, whilst accepting that some displayed 'slovenly' standards of artistic competence, claimed that others, notably Allectus's later coins, portrayed 'a recognisable and seaworthy vessel'. Seen in the light of this analysis, the image on Carausius's silver denarius (*colour plate 8*) might well be accepted as slovenly, while that on Allectus's billon quinarius (*colour plate 9*) might be considered more realistic. Dove develops his argument to propose that this more realistic image represents a new design of warship more suited to local conditions and the strategic needs of the defence of the 'Saxon Shore' against the inroads of the Germanic pirates. Because of the impracticability of keeping fleets of liburnians continually at sea, the coast would be patrolled by a new type of scout vessel. These scout vessels would have been built in a local shipbuilding tradition, which Dove believes to have been that of the Celtic skin-covered boats which survives today in the form of the Irish *curragh*.[10]

The idea that a new design of warship emerged in northern waters in the late third century has gained credibility from the recovery at Mainz in 1981-2 of a number of wrecks which do indicate a significant departure on the part of the Romans in the design of warships intended for use at least on the Rhine/Danube frontier, if not in British waters (*colour plate 11*). Of the two types identified, Mainz A is a new type of light warship about 21m long with an oarcrew of 30. The wrecks are dated to the fourth century AD, but citing the evidence of coins of Postumus, on which he identifies an image of the new warships, Höckmann dates their appearance to *c.*260.[11] What is significant is that for these warships the well-tried Mediterranean practice of shell-first construction using locked mortice-and-tenon plank fastenings was abandoned in favour of a different, possibly local, method of construction, which involved fastening the edge-to-edge planking to floor and side frames with clenched iron nails.[12] This is, therefore, not Dove's skin-covered style of construction. Höckmann identifies these ships as *lusoriae*, but John Haywood, doubting whether the *lusoria* designated a specific ship type, has argued that the Mainz A ships fit the description of Vegetius's *scafae exploratoriae*. Following Dove, he interprets Vegetius as specifically associating this class of vessel with Britain. He also suggests that depictions of the Mainz A ships feature on the coins of Carausius and Allectus.[13]

Haywood's hypothesis to a large extent follows on from Dove's. It is that, after two centuries of naval operations in the north with triremes and liburnians, the Romans abandoned Mediterranean-style warships for a new design more suited to local conditions and new threats. The old warships, he believes, were not very manoeuvrable in river channels, nor very seaworthy in the open waters of the Channel and North Sea. They were grossly expensive in terms of manpower, both to build and to operate. Moreover the challenge now came from raiding Germanic tribes in their 'light, fast, seaworthy ships'.

According to Haywood, the Romans' 'lumbering' liburnians would have been unable to cope with these raids. He accepts that, once they had engaged the pirate ships, the liburnians would have been more than a match for them. The question for Haywood was the ability of the liburnians to bring them to battle in the first place. He is quite correct to emphasise the difficulty of engaging an enemy fleet on the open sea. However, Haywood's assertion, for that is what it is, that liburnians 'would have had a very poor chance of catching the pirates' implies that they would have been slower and less handy than the new-style Mainz warships. Although he quotes Höckmann as suggesting that the Mainz warships might have been able to achieve rowing speeds of up to 6.5 knots, he does not mention that this is Höckmann's estimate of their sprint speed over the ground when travelling downstream. What counts in interceptions at sea is speed through the water. For this Höckmann's conclusions are rather different and he is quite explicit in his view that the new-style warships would have been slower through the water than the liburnians they replaced. In essence what Höckmann offers is something of a Dutch auction, starting with the calculation that an Athenian trireme was recorded as achieving an estimated speed of around 7.5 knots on passage from Piraeus to Mytilene in Lesbos. The circumstances of this passage were unusual and he suggests that the normal operational speed of a trireme would be 'scarcely more than 6 knots'. He then suggests that a two-tiered ship such as a liburnian could 'hardly have exceeded 5 knots'. On that basis he estimates the speed of a ship with a single tier of oars such as the Mainz A warships at about 4.5 knots. Whatever one thinks of Höckmann's broad-brush approach to the assessment of speed potential, it has the merit that it fits with the fact that the longer the waterline length of a hull, the greater its speed potential. Höckmann's conclusions are scarcely to be reconciled with a claim that the design of the new warships was a response to the need for greater speed to intercept raiding Germanic vessels in the Channel and southern North Sea.[14]

Haywood's doubts about the seaworthiness of liburnians in the waters of the Channel and the North Sea echo Dove's earlier claim that 'galleys are not good sea boats', but neither advances any evidence to support such doubts. Unfortunately this is a topic for which few objective data are available. Moreover, 'seaworthiness' is a complex subject and covers a wide range of desirable qualities. However, a key quality is transverse stability, i.e. the ability of the ship to resist capsize. Marsden's hydrostatic study of the reconstruction of the Mainz ships did include an assessment of their stability; he concluded that they would be stable and would be able to carry their estimated maximum load with a reasonably safe freeboard. At maximum load that freeboard would be less than half a metre, reasonable for river work, but a little less than might be desirable for an open boat on the open waters of the Channel and southern North Sea. In fact he states that the behaviour of the vessel while being rowed or sailed would 'depend largely on the seamanship of the men rather than on the stability of the vessel'.[15]

There is in fact no rational reason for believing that Mediterranean-style warships were inherently unsuited on grounds of seaworthiness to conditions in the Channel and North Sea, even if the local tidal regime does create a maritime environment different from that of the Mediterranean. Höckmann sees the new-style warships essentially as a response to new conditions on the riverine frontier of the Rhine and Danube, rather than to the need for a new sea-going design to intercept Germanic raiders at sea. Of course one advantage of the new warships was that they were cheaper to build and man. But the issue was the need for effective river patrols in the light of the greater threat of breaches of the Rhine/Danube frontier by Germanic tribes; with the smaller crews of the Mainz A ships, compared with those of the liburnians, the frequency of the patrols could be tripled.

There is some archaeological evidence that, even before the Mainz ships, light river patrol boats were in use on the Rhine and Danube. In 1986 two Roman ships built with the Mediterranean technique of shell-first construction with locked mortice-and-tenon joints were found at Ingolstadt, Germany, close to a small tributary of the Danube. Designated Oberstimm 1 and 2, they were equipped for both sailing and rowing with an oarcrew of 18–20. Reconstructed, the length overall is put at 15.7m with a beam of 2.7m and a depth of 1m. Their construction is dated to the end of the first century; oak piles driven through both hulls to revet the bank and dated to the beginning of the second century AD provide a *terminus post quem* for their going out of use.[16] Thus they would belong to the period when Domitian and Trajan were emperors and they may well have been in commission at the time that Trajan was waging the Dacian Wars. They are interpreted as military vessels, although their precise function is not certain, whether as troop ships, patrol vessels or as communication vessels between the Roman forts on the Danube. Perhaps they may have fulfilled all three functions, although their size would impose limitations on their usefulness as troop carriers. While to suggest that these vessels were involved in the Dacian wars would be to exceed the scope of the evidence, nevertheless they may provide an important clue as to the nature of the auxiliary craft used by the Romans in these campaigns.

The lower Rhine has also provided examples of the use of mortice-and-tenon joints in shipbuilding in the Roman period. The Vechten boat, originally discovered in 1893 and dated to the first century AD, was republished by Maarten de Weerd some 15 years ago. Smaller than the

Oberstimm boats with a reconstructed length of 12m, beam of 30m and depth of 1.5m, it too has been interpreted as a military vessel. The drawings published by de Weerd include rowing thwarts, though whether the vessel could also be sailed is not certain. Another vessel built in the Mediterranean style, also published by de Weerd, is Zwammerdam 2a; this is also interpreted as an oared military vessel. This is dated to the second/third century AD.[17]

Seen in the context of these earlier vessels, the originality of the Mainz ships could well be their adoption of local shipbuilding methods for an already existing class of river warship, rather than in their evolution to replace the sea-going liburnian. All in all the evidence, such as it is, for Roman-period warships in northern waters points to the deployment of Mediterranean-style vessels at least until the end of the third century AD. The Arras Medallion would be consistent with the presence of liburnians in Constantius's successful invasion of Britain in 296, while the contemporary County Hall Ship demonstrates that mortice-and-tenon methods of construction were still in use in Britain at that time. On the other hand the Mainz ships demonstrate the adoption at about the same time of a new design using local methods of construction. Höckmann's proposal, that they were a response to the changing defence needs in the riverine context of the Rhine/Danube frontier, is based on a well argued analysis of those needs and of the capabilities of the new ships. The attempt by Haywood to extend that hypothesis to the use of the new design in the defence of the 'Saxon Shore' depends on unjustified assertions about the sluggishness and unseaworthiness of liburnians. Once one discounts such assertions the evidence for a new-style of warship in British waters in the late third century rests on Marsden's perception of a change in the iconography of the coins of Carausius and Allectus. In his earlier attempt to interpret that iconography as representing a new design of hide-covered warships, Dove did confess to 'an element of toga-trailing'.

Naves longae: *performance*

Classical sources suggest that under oars Greek triremes were very fast indeed and faster than under sail. Morrison examines a number of passages recorded by Greek authors which appear to point to sustained speeds under oar in the range of 7.0 to 7.5 knots. In fact in one case, that of the statement by Xenophon that the passage from Byzantium to Heraclea – 129 nautical miles – was 'a long day's voyage for a trireme under oar', he concludes that this might indicate an average speed as high as 8.6 knots for the passage. The basis of this estimate is a 17-hour day including a 2-hour lunch break. He notes that marginal changes in his assumptions about the length of the day and, in particular, about the length of the lunch break could have a significant effect on his estimate of the average speed, bringing it to as little as 7 knots.[18]

Moreover, the context of Xenophon's remark – it is no more than that – suggests that it should not be given undue weight. He is narrating the return home of the Greek army in 400-399 BC along the Black Sea coast of Turkey from their campaign in Persia with Cyrus, a campaign in which Xenophon had played a leading role. By various routes, some in ships following the coast, others overland, they have reached a place on the coast known as Calpe Harbour. Calpe is midway between Byzantium and Heraclea; in his description Xenophon contrasts its advantages as a natural and uninhabited harbour with the fact that the whole coast between Heraclea, a Greek colony, and Byzantium was inhabited by Bithynian Thracians who 'are said to abuse outrageously any Greeks they may find shipwrecked or may capture in any other way'. What Xenophon seems to be saying is that on this very long haul along a hostile coast between Byzantium and Heraclea, where there was 'no city, either friendly or Greek' to turn to in case of need, Calpe Harbour might be a useful refuge. Such a refuge was absolutely critical for oared warships; the crews had to come ashore each night to eat and bivouac. The precise length of time needed for a direct passage by trireme between Byzantium and Heraclea is irrelevant to the point and Xenophon may not have known it.

A more persuasive case examined by Morrison, drawing on an actual voyage reported by Thucydides, occurred in 427 BC when, after the suppression of a rebellion in Lesbos, the Athenian Assembly ordered that the rebels should be put to death. The next day they revoked this decision, but a trireme had already been sent to Mytilene in Lesbos ordering the Athenian commander to carry out the sentence. A second trireme was sent and the Mytilenian representatives in Athens promised the crew great rewards if it arrived first. Thucydides reports that on passage the crew of the second ship did not stop for meals and that during the night they took turns to sleep, some sleeping while the rest continued rowing. The second ship did not overtake the first, but did arrive in time to prevent the executions.

The distance between Piraeus (the port of Athens) and Mytilene is about 184 nautical miles. Thucydides does not give any precise timings for the voyage of either ship, but it is clear from his account that the first trireme arrived on the third day after the original decree of the Assembly and the second arrived only shortly afterwards. On this basis the passage of the first ship, including breaks for meals and an overnight bivouac ashore, might have taken in the order of 48 hours and that of the second 24 hours. This would give the second ship an average speed close to 7.7 knots. Of course, one might suppose that this second voyage lasted as long as 30 hours, which would return an average of just over 6 knots. However, the second ship cannot have left much before midday. Before its departure, the Assembly had to meet and reach its decision, the crew had to be mustered and the ship victualled (Thucydides reports that the Mytilenian representatives, in addition to their promises of rewards, provided wine and barley bread for the crew). Its arrival in Mytilene was sufficiently early in the day to prevent the massacre just as it was about to start. All in all a passage time in the order of 24 hours seems likely.

Another case, remarkable because it involved a fleet, is that of the passage in 411 BC of 73 ships from Chios to Rhoeteum on the Hellespont under the Spartan admiral Mindarus in a direct challenge to the Athenians during the Peloponnesian War. For a variety of reasons, but largely because the commander will wish to keep his fleet in an orderly formation and will adjust the fleet speed to do so, fleets will travel more slowly than the individual ships comprising it would under similar conditions. Mindarus's passage took two days and followed the highly indented coastline of Western Turkey. The crews stopped for a midday meal and to bivouac overnight. Overall the length of the coastline route is some 190 nautical miles. Morrison estimates that the larger part of the passage was completed on the second day, some 124 nautical miles and, from the detail given by Thucydides, he concludes that the passage time would have been some 18 hours, giving an average speed of 6.9 knots. However the validity of this assessment does depend significantly on the assumption that the fleet followed the coastline closely; it would have been possible significantly to reduce the length of the passage on the second day – and on the first – by cutting across the large bays which are a feature of this coastline.[19]

All in all, drawing on the cases he examines, Morrison's conclusion is: 'It looks as if 8 knots was a possible average speed for an oared warship in a hurry, but that the normal speed was less'.[20] Sea trials of the replica Athenian trireme, *Olympias*, were carried out in 1987, 1988, 1990, 1992 and 1994. They certainly confirm the manoeuvrability of the trireme. Entering a turn at 6.1 knots with one side rowing she was turned through 360° in 62m (1.9 ship lengths); with both sides rowing and starting the turn at 7 knots, her turning circle was 110m (3.4 lengths). Morrison remarks that these figures are comparable with modern warships. Under sail her performance was also impressive. She was found to be safe and easy to control; her tendency to weather helm could be controlled by brailing up part of the main sail. Running before the wind she rolled up to 12°, a characteristic found in most sailing ships. On the wind she was stiff in the seaman's sense of the term, of being able to stand up to her canvas. She was sailed to within 65° of the apparent wind, with 5° to 7° of leeway; this equates to a track made good against the true wind of 85°. It is considered that the ship could probably be sailed as close as 60° to the apparent wind, but a polar diagram published by John Coates and his colleagues shows that, closer than 85° of the true wind, water speed fell off sharply. Speeds under sail clearly varied with the strength of the wind and the point of sailing, best results being recorded with the wind astern or on the quarter. In following and quartering winds of about 15 knots, speeds over 7 knots were recorded. In 1992 a gust of 20 knots in a following wind produced the highest speed recorded in the trials of 10.8 knots.[21]

Speeds recorded under oar did not match those expected in the light of the documentary sources, though as the trials proceeded from year to year they did improve. Best sustained short-distance speeds ranged from 5.67 knots in 1987 to 7 knots in 1992, with peak bursts of 6.95 knots and 8.9 knots. However, passage trials returned best figures ranging between 5.4 knots in 1990 and 5.77 knots in 1992. The last figure was achieved with a depleted crew of 154 out of 170 rowers and it is considered that a full crew might have reached an average as high as 6 knots. Even so it is nowhere near the averages suggested by the ancient sources. Morrison identifies two reasons for this discrepancy. First, the trials showed up inadequacies in the design of the reconstructed rowing system. In particular the space available to the oarsmen restricted their ability to take a full stroke. The design of the replica had been based on ancient documentary evidence that the *interscalmium* (the unit of length between one tholepin and the next fore or aft) was two cubits. Among the many values of the cubit known from the ancient Greek world, the value current in fifth- and fourth-century Athens of 0.444m was adopted, giving an *interscalmium* of 0.888m. In 1990 archaeological evidence came to light for the continued currency at this period of an archaic cubit 0.49m, which points to an *interscalmium* of nearly 1.0m. Based on this evidence, modifications to the rowing system have been designed which it is hoped would enable rowers to pull at maximum efficiency. However, it would not be practicable to incorporate these modifications into the existing hull and testing their effectiveness must await the commissioning of a new replica.

The other factor which has been advanced to account for the discrepancy is that modern oarcrews simply are not ancient Greek rowers. In the modern context it is not possible for crews to be kept together and to work together long enough to achieve the standards of performance and stamina, which are evidenced by ancient accounts. The sources make it clear that pulling an oar in a trireme was a specialist activity and that the required skill and stamina came only after long training.

Finally it must be pointed out that windage was a significant factor in performance, both under sail and oars, the large stern feature virtually acting as an air brake. The best passage speed under oars of 5.4 knots in 1990 was achieved with a 20-knot following wind over a 14-nautical-mile-leg on a passage from Poros to Nafplion. On the return voyage into a strengthening head wind the average dropped to 4.6 knots over a 31-mile leg. On another occasion, with a head wind gusting to 20 knots, speed is reported to have dropped to 0.5 knots. Morrison states:

> It was very clear that, with the whole crew rowing into a strong wind, there was a limited amount of time before exhaustion would set in and the ship would be in danger, especially off a lee shore. The conservation of the human engine of oared warships is a factor of ancient seafaring almost entirely ignored by present-day historians, although it was obvious enough to Herodotus when he wrote about the state of the Persian fleet at Salamis.

Naves longae: *crews and training*

The most significant element in the complement of the ancient warship was the oarcrew. In the very largest ships the numbers of oarsmen would have been quite staggering For the 40-file leviathan built for Ptolemy IV more than 4000 oarsmen were recorded as required for her trial, together with a deck crew of 400 and 2,850 soldiers, together with an unspecified, but large, number of stewards.

At a more realistic level the oarcrew of Athenian triremes is well documented in Athenian records as numbering 170. For warships of other ratings, estimation of the size of the oarcrew is more a matter of detective work which inevitably must leave a measure of uncertainty. Basing his assessment on a first-century BC/first-century AD graffito which, uniquely among images of ancient ships, is labelled by the artist as to its rating (it is a four), Morrison estimates that it would have been powered by a total of 88 oars, configured in two tiers on each side. This, since there were two men to each oar, gives a total oarcrew of 176 (*14*). The fives in the Roman fleet at the Battle of Eknomos in 258 BC in the first Carthaginian War were recorded as having oarcrews numbering 300, while the flagship of Pleistarchos, a six, lost in a storm in the Black Sea in 302 BC was said to have had a ship's complement of not less than 500. After making allowances for deck crew and marines, Morrison suggests for this six an oarcrew of 360.[22]

With the exception of the well-attested case of the Athenian trireme, there must be some degree of imprecision about these figures; in particular, there can be no assurance that these were standard figures for the oarcrews for specific classes of warship throughout the classical period. Even so, bearing in mind that there would be structural limits to the length of the ship, which would have been why ships with multiple files of oarsmen evolved anyway, the figures given may be taken as a reasonable indication of the order of the increasing size of the oarcrew as the number of files of rowers increased.

Apart from the oarcrews, ancient warships also carried officers, deck hands and marines. Again for the Athenian trireme these are documented with some precision in Athenian records. Alongside the trierarch, or commander, the officers were the helmsman, the rowing master and the bow officer, together with a purser, shipwright and piper. Deck hands were organised in two groups of five, one working forward and the other aft. There were ten marines, together with four archers. This gives a total complement for an Athenian trireme of 200 men plus the trierarch. Morrison suggests that the role of the archers was to sit beside the trierarch and the helmsman as their bodyguard. For the Athenians the main objective in a naval battle was to disable enemy ships by ramming them; the number of marines was therefore kept to a minimum and their function was to defend the ship if, after a ramming attack, she was unable to back off. However, as with the evolution of ships and of tactics, grappling and boarding became more important, so the number of marines carried grew. For example, in the case of the Rhodian navy, operating fours as their capital ships from the third to the first centuries BC, the total number besides the oarcrew had grown to 45, including some twenty-eight marines, six of them archers and two catapult men. The number of fighting men on fives and sixes was even larger. We have already noted that oarcrews numbering 300 were recorded on board the Roman fives at the Battle of Eknomos; this was together with 120 other personnel recorded, of which Morrison suggests 80 might have been the military complement. As for the six of Pleistarchos, wrecked in the Black Sea, for which we noted an oarcrew estimated at 360, a total complement of not less than 500 was reported, of which 90 or 100 might have been military personnel. Apart from an increase in the number of marines, other specialist officers also began to appear in ships from the Rhodian navy onwards, including the ship's doctor and the masseur – possibly better described as the team physiotherapist!

For their warships the Romans grafted onto the command structure, common elsewhere, officers whose origins are to be found in the hierarchy

14 The Alba Fucens first-century BC/first-century AD graffito of a warship. The label *navis teteris longa* designates it as a four. Morrison assumes that the drawing is broadly to scale and on that basis calculates that the length of the rowing area indicated by the cross-braced openwork could accommodate 22 oars at each of two levels. *Notizie degli Scavi, 1953,* 120

of the legion. Thus while in the Roman navy one can find the equivalents of the trierarch, the helmsman, the rowing master and the bow officer, and even of the medic and the 'team physiotherapist', there operated alongside these a set of military ranks which created what was in essence a dual command structure. Each ship was in effect treated as a century in the Roman army and had in addition to the naval officer structure a military structure headed by a centurion and his subordinates. It seems that, while the maintenance and navigation of the ship fell to the naval hierarchy, the overall command of the military operation was the responsibility of the military.[23]

Training was critical, particularly of the oarcrews, for effectiveness in battle. The trials of *Olympias* demonstrated that even for present-day experienced rowers, rowing an ancient warship presented massive challenges in achieving a coordinated stroke. A particular problem was that the oarsmen at the two lower levels were, in effect, rowing blind, unable as they were to see the outboard end of their oars. It may well be that in battle the upper file too suffered the same handicap; screens would have been erected to protect them from missile attack. In battle it was the normal technique to reverse away immediately after ramming an enemy vessel; to achieve this, the oarcrew had to reverse their stroke together. Experience with *Olympias* suggested that reversing might best be achieved if the whole oarcrew turned round and started rowing with the oar of the man behind him. However, timing would be everything; an ill-timed order could have half of the oarcrew falling over with the impact of the collision.

In battle the ability to ship oars smartly would also be critical. On occasions ships would attempt to disable each other by passing close and breaking the oars on one side. To be effective such a manoeuvre would require the oarsmen on the engaged side of the attacking vessel to ship oars just before impact; the defensive response would also be to ship oars at the critical moment. All such manoeuvres would have required well drilled crews who knew what they were about. Julius Caesar had the oarsmen summoned from Provence for his campaign against the Veneti trained during the winter of 57/56 BC.[24] Initial training may well have taken place on dry land, while the new warships required for the campaign were being built. Such at least was the method adopted for training new crews by the Romans for the first Carthaginian War and by Agrippa as naval commander for Octavian in the Civil War. The technique was to employ a mock up of the oar system. Sitting as they would at their oar benches, the crew were drilled to respond to the commands of the rowing master. This would have been followed by rowing exercises at sea, practising manoeuvres and perhaps competing in rowing matches.

Naves longae: *maintenance*

On landing in Britain in 55 BC Caesar had his warships hauled ashore and left his transports at anchor. Four days later a violent storm, which was associated with a tidal surge, damaged many of the transports and swamped the beached warships. The next year he left both warships and transports at anchor; however, he later had the whole fleet hauled ashore. The reason for beaching the ships in 54 BC is clear from Caesar's account. Once again that year a storm had struck the fleet at anchor, wrecking 40 vessels and damaging most of the rest. They were brought ashore for protection, both from the weather and perhaps – given the mention of a fortification – from attacks by the Britons. But why were the warships, and only the warships, hauled ashore in 55 BC?

Ancient practice appears to have been to bring warships ashore in the winter and to keep them under cover and it would have been during this period that general maintenance was carried out. In fact the sea was generally regarded as closed during the winter months. However, there are records of warships being hauled ashore during campaigns. While this might be to carry out repairs, it seems that one particular reason for beaching warships was to let them dry out. The Athenians in particular distinguished between 'fast' triremes and others and one factor in that distinction is said to be that regular drying out was required to maintain maximum performance.[25] When Caesar brought his warships ashore in 55 BC, it could have been to protect them from excesses of the weather at an anchorage with which he (and his mariners) were unfamiliar. It might equally be as the result of normal practice to keep the warships as dry as possible.

Naves longae: *conclusion*

The British tribesmen opposing Caesar's landing in 55 BC had seen nothing like the warships which were part of his invasion fleet. They were highly sophisticated oared warships, which had evolved in the Mediterranean over five or more centuries, in which oar systems had developed to maximise the size of the oarcrew. Their normal method of attack was by ramming, but over time the numbers of deck soldiers carried had increased as the importance of using missiles had grown, with the increasingly practical option of boarding attacks. There is good evidence that such vessels continued to be used in British waters at least until the end of the third century AD. Even though the sources are silent on the make up of Claudius's invasion fleet of AD 43 we may be reasonably sure that it included Mediterranean-style warships. Certainly in the late first century AD Agricola, the Roman governor of Britain, deployed his fleet in support of his campaigns in Scotland and from the incident of the three hijacked liburnians we know that it included Mediterranean-style warships.

By the end of the third century a new style of warship, exemplified by the Mainz ships, constructed in a local shipbuilding tradition, had emerged on the Rhine/Danube frontier. Höckmann has plausibly argued that this new design was a response to the need to provide effective river patrols in defence of the frontier against Germanic incursions. The argument that these ships were also used as part of the Saxon Shore defensive system along the coastline of northern Gaul and eastern Britain, which dates to about the same time, is much less persuasive. Both Carausius and after him Allectus issued coins with depictions of warships. While some of these coins, notably those of Carausius, are of a poor artistic standard and difficult to interpret, others, such as Allectus's billon quinarius, offer a more realistic representation. Whether the image on these latter coins represents a new design of warship, or simply a new conventionalisation of the way warships were to be depicted, must remain an open question – at least until relevant archaeological evidence from a maritime, as opposed to a river, context is brought forward. Whatever ships were deployed by Carausius and Allectus in the defence of the Saxon Shore, the Arras medallion seems to make it clear that the warships in Constantius's invasion fleets were traditional Mediterranean-style warships.

4

SUPPLY SHIPS – TROOP SHIPS

Naves onerariae

Formidable fighting machines though they were – engaging in battles which swung the destinies of empires, from Salamis of 480 BC, which ended the ambitions of Xerxes, ruler of the Persian Empire, to Actium, which in 31 BC settled the struggle between Augustus and Antony for the mastery of the Roman world – the ancient oared warships of the Mediterranean suffered from one major disadvantage: they could not operate independently, either of the shore or of support ships. Because their hulls were crammed with rowing benches, with little room for anything else and certainly with no sleeping accommodation, their crews had to come ashore each night to feed and to bivouac. Moreover, the room on board limited the amount of food and water that could be carried and crews had to rely on the willingness of the local inhabitants for supplies. Alternatively warship crews could rely on supply ships, which were either towed or made their own way under sail.

Supply ships were also needed for major invasion operations such as those of Julius Caesar and Claudius against Britain. Oared warships simply did not meet the requirement to transport the large numbers of troops and the substantial amounts of equipment needed for an invasion campaign. In his account of his expeditions to Britain Caesar clearly sets out the role of the *naves onerariae* or transports, as being distinct from that of his warships. For his first campaign he requisitioned transport ships from the neighbouring coasts and allocated them to the legions and to the cavalry, while the warships he had had built for the Venetic campaign were allocated to staff officers. On arrival at the beachhead it was the warships which were deployed to bring covering fire to support the legionaries disembarking from the transports. When the landing was complete, he ordered the warships to be hauled ashore, while the transports were left at anchor. For the campaign the following year he ordered the construction of new warships and transports to supplement his existing fleet. The new transports were built to a modified design to be more suited to local conditions and to the conveyance of draught animals and heavy equipment.

It is Caesar's description of his requirements for these new transports that gives us our first glimpse of Roman transport ships in northern waters:

> He set forth the plan and pattern of the new ships. For speed of loading and for purposes of beaching he would build them somewhat lower than those which we are accustomed to see on our own sea – the more so because he had learnt that by reason of the frequent turns of the tides the waves off Gaul were generally smaller. For the transport of cargo, and of the numerous draught animals, he would have the ships somewhat broader than those we use on the other seas. All of them he ordered to be fitted for oars as well as sails, to which end their lowness of build helped much.

The point about the oars is significant as the implication is that the transports which he had requisitioned from the Gauls for his first expedition were sailing ships. Moreover the oars turned out to be a very useful modification: during the crossing to Britain in 54 BC the fleet was becalmed and the legionaries had to take up the oars to reach the coast.

We have another account of supply ships built for an expedition in north European waters, this time that of Germanicus's ill-fated naval expedition from the Rhine to the Ems in AD 15. Tacitus described the construction of the ships:

> A thousand vessels were considered enough, and these were built at speed. Some were short craft with very little poop or prow, and broad-bellied, the more easily to withstand a heavy sea: others had flat bottoms, enabling them to run aground without damage; while still more were fitted with rudders at each end, so as to head either way the moment the oarsmen reversed their stroke. Many had a deck-flooring to carry the military engines though they were equally useful for transporting horses or supplies. The whole armada, equipped at once for sailing or propulsion by oar, was a striking and formidable spectacle, rendered still more so by the enthusiasm of the soldiers.[1]

It is possible to discern in Tacitus's account three or possibly four types of ship, although it must be said that it would not be inconsistent for the features he mentions to be incorporated into a single ship; a 'broad-bellied' craft could well be built with a 'flat bottom' and be fitted with the 'deck-flooring' required to transport 'military engines'. It is possible that all the ships, rather than just some of the fleet, were been fitted with two rudders, not at each end, but on each quarter, since that appears to have been normal practice at the time. What is clear from this passage is that the design of ships was dictated both by their role as military supply ships and by the needs of the local maritime environment. Their profile was designed to withstand heavy seas and they could take the ground without damage. Like Caesar's modified transport ships 70 years earlier, they could be propelled both by sail and by oar.

Although both Caesar and Germanicus had set ideas as to what they required of their supply ships, it is hardly likely that they would have created a wholly new shipbuilding tradition. In essence a shipbuilding tradition may be defined as a set of visual concepts, skills and technologies shared by boat-builders, evolving as it is passed on from one generation to the next, like any other cultural element of human society. While such traditions will normally find their expression in craft which have a close resemblance to one another, that does not preclude the possibility of using the resources of the tradition to build specialist craft. Thus when Caesar and Germanicus had set out their requirements for their supply ships, we may envisage that their shipwrights drew on and modified the techniques of their shipbuilding tradition to achieve the required results, rather than seeking a new solution to every construction problem that arose.

So, a key question is: which tradition was exploited to build the supply ships which the Romans would have used in their military campaigns in north-west Europe? There are, it would seem, three possibilities. First, they could, like the warships, have been built on the Mediterranean pattern, shell-first with the characteristic edge-to-edge planking fastened with mortice-and-tenon joints. Second, they might have been built with hulls fashioned from hides over a wooden or wicker framework. Such vessels are attested in the British Isles in the Roman period and survive today in the form of the Irish *curragh* and the Welsh coracle. Thirdly, they might well have been built in the wooden shipbuilding tradition which maritime archaeologists have designated the Romano-Celtic tradition.

Naves onerariae: *the Mediterranean tradition*

Excavation campaigns by maritime archaeologists in the Mediterranean over the past half-century have recovered a wide range of ancient wrecks of cargo ships. The typical method of construction was the same as that used for the ancient Mediterranean warships which we described in Chapter 3 – shell-first with the hull made up of planks laid edge to edge and secured with locked mortice-and-tenon joints, with the framing timbers inserted subsequently.[2]

Although the basic techniques of construction were the same, these cargo ships had evolved into specialist craft to meet the needs of the burgeoning trade across the Mediterranean. The shipwrights focused on producing vessels which had a good cargo-carrying capacity, resulting in broad beamy craft, which could be handled with a minimum crew. The wreck recovered off Kyrenia, Cyprus, and dated to *c.*300 BC is that of a trading coaster around 15m long with an estimated cargo capacity of 30 tons; from this ship the excavators recovered cups and other personal utensils in sets of four, suggesting a crew of four. In the scale of things the Kyrenia ship was very small and much bigger vessels are recorded; according to Lionel Casson, from the fifth century BC merchant vessels with a cargo capacity of 100 to 150 tons burden were normal, while freighters of up to 500 tons were not uncommon. By the end of the second century AD the Roman imperial government was encouraging the building of freighters of a minimum size by granting exemptions from compulsory public service to owners of vessels with a burden in excess of some 340 tons. Moreover, as the need grew of the imperial authorities to bring to Rome huge quantities of grain to feed the citizenry, even larger ships are recorded with a capacity in excess of 1,000 tons. One such mega grain ship, the *Isis*, was described by a second-century AD eyewitness as being 120 cubits (55m) long, with a beam of more than a quarter of that (13.75m plus) and a depth of 29 cubits (13.25m) from keel to deck. Casson estimated the cargo capacity of this ship as between 1,200 and 1,300 tons.[3]

Evidence of the means of propulsion of ancient ships rarely survives to be excavated. A wealth of ancient images, however, has survived to confirm that these ancient cargo ships were sailing ships, rather than rowing ships. This perhaps is what one would expect if the evidence of the Kyrenia ship is to be credited as pointing to minimum crews for cargo carriers. Except for the smallest ships, such as the Kyrenia ship, the normal rig consisted of two masts, a main mast and a smaller foremast, termed an *artemon*, stepped over the bows much like the bowsprit of late medieval and early modern-age sailing ships. The largest ships would have carried a third mast stepped aft, a mizzen. The characteristic sail was a square sail, although both the lateen and the spritsail are shown in the iconography of the classical period.

That Mediterranean-style supply ships accompanied Brutus's fleet on its passage in 56 BC from the Mediterranean to the Atlantic coast of Gaul in support of Caesar's campaign against the Veneti is possible, likely even, given the inability of the warships to operate for a prolonged period without re-supply. However, valid though such an assumption may be, there appears to be no documentary evidence to support it. Moreover, the archaeological evidence for the use of Mediterranean techniques in shipbuilding north of the Alps is scanty. As we saw in Chapter 3, this is limited to the County Hall ship, together with Oberstimm 1 and 2, Vechten and Zwammerdam 2a. None of these wrecks has been unequivocally identified as a cargo-carrier, the sort of vessel that might have been suited to operate as a supply ship to warships on active service or a military transport in major amphibious operation. Thus while some of the transports in Caesar's invasion fleets may have come from the Mediterranean in support of the warships of Brutus's fleet, there is no evidence that Mediterranean construction techniques were employed in the locally-built supply ships used by Caesar or any of his successors.

Naves onerariae: *the hide boat*

It is well established in documentary sources that, during the Roman period and earlier, quite large craft were used in British waters with hulls constructed from hides covering some form of wooden or wickerwork framework. In his encyclopaedic *Natural History*, Pliny the Elder quoted a writer of the third century BC, Timaeus, as reporting that Britons used sea-going ships 'made of withies covered with stitched leather'. Ultimately the source for Timaeus's report was a fourth-century BC Greek, Pytheas, who made a ground-breaking voyage from his home city of Marseilles to the British Isles and reported, among other things, on the trade in tin with Cornwall.

During the Roman Civil War, Julius Caesar records that he had built hide boats for a river crossing 'of the kind that his experience in Britain in previous years had taught him to make. The keels and first ribs were made of light timber, the rest of the hull was wattled and covered with hides'. One early medieval source, *The Voyage of St Brendan*, gives a remarkably detailed account of the way in which Irish monks built their hide boats:

> Brendan and his companions made a coracle, using iron tools. The ribs and frame were of wood, as is the custom in those parts, and the covering was tanned ox-hide stretched over oak bark. They greased all the seams on the outer surface of the skin with fat and stored away spare skins inside the coracle, together with forty days' supplies, fat for waterproofing the skins, tools and utensils. A mast, a sail, and various pieces of equipment for steering were fitted into the vessel; then Brendan commanded his brethren in the name of the Father, Son, and Holy Spirit to go aboard.[4]

Hide boats have been in use, not only in the British Isles in the Roman and early medieval periods, but also in many other regions of the world and down to the present day. They are best known today in the form of the kayak used in arctic waters and of the Irish *curragh* and the Welsh coracle, though modern versions of the last two have adopted waterproof cloth as a substitute for hide. Across the world, the regions where versions of hide boats have been reported include the Americas, Arabia, India and Siberia. Some scholars have seen in rock carvings found in Scandinavia evidence for the use of hide boats and go so far as to argue that the Nordic clinker-built hulls of the Viking age ultimately derive from these craft. No ancient hide boat has ever been found, no doubt because of the biodegradable nature of the materials of which they were constructed. Models and other representations of watercraft have been identified as hide boats, with varying degrees of confidence. Often, as in the case of the Scandinavian rock carvings, the interpretation can be no more than speculative. In other cases, such as that of the gold model from Broighter, now in the National Museum of Ireland, which McGrail suggests 'probably represents a sea-going hide boat', the identification may be more certain (*colour plate 12*). Perhaps the most convincing representation is Captain Thomas Phillips's seventeenth-century 'Draught of a Portable Vessel of Wicker, ordinarily used by the Wild Irish' (*15*).[5]

Hide boats were capable of being built in quite significant sizes. McGrail tabulates the range of dimensions reported for various types of hide boats: the maximum length overall for the 'boat-shaped *curach*' is shown as 7.6m, that of the *umiak/baidara* as generally 10.7m. The largest *umiak* ever recorded was *c.*18m. In that context the *curragh* in Captain Phillips's drawing must be at that limit. Scaling off the human figures shown in the drawing suggests a length overall for this vessel of 17m, possibly even 20m.[6] Hide boats would have offered significant advantages. They were light and relatively quick to build. While the hull could be easily holed, it could equally readily be repaired. However, at sea, this could be a major incident and might well lead to the loss of the ship, as Tim Severin and his crew learnt when their reconstruction of the *curragh* of St Brendan was holed by an ice floe in the North Atlantic. It was not until the next morning that Severin was able to locate the leak; two of his crewmen then had the excruciating task of sewing on a leather patch in a water temperature of zero degrees centigrade – from the outside of the hull![7]

Appropriate designs could carry considerable loads. Their very lightness meant that they were outstandingly buoyant, which would have improved their carrying capacity. While smaller inshore versions would have been intended for a few fishermen, with their gear and catch, the large *baidari* of Siberia could carry up to 20 men or ten tons of cargo and the largest of the Indian round boats carried 50 men or 40 bags of grain. These are likely to have been for relatively short river or inshore voyages. However, Pliny's report of the use of hide boats by the Britons confirms their use as sea-going carriers of tin; clearly economic amounts were being carried, perhaps several tons per vessel, though obviously the figure cannot be quantified. On his ocean voyage, St Brendan is said to have taken 17 monks with him and the need to make allowance for stores and living room suggests that his would have been one of the larger hide boats.

The fact that in his reconstructed *curragh* Severin was able – in two seasons – successfully to cross the Atlantic argues that the sea-keeping qualities of hide boats, at least in the larger versions, were not to be underestimated. In rowing tests of Severin's *curragh* quite good results were achieved, between 3 and 3 knots depending on the size of the oarcrew. Performance under sail, however, was unimpressive. The average day's run was 40 sea miles and a cruising speed of 2-3 knots was considered normal in winds of Force 3 to 4. On the wind she could not do better than make good a course at 90° to the true wind, largely because of leeway of 30°. Severin reports that to attempt to continue to reach across the wind in Force 6 and above was dangerous and that it was safer to turn downwind. While major modifications to her design might have improved her resistance to leeway, this would in all probability have involved anachronistic features such as leeboards.[8] Such performance results are not wholly out of keeping with what might be achieved by most ancient ship types, though some might do better. The ultimate disadvantage of the hide boat is that the hide contributes nothing to the structural strength of the hull. This imposes a practical limit – McGrail suggests that this might have been in the order of 18m – to the overall length attainable with this method of construction.

Naves onerariae: *the Romano-Celtic tradition*

In Book III of his account of his campaign in Gaul, Caesar compares the ships of the Veneti with his own warships:

> Not so the ships of the Gauls, for they were built and equipped in the following fashion. Their keels were considerably more flat than those of our own ships, that they might more easily weather shoals and ebb-tide. Their prows were very lofty, and their sterns were similarly adapted to meet the force of waves and storms. The ships were made entirely of oak, to endure any violence and buffeting. The cross-pieces were beams a foot thick, fastened with iron nails as thick as a thumb. The anchors were attached by iron chains instead of cables. Skins and pieces of leather finely finished were used instead of sails, either because the natives had no supply of flax and no knowledge of its use, or, more probably, because they thought that the mighty ocean-storms and hurricanes could not be ridden out, nor the mighty burden of their ships conveniently controlled, by means of sails. When our own fleet encountered these ships it proved its

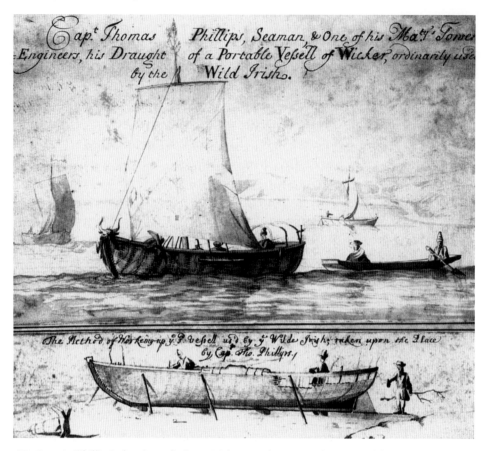

Capt Thomas Phillips, Seaman, & One of his Ma.^t.^s Tower Engineers, his Draught of a Portable Vessell of Wicker, ordinarily used by the Wild Irish.

The Method of Worke.ing.up y.^e Vessell us.'d by y.^e Wilde Irish; taken upon the Place by Cap. Tho. Phillips.

15 Captain Phillips's drawing of a large Irish curragh. *Pepys Library, Magdalene College, Cambridge*

superiority only in speed and oarsmanship; in all other respects, having regard to the locality and the force of the tempests, the others were more suitable and adaptable. For our ships could not damage them with the ram (they were so stoutly built), nor, by reason of their height, was it easy to hurl a pike, and for the same reason they were less readily gripped by grapnels. Moreover, when the wind began to rage and they ran before it, they endured the storm more easily, and rested in shoals more safely, with no fear of rocks or crags if left by the tide; whereas our own vessels could not but dread the possibility of all these chances.

This account is remarkably specific, especially in terms of the description of the underwater profile and the timbers and iron fastenings of the Venetic ships. Maritime archaeologists have seen this as a description of a style of shipbuilding which they have designated the Romano-Celtic tradition. The remains of ships and boats built in this tradition and dated to the Roman period have been found in London, at St Peter Port, Guernsey, South Wales, in the Netherlands and at various places along the Rhine, while Caesar's narrative suggests that the range of the type extended to the Atlantic coast of Gaul (*colour plate 13*).

The key features of ships of the Romano-Celtic tradition include a hull constructed of stout planks laid edge to edge and secured to very characteristic 'massive and closely spaced framing timbers' (*colour plate 14*). These frames are either asymmetric grown timbers spanning the bottom and one side of the hull, alternately port and starboard; as in craft excavated at Zwammerdam in the Netherlands, at Bevaix on Lake Neuchâtel in Switzerland and Krefeld-Gellep in Germany; or separate floor and side timbers, as in Blackfriars 1 (London) and St Peter Port 1 (Guernsey); or a combination of the two, as in the Barland's Farm Boat from South Wales (*colour plate 15*). The hulls are either flat-bottomed without a keel or with a central plank keel, thicker than the remaining planking.[9]

An important characteristic is that the planking was fastened to the framing timbers, not edge-joined, a feature which is shared by all representatives of the tradition and clearly marks them out from craft built in the Mediterranean tradition. During the Roman period the planking was secured exclusively by massive iron nails which passed through both frame and plank and were bent back on themselves so that the point was hammered back into the wood. The iron nails recovered, for example, from Blackfriars 1 are huge and are fully consistent with Caesar's 'iron nails as thick as a thumb'. Detlev Ellmers has argued that the introduction of such iron fastenings did not come about with the Roman occupation of Gaul, but with the establishment of the Celtic *oppida* culture in the second and first centuries BC. Caesar's observation confirms Ellmer's argument that such iron fastenings were in use in Celtic shipbuilding before the Romans came to Gaul.[10] In fact the use of iron fastenings may go back earlier. Béat Arnold proposes that iron fastenings for Romano-Celtic ship construction were in use earlier, although 'there are no examples of Iron Age boats assembled by nailing'. Evolving from Bronze Age craft, such as North Ferriby 1 and 2 and the Dover boat, he sees the shipbuilding methods north of the Alps gradually abandoning the use of stitching with transverse timbers through mortised cleats, in favour of the use of nailing with a strong framework to cross-brace the hull. As a parallel, he points to the use of turned and hooked iron nails to fix iron tyres to wooden wheels by the middle of the first millennium BC.[11]

Two sub-groups have been identified within the Romano-Celtic tradition, craft built for use on inland waterways and vessels intended for use in estuaries and the open sea. There are three, possibly four, excavated representatives of the sea-going sub-group – Blackfriars 1, St Peter Port 1 and the Barland's Farm Boat. The fourth is the Bruges boat, found in 1899, in which Peter Marsden sees close similarities with Blackfriars 1. It is of course with this sub-group that Caesar's description of the ships of the Veneti is to be associated.[12] The two sub-groups display marked differences in shape, perhaps the most obvious being the flat-bottomed box-like profile of the inland group and the fuller, more rounded section of the sea-going sub-group. Moreover, the Mainz warships which we looked at in Chapter 3 display constructional techniques which are consistent with the Romano-Celtic tradition; however, while these craft are clearly intended for river use, their rounded profile distinguishes them from other Romano-Celtic river finds. Possibly this is because of their military role. Recently, McGrail has questioned whether all these different ships and boats can legitimately be seen as representing a single tradition.[13]

Another significant feature of the Romano-Celtic tradition is that the single mast step was located in the forward part of the ship, at a marked distance forward of amidships. In Blackfriars 1 it is about one-third of the length of the vessel from its bow. This is also true of St Peter Port 1 and the Barland's Farm Boat (*colour plate 14*). Iconographic confirmation that this was a common feature of the Romano-Celtic tradition is given by a mosaic of *c*.AD 250 from Bad Kreuznach, which shows the mast stepped approximately one third back from the bow (*colour plate 16*). Masts stepped in a similar position are also a shared feature of Romano-Celtic inland craft, but these may be towing masts; this position is appropriate for a mast used for towing a vessel from a river bank. However, the masts on the sea-going ships were certainly used for setting sails, and it is not inconceivable that sails were also set on the masts of the inland sub-group, which may indeed have served the dual function of towing and sailing mast.

The position of the mast is noteworthy for any assessment of sailing performance, particularly windward ability, since it impacts on directional stability or hull balance. Hull balance manifests itself at the helm. When under way, a sailing ship has either weather helm, lee helm or neutral helm (*16*). When the helm is released, a vessel with weather helm will turn into the wind, while one with lee helm will turn downwind. A vessel with neutral helm will maintain its course when the helm is released. At least on fore-and-aft rigged vessels a modest amount of weather helm is generally considered desirable to give feel to the helm and in a sudden gust the ship will turn into the wind, thus reducing the pressure on the sail/s. Excessive weather helm can be tiring, while lee helm is considered dangerous, since in a blow the ship will tend to turn down wind with a consequent increase in wind pressure on the sail/s.

This could lead to a loss of control and in extreme conditions damage to the sail/s and rigging.

However, work with reconstructions of Viking ships and traditional Norwegian working craft has led to the understanding that with ships carrying a single square sail a neutral helm is highly desirable. 'They must be able to keep the balance *in all wind directions and wind forces* with their rudder in a neutral position'. Theoretically speaking such craft have the Centre of Effort (CE) of their rig in exact equilibrium with the Centre of Lateral Resistance (CLR) of the underwater body of their hull. This is achieved – on all points of sailing – by the combination of a single square sail rigged on a centrally located mast. However, traditional Norwegian working craft have proved very sensitive both to the tuning of the rig – whether the mast is raked or not – and to the distribution of ballast within the hull.[14]

By contrast, no vessel rigged with a square sail on a single forward-located mast can achieve a neutral helm on all points of sailing. This has led maritime archaeologists to consider other possibilities for the rig of Romano-Celtic sailing ships. In their reconstruction of the Barland's Farm Boat McGrail and Roberts adopted a fore-and-aft sail (a 'single dipping lugsail'), since they considered that their calculations showed that it gave a better balanced rig than a square sail (*colour plate 15*). For Zwammerdam 2 (a member of the inland sub-group) de Weerd illustrates a reconstruction with a spritsail and jib (foresail), the latter somewhat unexpected since it is unknown until modern times. For Blackfriars 1, Marsden considered the possibility that she might have had a spritsail. However, after a detailed consideration of the evidence he opted for a square sail, essentially as a trade-off in which some loss of directional stability was accepted against the need to rig the mast as a crane at the forward end of the hold to load and discharge cargo. This would have had the effect of inducing heavy lee helm when sailing close to the wind; however, when running downwind or with the wind on the quarter Blackfriars 1 is likely to have displayed good directional balance. This would have restricted vessels of the Blackfriars 1 type to sailing with favourable winds.[15]

No excavated find of a Romano-Celtic vessel has yielded any direct evidence as to its sail type. The best of the known evidence is from two images from Germany, the third-century AD mosaic from Bad Kreuznach and a grave monument of the second to third century AD from Jünkerath (*17* and *colour plate 16*). The Broighter gold model, dated to the first century BC (*colour plate 12*), shows a yard which would have supported a square sail, but the mast is centrally located and the model is unlikely to represent a Romano-Celtic vessel, being more probably a hide boat. Images do appear on pre-Roman native coins which appear to show single-masted square-rigged ships, but the

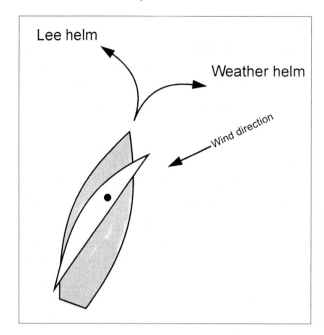

16 A vessel exhibiting lee helm will turn in the direction of the 'lee helm' arrow when the helm is released, i.e. away from the wind; a vessel with weather helm will turn towards the wind, when the helm is released, i.e. in the direction of the 'weather helm' arrow

detail is unclear. These also tend to show the mast stepped amidships and there may be some doubt as to whether they represent Romano-Celtic ships. The interesting thing about the images from Bad Kreuznach and Jünkerath is that they clearly show sails with two horizontal battens running from side to side beneath the yard; a boom is shown at the foot of the sail in the Bad Kreuznach depiction. Battens such as these are characteristic of the lugsails seen on Chinese junks. In fact Ellmers has suggested that the image from Bad Kreuznach shows a Chinese-style lugsail and the details of the image are strikingly similar even down to the control lines running to the end of the yard, battens and boom. In spite of this detail, however, it is probably unwise to take this image as evidence of a lugsail. The interpretation depends on the fact that the sail is depicted asymmetrically rigged on the mast. Ellmers himself noted that evidently the artist 'was used to the appearance of typical Mediterranean ships' and it is clear that his depiction leaves much to be desired; the hull actually looks somewhat akin to a sauce boat. On the other hand the sail on the Jünkerath gravestone is without doubt a battened square sail.[16]

In the last analysis the fact of a forward-located mast cannot be taken as evidence of a fore-and-aft rig. A mast stepped forward of amidships is not unique to the Romano-Celtic tradition, being present in a number of early *cogs*. It is also a feature of modern square-rigged craft such as the present-day Bangladeshi *balam* (*18*) and the Humber keel (*colour plate 17*). These examples of square-rigged vessels from the modern era are sufficient to show that a single forward-located mast is not incompatible with a square rig. Although the absence of direct excavated evidence must make any conclusion speculative, my own view coincides with Marsden's; the probability is that Romano-Celtic sea-going ships were square-rigged and as a result were poor performers on the wind. Normal practice would have been for their crews to await a favourable wind before setting sail.

It only remains to consider the dimensions and in particular the load-carrying capacity of Romano-Celtic sea-going ships. So little remains of the Bruges boat that it can offer little that is specific. The two eyewitness accounts differ as to her dimensions. One estimated the length of the hull at about 7m and recorded the discovery of the mast probably originally 5 or 6m long; the other reported the length of the hull as about 15m and the beam as about 4 or 5m. He thought that the mast could have originally measured 7 or 8m in height. Marsden's reconstruction of the cross-section gives a beam close to 5m and a contemporary sketch of the mast indicates a height of at least 9.3m. While he does not commit himself to a figure for the length of this vessel, his figures for the mast height and beam would confirm the estimate of the second witness, making the Bruges boat somewhat smaller than Blackfriars 1 (length 18.5m, beam 6.12m, depth 2.86m). St Peter Port 1 is by far the largest of the group (length 25m, beam 6m, depth 3m plus). The smallest is the Barland's Farm Boat (length 11.4m, beam 3.16m, depth 0.9m). McGrail considers that the latter was basically suited to work the waters of the Bristol Channel, the Severn estuary and the adjacent rivers. Estimates have been published of the load-carrying capacity of the Barland's Farm Boat and Blackfriars 1. For the former, depending on the draft, a figure of between around 4.5 and 6.5 tons is suggested. For Blackfriars 1, Marsden estimated a maximum of 63.7 tons. Although no estimate has been published for St Peter Port 1, it would not be unreasonable to assume a capacity in the order of 90 tons.

Naves onerariae: *conclusions*

It would seem improbable that Mediterranean shipbuilding techniques were used to build the transports required for the cross-Channel expeditions of Caesar and his successors. None of the attested examples of the use of these techniques north of the Alps can be demonstrated to be a cargo-carrier. The absence of excavated finds cannot of course be a clinching argument. However, the many examples of contemporary load-carriers built in the Romano-Celtic tradition and the considerable evidence for the use of hide boats suggest lively native traditions, which the Romans would have been able

17 Grave monument of the second/third century AD from Jünkerath, Rheinland-Pfalz, Germany. *Photograph reproduced by kind permission of the Rheinisches Landesmuseum, Trier*

to exploit. While the Romans would have considered it necessary to continue to employ in the north the complex and expensive Mediterranean techniques for the specialist construction of their warships – at least until native techniques were adopted for the Mainz river patrol vessels in the third or fourth century – they would have had every incentive to exploit the skills of local ship-wrights for the more prosaic task of building transports. But were those local shipwrights building in the Romano-Celtic manner or were they building hide boats? One striking aspect of Caesar's account of the construction of his fleet for the campaign of 54 BC was the speed with which it was built. Some 628 vessels, including 28 warships were built in the winter of 55/54 BC. In this regard hide boats might have offered a significant advantage. As we noted above, they were relatively quick to build. However, it cannot be claimed that only by using hide boats would it have been possible to achieve this speed of construction. In 1066 William the Conqueror assembled his fleet of several hundred ships in a similar timescale, certainly building some of them and the evidence of the Bayeux tapestry shows that these were not hide boats.

Caesar's account of his British expeditions gives specific figures as to the size of his expeditionary force and the numbers of ships used on each occasion. These give a valuable insight into the average number of legionaries involved on

18 A *balam* from Bangladesh under sail and 'apparently making some way to windward'.
Photograph by Dr. Basil Greenhill; reproduced by kind permission of Mrs Ann Greenhill

the one hand in a lightly equipped exploratory raid and a more serious invasion task force on the other. In 55 BC Caesar assembled about 80 transports to convey two legions across the Channel; of these 12 were lost at anchor in a storm off Deal. In addition 18 transports were reserved for the passage of an unspecified number of cavalry, who in the event failed to arrive. If one takes a legion as comprising a maximum figure of 6,000 men, these figures suggest that the average capacity of the transports was 150 men. Even at a lower and possibly more likely figure of 5,000 men a legion, we are still looking at an average capacity of 125. These figures are neatly confirmed by an incident on the return voyage from the first expedition: Caesar mentions that two transports did not make the same harbour as the rest and records that about 300 men landed from these two ships.

The following year Caesar had available some 600 newly built transports, of which 60 were prevented by adverse weather from arriving at the port of departure. To the net figure of 540 newly-built transports is to be added the figure of some 86 remaining from the previous year, after taking account of the loss of the 12 in the storm off Deal, making some 626 transports in total. This time Caesar took with him five legions, say 30,000 men, and 2,000 cavalry. However one works the figures, the average number of legionaries per infantry transport was considerably less than the previous year. A study of the carrying capacity of the cavalry transports suggests that each might have accommodated ten to fifteen horses and their attendants. If we apply these figures to calculations of the number of infantrymen per ship, it appears that for Caesar's second expedition each infantry transport carried an average of between 60 to 70 men. These figures assume a maximum of 6,000 men in a legion and clearly would be lower if the legion were smaller, for example 50 to 60 men per transport for a legion of 5,000 men.[17]

If we compare these figures with that of up to 150 men per ship for Caesar's first expedition, we are inevitably drawn to the conclusion that there was a real and significant difference between the two expeditions. A further indication of the lower number of legionaries per transport in 54 BC is given by the details of Caesar's return from Britain that year, when in addition to the legionaries, he brought back 'a large number of prisoners'. This, together with the fact that he had again lost ships at anchor in a storm, some 40 in number, determined him to make the passage back in two waves. Although he claims that no ship carrying troops was lost in either year, very few of the returning empty ships or of the 60 replacement ships, which he had had built for him in Gaul after the storm, made it to Britain for the second crossing. Caesar, therefore, crammed his troops into the few ships available to him, perhaps reaching or exceeding the loading of the previous year. To do so he may well have been compelled to abandon much heavy equipment.

In fact, the undertaking in 54 BC was a much more serious affair than that of 55 BC, involving significantly more back-up in terms of supplies and resources than that of the previous year. In specifying the design of the new ships he commissioned for the expedition of 54 BC, Caesar mentions the need to accommodate cargo and numerous draft-animals, which had not been taken the previous year, when the legionaries had been travelling light. The conclusions that we can draw can be applied to any Roman invasion fleet in northern waters at the turn of the millennium. They are:

1. While a lightly equipped expeditionary force might be accommodated within a loading of up to 150 men per ship, a loading of 60 to 70 men per ship seems more likely for a fully equipped invasion army.
2. Cavalry would require one (suitably adapted or designed) transport for every ten to fifteen horses.

It is considerations such as these which would eliminate the use of hide boats for the transports of Roman invasion fleets. As we have seen, appropriate designs of hide boast could carry considerable loads. However, the limitation of their overall size, 18 to 20m, would make it questionable whether they were the heavy load-carriers which the Roman army would have required. Only ships of the Romano-Celtic tradition could have fulfilled that requirement.

5

CAESAR: AN OLD CONTROVERSY REVIEWED

Harbours, estuaries and landing places

In his *Gallic War* Caesar names his port of embarkation in Gaul for the invasion of 54 BC as the *Portus Itius* (or the Itian harbour). The geographer Claudius Ptolemy, writing in Greek, gives coordinates for an 'Itian promontory', while Strabo mentions the 'Itian (promontory), which the divine Caesar used as his naval station, for his crossing to the island'. But Caesar is the only ancient author to use the name *Portus Itius*. As for his crossing the previous year, he is not as specific, indicating only that he set sail from the territory of the Morini, 'from which was the shortest passage across to Britain'. He does not name his bridgehead in Britain in either year, perhaps for the good reason that in those days the only topographical feature in Kent at all well known to the Roman world was *Cantium* – perhaps the South Foreland.[1] Nevertheless the reference to the 'shortest passage' suggests that he crossed by the Dover Strait and there is in his account plenty of circumstantial detail which makes it possible to identify with a high level of certainty, where he embarked and where he landed in both years.

Let us look first at the essential elements of that detail. In his *Gallic War* Caesar tells us that in preparing for his first raid in 55 BC he recognised that he was deficient in intelligence, in particular about the lie of the British coast and about harbours which could accommodate his fleet. Although he summoned merchants to his headquarters to interrogate them, he learnt nothing from them. So he sent an officer, Gaius Volusenus, with a ship of war to reconnoitre 'everything'. Volusenus returned five days later with his report to Caesar. Meanwhile, a number of British tribes, who had learnt from the merchants about Caesar's intention to invade, sent embassies to him to offer hostages and to declare their willingness to accept the dominion of Rome. In response to these overtures, Caesar sent a Gallic chieftain by the name of Commius, who had connections with British tribes, with a small detachment of cavalry, to pave the way by visiting as many tribes as he could, to announce Caesar's impending arrival and to urge them to seek the protection of Rome.

A fleet of about 80 transports and an unspecified number of warships was assembled – enough, Caesar thought, to transport two legions – and, taking advantage of a spell of fair weather, set sail about the third watch.[2] Arriving off the British coast about the fourth hour of the day, Caesar saw the armed forces of the Britons arrayed on the cliff tops and, noting the ease with which weapons could be hurled from the cliffs onto the shore, he decided that this was no place to disembark. So he anchored until the ninth hour to wait for the rest of the fleet to assemble. He summoned his senior officers to join him and, it seems, only now shared with them Volusenus's intelligence. In giving his instructions to his officers, Caesar was at pains to stress the need, because of the exigencies of a developing tactical situation and the uncertainties of pilotage, for a rapid response to any order he might give. Taking advantage of a favourable wind and tide, the fleet moved on 7 (Roman) miles from the spot where they had anchored to land on a shore which Caesar describes as even and open.[3] The landing was opposed. The Britons, seeing what the Romans were about, sent their cavalry and charioteers on ahead to intercept them as they landed, while the remainder of their forces followed on. At first, confronted by the British onslaught, the Roman legionaries hesitated to disembark. Caesar deployed his warships to some effect to bring their artillery to bear on the British forces. It was at this point that Caesar reports that the standard-bearer of the Tenth Legion led the way by leaping into the water with the celebrated cry that he at any rate would do his duty to Rome and his commander.

The Romans had arrived without their cavalry. When the main fleet of some 18 transports left Gaul, 18 others had not yet arrived at the assembly point, being detained by a contrary wind at a point some 8 Roman miles away. Caesar sent the cavalry to embark on these ships at a place he describes as the 'further' or 'upper harbour', instructing them to follow the rest of the fleet. It is possible that he allotted these ships to the cavalry because they would have been able to get there faster than a detachment of infantry. However, they clearly did not move as fast as Caesar had expected, since he expresses displeasure that they 'took somewhat too long to dispatch the business'. Caesar in fact gives a hint that the cavalry transports left soon after the main fleet, but failed to arrive. What he says is that, immediately after their landing, having defeated the Britons opposing their disembarkation, the Romans were unable to follow through their pursuit of the enemy, because the cavalry transports had not been able to hold their course and reach Britain. However that may be, they eventually did set sail with a gentle breeze on the fourth day after the landing in Britain of the main contingent. As they were approaching the bridgehead in Britain a violent storm arose, which prevented them from holding their course: some were driven back to the harbour from which they had started; others were carried to 'the lower, that is, to the more westerly part of the island', where they anchored. However, when these ships began to be swamped, they stood out for an unpleasant night at sea, before they too were able to make their way back to Gaul.

The same storm wrought much damage on the main fleet. The warships, which had been hauled ashore, were swamped. Several of the transports, which had been left at anchor, were wrecked, while others lost so much tackle as to make them unserviceable. It seems likely that they dragged their anchors and that much of the damage was caused by the resultant collisions and by ships going aground. Caesar explains that it was the night of the full moon, saying that the Romans had not been aware that this causes the highest tides.[4] After cannibalising the most seriously damaged ships and summoning materials from Gaul, the Romans were able to make all but 12 of the transports seaworthy. With these the return voyage was achieved just before the equinox. Taking advantage of a spell of fair weather (again), the fleet weighed just after midnight. Although all the ships arrived in Gaul, two were unable to make the same harbour as the rest and were carried some distance further down the coast.

The next year Caesar planned a much larger campaign, involving five legions and 2,000 cavalry. After inspecting the 600 or so new transports and the 28 warships which he had commissioned over the winter, he ordered them to be assembled at the *Portus Itius*, which, he had learnt, offered the most convenient passage to Britain, about 30 (Roman) miles. The departure for Britain was delayed by a persistent north-west wind for around 25 days. At last the fleet was able to weigh anchor around sunset and set sail 'with a gentle south-westerly'.[5] This failed at about midnight and the fleet drifted with the tide. At sunrise Britain was sighted left behind on the port side. The tide turned again and the fleet rowed to reach the shore by about midday. Caesar describes the landing place as 'that part of the island where (as he had learnt in the previous summer) was the best place for disembarkation'. The Britons had gathered their forces in large numbers, but, seeing the size of the fleet of over 800 vessels, had taken fright and withdrawn. Caesar pressed on after them into the interior early the next morning, leaving a small detachment of legionaries and cavalry to guard the fleet, being reassured that it had been left at anchor 'on a soft and open shore'. He caught up with and defeated the Britons at a place 12 (Roman) miles from his bridgehead. The next night, however, there was a severe storm in which nearly all the ships dragged their anchors and were driven ashore. Some forty vessels, out of a total of over 800 which had arrived off Britain, were destroyed. To repair the rest, Caesar detached specialist craftsmen from the legions and summoned others from Gaul. He had the ships beached and protected by an entrenchment connected to the bridgehead camp. He ordered Labienus, the commander of the legions left in Gaul, to build as many replacement ships as possible – in the event he managed to build 60. Because of the huge number of captives to be taken back to Gaul as well as the loss of ships in the storm, Caesar decided to make his return voyage in two stages, using what remained of his original fleet and the replacements constructed for him by Labienus. However, few of these ships made it back to Britain from Gaul for the second trip and after waiting some time for them to arrive and with the equinox imminent, Caesar packed his troops into the few ships available to him. He weighed anchor in a complete calm at the beginning of the second watch and reached Gaul at dawn.

Theories and hypotheses

In spite of this detail – perhaps because of it – the nineteenth and earlier centuries saw the publication of a riot of irreconcilable hypotheses by scholars and amateurs as to the identity of the *Portus Itius* and the location of Caesar's bridgehead in Britain. Among the distinguished historians, geologists, astronomers and others who contributed their pet theories were the Astronomer Royal, Sir George Airy, formerly Lucasian Professor of Mathematics at the University of Cambridge; the geologist George Dowker; the historian Edwin Guest; the philologist William Ridgeway; the barrister Thomas Lewin and Emperor Napoleon III. Among the claims advanced were that Caesar's fleets had set sail from places as far south as the Somme estuary and as far east as St Omer; and that his legions had landed at places as far apart as Pevensey and Richborough (*19*). One enthusiast, the Rector of Banham, Norfolk, went so far as to 'show beyond reasonable doubt' that he crossed from the Netherlands to land in Norfolk.

Airy, apparently inspired by the later invasion of William the Conqueror, argued for identifying the *Portus Itius* with the Somme estuary and placing Caesar's bridgehead at Pevensey. He placed the 'further' harbour from which the cavalry sailed in 55 BC at the mouth of the Authie. Ridgeway agreed with him in placing the Roman landings at Pevensey, but thought that the fleet sailed in both years from Wissant. In that case the cavalry harbour would have been at Sangatte. Another advocate for identifying the *Portus Itius* with Wissant was Guest. Henry claimed that the so-called *Camp de César* – a group of mounds in the vicinity of Wissant – were fortifications erected by the Romans to protect the *Portus Itius*. Lewin, who had Caesar sailing from Boulogne, which put the cavalry port at Ambleteuse, argued that he landed on Romney Marsh, either at Lympne or Hythe. Napoleon III, who also spoke for Boulogne on the grounds that this was the port selected by his uncle in 1804 for the embarkation of the troops intended for the invasion of England, maintained that the Romans landed in both 55 and 54 BC on the East Kent coast between Walmer and Deal. Dowker, who considered that the Romans landed near Sandwich on his first expedition, is the only scholar I have come across to make the case for his second landing to have been at Richborough. As a geologist, his important contribution to the debate was to outline the changes that have taken place in the configuration of the East Kent shoreline and the land immediately behind it since Roman times.[6]

The modern consensus was established by T. Rice Holmes in a robust and exhaustive analysis of these and other theories, in which he forcefully demolished those hypotheses which he found wanting, often by exposing internal inconsistencies within them. For example, Airy had claimed that the distance by sea from the harbour entrance at Boulogne to that at Ambleteuse was 5.5 (Roman) miles rather than the 8 as recorded by Caesar. Holmes responds with the argument that Caesar was speaking of the distance by land, adding with some amusement that, on the preceding page, Airy had maintained that Caesar's estimates of distances at sea were valueless.[7] Holmes was not immune to using a circular argument. His 'proof' that in 54 BC the Romans landed near Sandwich amounts in essence to the statement that only a landing place near Sandwich could have been 12 (Roman) miles from the site of the engagement the next day with the British forces, which he would show was on the Great Stour. When he comes to it, to support his argument that this action took place on the Great Stour at or near Canterbury, he argues that he has already demonstrated that the 12 miles is to be measured 'from a point in the neighbourhood of Sandwich'.[8] As a polemicist, Holmes's approach was nuclear; he was not a man to be content with one good argument when half a dozen would do. To disprove Airy's extraordinary notion that Caesar sailed from the Somme and landed at Pevensey, Holmes deploys a total of 19 arguments, nine against the Somme and ten against Pevensey. To retail them all would be too tedious. However, a flavour of them may be had from the following:

1. Airy dealt with the fact that the Somme is not in the territory of the Morini, by arguing that, although Caesar set out in the direction of that territory, he did not arrive there. Holmes demonstrates that this is to misunderstand Caesar's Latin.

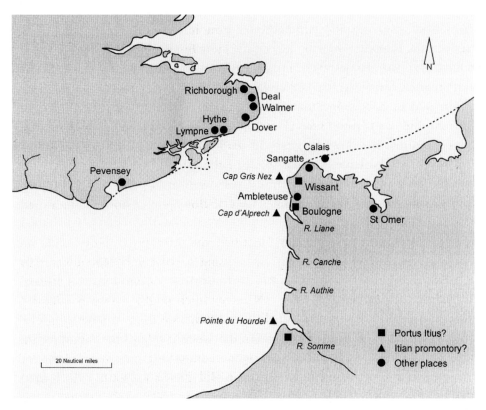

19 The places variously proposed as the harbours of embarkation and disembarkation of Caesar's expeditions to Britain in 55 and 54 BC before they were identified by T. Rice Holmes

2. Airy argued that Strabo's description of the Itian (promontory) places it near, not in, the territory of the Morini. Holmes demonstrates that this is to misunderstand Strabo's Greek.
3. Airy claimed that, when Caesar said he left Britain at the end of his second campaign in a flat calm (*summa tranqullitate*), he meant that he left with 'a stiff north-west wind'. One scarcely needs Holmes's page of circumstantial refutation.

In fact, as we shall see, a single good argument – which in fairness Holmes does deploy – will destroy not only Airy's theory, but also any interpretation which puts Caesar's bridgehead in Britain west of Dover.

The Portus Itius

Leaving aside Holmes's various demolition jobs, the logical place to start is with the *Portus Itius*. Boulogne, known by its later Roman name of

Gessoriacum, was an important harbour in the imperial period and one of the bases of the Roman Channel fleet, the *Classis Britannica*. The fact that Caesar referred to the *Portus Itius*, rather than to *Gessoriacum*, has inspired the argument that the two are different places. Further evidence for this view might perhaps be seen in Ptolemy's *Geographia*. This encyclopaedic work gives the longitude and latitude for places throughout the known world. It lists the Itian promontory at 22° 15′; 53° 30′ and *Gessoriacum* at 22° 30′; 53° 30′.[9] Assuming that Ptolemy's degrees implied the same linear length as ours this puts the Itian promontory 8.9 nautical miles west of *Gessoriacum*. This appears to be a nonsense; 8.9 nautical miles west of Boulogne is, however measured, several miles out to sea.

As we have noted, Strabo identified the Itian promontory with the 'naval station' used by Caesar in his crossing to Britain.[10] Not unnaturally, searchers for Caesar's embarkation harbour have been keen to identify promontories on the north coast of France which might qualify as Ptolemy's Itian promontory. Perhaps one of the oddest identifications still being offered is the Pointe du Hourdel, which marks the western side of the mouth of the Somme (*20*). This is included in an online edition of a translation of the full text of Ptolemy's *Geographia* published on Bill Thayer's website, which gives the latitude of the Itian promontory as 52° 30′, rather than 53° 30′. This places Itian promontory nearly 61 nautical miles south of *Gessoriacum* and certainly outside the territory of the Morini. While the location of the Itian promontory here would bring comfort to the soul of Sir George Airy, this reading of Ptolemy's coordinates seems to be an error in transcription. It is simply not consistent with Strabo's evidence that the promontory and Caesar's naval station were located in the land of the Morini or with Caesar's statement that the *Portus Itius* offered 'the most convenient passage to Britain'.[11]

Advocates of the claims of Wissant to be recognised as Caesar's port of departure have argued that the *Portus Itius* is to be identified as Cap Gris Nez. In fact Ridgeway argued perhaps erroneously that advocates of both Wissant and Boulogne had identified Cap Gris Nez as the Itian promontory. The charismatic nature of this feature was enough to convince Edwin Guest: 'Cape Grisnez, there can hardly be a doubt, was the Itian promontory, and if so, the great port which lay beneath it must have been the Itian Port'.[12]

However, the most likely candidate as the Itian promontory is Cap d'Alprech, which stands on the southern bank of the Liane estuary, immediately to the west of Boulogne. While not as outstandingly conspicuous as Cap Gris Nez – it is conceivable that it has been much diminished by erosion since Roman times – it does stand at the same latitude as Boulogne, even if the differences in the longitude given by Ptolemy suggest that they are further apart than they are. Holmes, who takes the reading for Ptolemy's latitude for the Itian promontory to be 53° 30′, the same as for Boulogne, speaks of Ptolemy's 'slight error in longitude'. However, this 'error' must be put into context. The coordinates for the locations listed in Chapter VIII of Book II of his *Geographia*, the one which includes *Gessoriacum* and the Itian Promontory, show that normally Ptolemy did not discriminate by less than a sixth of a degree, i.e. by less than 10 minutes of latitude or longitude. Occasionally, as in the case of the Itian promontory, coordinates are expressed in terms of a quarter of a degree (15 minutes). Within the limits of the accuracy of the system which he had adopted, the position which Ptolemy assigns to the Itian promontory is that of Cap d'Alprech. If one goes along with Holmes's reading of the latitude, then there is little doubt on the basis of the combined testimony of Ptolemy and Strabo that the *Portus Itius* was the estuary of the Liane. It also fits Caesar's description of it as offering 'the most convenient passage to Britain, about thirty (Roman) miles from the continent'.

At this point, one must pause to consider that the Latin word *portus* means, not 'port', but 'harbour' or 'haven'. There is, therefore, no need to suppose that in writing of the *Portus Itius* Caesar is referring to some established port with associated installations and settlement. Nor is there any reason for him to have named the harbour of his embarkation in 55 BC after whatever settlement there may have been on the future site of the city of *Gessoriacum*. He was referring to the superb natural harbour then offered by the estuary of the Liane.

Associated with the identification of the *Portus Itius* is the question of whether Caesar led both expeditions from the same harbour. In 55 BC he does not give a name to his port of departure, and certainly does not call it the *Portus Itius*. He says only that he left from the territory of the Morini, 'from which was the shortest passage across to Britain'. In naming his embarkation port the next year as the *Portus Itius*, he says that 'he had learnt that this harbour offered 'the most convenient passage' to Britain'. Scholars have endeavoured to distinguish between the 'shortest' and the 'most convenient' passage; for myself I have to say that I have not found such distinctions particularly enlightening. There is, however, a strange parallelism of expression between the phrase 'he had learnt' and the phrase used to describe the landing place Caesar chose for his second campaign: 'that part of the island where (as he had learnt in the previous summer) was the best place for disembarkation'. The verb (*cognoverat*) is the same and so too is the grammatical structure of the two Latin phrases. Did Caesar learn that the *Portus Itius* offered the most

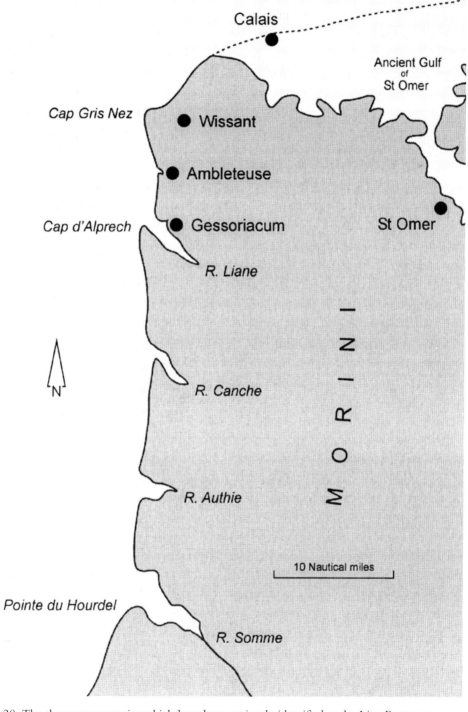

20 The three promontories which have been variously identified as the Itian Promontory

convenient passage to Britain as a result of his experience the previous year and does that imply that that experience led him to choose *Portus Itius* instead of a different harbour which he had used the previous year? Certainly it can only have been his previous year's experience that led Caesar to choose his landing place in Britain in 54 BC and Holmes, among others, considered that he chose a new one.

Ultimately whether the invasion fleets sailed from the *Portus Itius* in both years is a question which cannot be solved by an examination of Caesar's text alone. Taken together, Ptolemy and Strabo give good documentary evidence for identifying the *Portus Itius* as the estuary of the Liane, protected from seaward by the Itian promontory, or Cap d'Albrech. If we adopt this as a working hypothesis, other things fall into place. The estuary would certainly have been large enough to accommodate the Roman invasion fleet described by Caesar. The estuary of the Liane is 30 (Roman) miles from the South Foreland.[13] A north-westerly wind would prevent a fleet from sailing from the Liane to Britain. A south-westerly, particularly with a favourable tide, would be a fair wind for a passage to the South Foreland. All this is sufficient to establish with a high degree of probability that the embarkation harbour in 54 BC was the estuary of the Liane. But to establish that the expedition the previous year also left from the Liane, it is necessary to show that no other harbour on the French coast could reasonably have served the expedition of that year.

In fact, in spite of all the ink spilt in the debate, such an elimination process is straightforward. Harbours to the south of Boulogne – the estuaries of the Somme, the Authie, the Canche – may be discarded on the simple grounds that they do not offer the shortest or even the most convenient passage to Britain. Indeed the Somme must be discarded on the grounds that it does not lie in the territory of the Morini. North and north-east of Boulogne, Ambleteuse would not have offered sufficient room to accommodate the fleet of 80 transports, plus warships, which left in 55 BC; moreover, if Ambleteuse had been the principal embarkation harbour, the 'further harbour', from which the cavalry transports sailed, would have had to be Wissant. Wissant, as we have seen, has had its advocates as the main invasion harbour. It has in its favour that it is known to have been used on a small scale as a place of embarkation for merchants and others during the Middle Ages, but it is hard to see how this stretch of sand between Cap Gris Nez and Cap Blanc Nez could ever have offered the large safe harbour required for the assembly of the invasion fleet even of 55 BC. It might just have served as a haven where the 18 transports held back by a contrary wind from the south might have found refuge, perhaps by sheltering in the small creek which formed the medieval harbour or perhaps by lying under the lee of Cap Gris

Nez, but that would have been an exposed anchorage, if the wind changed. Calais may be eliminated on the grounds that it did not exist in the Roman period, certainly not as a harbour. St Omer, which, although now several miles inland, stood at the head of the shallow gulf to the east of the high ground of the Boulonnais, scarcely offered the shortest passage to Britain. In the light of these considerations, no serious argument can be formulated for locating the *Portus Itius* anywhere other than in the estuary of the Liane, nor can it realistically be suggested that the expedition of 55 BC was launched elsewhere than from the *Portus Itius*.

Storm surge: the cavalry flotilla is driven back

The single argument deployed by Holmes which kills stone dead any notion that Caesar's invasion fleet of 55 BC landed west of Dover is that it would have been impossible for the storm which struck the cavalry flotilla to have driven some of its ships westwards, while allowing others to make it back to their original harbour in Gaul. As formulated, Holmes's argument is based on the assumption that at the time the wind was blowing from the north-east. With the wind in the north-east, a return to their harbour of departure from any point west of Dover would have meant the cavalry transports holding an impossible course to windward. However, Holmes's argument holds good whatever the direction of the wind.

Holmes did not have the information available to modern enquirers about the ships likely to have been available to the Romans, but he did talk to informants experienced in the ways of sailing ships, such as the Harbour Master at Dover and 'a distinguished admiral'. He points to the probable poor windward performance of the cavalry transports. He suggests that they would have made four points (45°) of leeway.[14] This estimate was derived by Holmes from Falconer's *Marine Dictionary* of 1815, which stated that a ship in a gale would make leeway varying between 5.5 and 6.5 points (62° and 73°). He reduced this figure to four points so as not to overstate his case. For the cavalry transports to reach the Authie from a point off Pevensey, as required by Airy's hypothesis, would have required a course made good over the ground of less than nine points (101.25°) off the wind. With four points of leeway, this would mean that the ships would have had to lie to within five points (56.25°) of the wind (*21*). Holmes advances similar arguments against the hypotheses for other bridgeheads on the south coast. Lewin, while arguing for a landing place on Romney Marsh, had nevertheless accepted that the cavalry harbour was Ambleteuse. For the cavalry fleet to have made Ambleteuse would have required a course made good of less than eight points (90°) of a north-east wind, which with four degrees of leeway, would have required a heading of less than four degrees (45°) of the wind, an even less likely heading than that assumed for Authie.[15]

Modern experience and research broadly confirm Holmes's argument. As we have noted in Chapter 4, Severin's reconstructed *curragh* sailing on the wind exhibited a leeway of 30°. This might seem better than Holmes's assumed 45°, but she still could not do better than an effective 90° to the wind, and this was in moderate conditions. Of course, the cavalry transports are unlikely to have been hide boats and I have suggested that they would have been the heavily built wooden craft of the Romano-Celtic tradition. But there is no reason for thinking that these could go to windward, any more than Severin's hide boat. Leeway might have been in the order of 20° to 30°, the better figure being characteristic of ships with deeper draft. With this constraint on performance, like Severin's *Brendan*, it seems unlikely that Romano-Celtic craft could ever do better than reach across the wind.

What is more telling is Severin's experience that in winds of Force 6 and above it became dangerous for his hide boat to reach across the wind and that the safe course was to run downwind. With any sailing craft, as the wind rises, its ability to go to windward is impaired. This is in part because, as sail is reduced, the action of the wind on the hull, rigging and superstructure, which contribute nothing to the windward drive of the sail, becomes an increasingly more significant factor in the total aerodynamic forces acting on the ship. It is also because the increasing weight of the waves, as the wind rises, makes it more and more difficult to drive the hull through them. Ultimately the only choice available is to turn downwind, either under bare poles or with reduced sail. There can be no question of making ground to windward. It is this inability to make to windward under storm conditions that means that it is inconceivable that some ships of the cavalry flotilla could have made ground westwards, while others made ground eastwards, whatever the direction of the wind.[16]

Holmes holds that the wind was blowing from the north-east. In my original assessment of the storm, I concluded that the wind was from the north or north-west. The critical piece of evidence in my view is that the tide was much higher that night than the Romans expected. Caesar's excuse (for that is what it is) that the Romans had not been aware that the full moon causes spring tides, is scarcely credible. In their campaign against the Veneti the Roman fleet had spent a summer experiencing the tidal conditions of the Atlantic coast of Brittany and Caesar himself gives an accurate account of the significance of the tidal pattern for the defence of the promontory strongholds of the Veneti. If Caesar himself was not aware of the difference between springs and neaps, his mariners must have been.

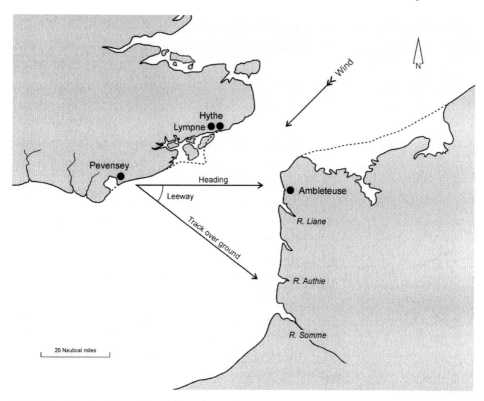

21 Holmes's refutation of Airy's hypothesis illustrated. The storm is blowing from the north-east. For the cavalry transports to return from Pevensey to their harbour of origin on the Authie requires a track over the ground of within 9 points of the wind direction. However, in the storm conditions the flotilla must have been making at least 4 points of leeway. To counteract this would have required a windward heading of at least 5 points of the wind – an impossible heading. Similar considerations refute Lewin's theory of a return from Romney Marsh to a harbour of departure at Ambleteuse

The reason why the Romans were caught out by the unexpected height of the tide during the storm can only be because there was a storm surge coinciding with High Water. Only a storm surge can explain why the warships which had been hauled ashore were swamped. A storm surge also goes a long way to explain the damage to the transports at anchor, for an unexpectedly high tide, associated with a strong wind would be a reason for them to drag their anchors. According to the *Dover Strait Pilot*, a storm surge would be created by a storm force wind from the north-west or north, together with an associated deep depression passing across the northern North Sea; this in extreme cases would raise the sea level by as much as 3m. The *Pilot* says that, 'if the peak of the surge coincides with High Water, severe flooding can result, as happened in the Thames estuary and on the Netherlands coast in January 1953' (*22*).[17]

Caesar tells us that the cavalry flotilla left Gaul with a gentle breeze, which may have come from the south-west or south, heralding a depression moving in to the north of the Channel. A storm force wind from the north or north-west would be consistent with this earlier, gentler wind as the warm front and then the cold front of a deepening depression passed over to the north. As each front passed over, there would have been a marked wind shift first to the west and then to the north-west or even north. This last wind shift would have prevented the ships from landing, but would have allowed some of the fleet to make the shelter of the South Foreland, while others made it back to Gaul. However, G.T. Meaden, writing as a meteorologist, has suggested that the centre of the depression followed a track to the south of the Channel, across northern Gaul, with the depression centred over north-east Gaul at the height of the storm. He has drawn a sequence of synoptic weather maps to illustrate this scenario (*23*). This would have produced a pattern of wind shifts over Caesar's theatre of operations quite different from those associated with a low tracking to the north of the Channel. The wind, blowing first from the south or south-east, would gradually strengthen, backing during the day through east and finally north-east. The highest wind speeds, he says, would have occurred during the afternoon and evening, reaching gale Force 8.[18] The starting point of Meaden's analysis was Holmes's study and, therefore, he followed Holmes's view that the wind during the storm was from the north-east. He reported that a search through the *Weather Logs* of the previous ten years had not revealed a weather pattern for the Dover Strait which 'met the same conditions as those of the great storm of 30 August 55 BC'. He noted that at this time of year most depressions weaken steadily as they cross northern France; he quoted a case recorded on 27 August 1977; in this example he noted that the timing of the backing of the wind corresponded to his model for Caesar's storm, but that this depression filled too quickly.

It cannot, however, be an objection to Meaden's analysis that a parallel case cannot be identified in modern times. While it is true that there was also a gale the following year, Caesar's storm of 55 BC must have been out of the ordinary. Whether the centre of the depression which caused it tracked north or south of the Channel is perhaps immaterial; it caused a storm surge which wrought havoc on his fleet. I would still subscribe to the view that it tracked north and note that Meaden's analysis does not meet the requirements for a storm surge set out in the *Dover Strait Pilot*, a storm force wind from the north-west or north, together with an associated deep depression passing across the northern North Sea. A storm-force wind (Force 10 is 48–55 knots) is significantly more violent than the maximum wind suggested by Meaden (Force 8 is 34–40 knots).

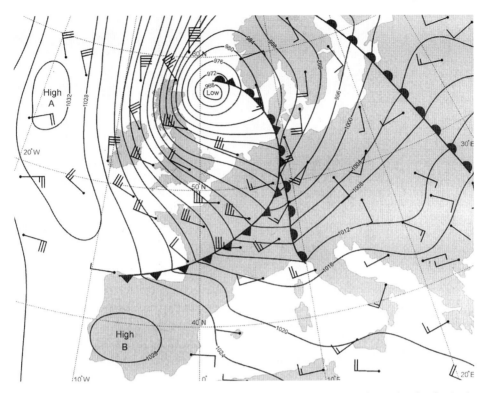

22 Synoptic Chart for midday on 31 January 1953. Wind direction is shown by the fletched arrows and wind strength by the number of bars in the fletch; for example, six bars indicates Force 12. A deep depression is centred over the northern North Sea and the northerly/north-westerly wind flow is made more violent by High A to the west and High B over south-west Spain. Winds over the Channel and southern North Sea are Force 6 and 7 and will increase to Force 8 and 9 later in the day. What, however, did the damage was the northerly winds of up to Force 12 to the north of Scotland driving the tidal surge southwards into the funnel of the Dover Strait. High Tide at Dover was just after midnight. *Crown Copyright, adapted from a chart kindly supplied by the Met Office*

The height of the storm seems to have been at night, but it had already set in while it was still light, when the fleet was 'in view of the camp'. When the moon is full, High Water at Dover is at approximately eleven o'clock morning and evening (GMT) and the tidal stream in the Strait changes from south-west to north-east an hour or so earlier. A possible reconstruction is that the fleet left Ambleteuse at around nine or ten o'clock in the morning to catch the tidal stream as it turned north-east. The wind would have been a gentle breeze from the south or south-west (south-east, if you follow Meaden). Six hours later the fleet would have been off the coast of East Kent; the tide turned to run to the south-west and the ships would have been fighting the tide to make their anchorage. About the same time or a little later the wind veered to the north-west (backed to the north-east), increasing in force. Even without the increase in the strength of the wind, the fleet would have been losing ground against both tide and wind and the appropriate tactic would have been to anchor until the tide and hopefully also the wind changed direction. The strength of the wind made that impossible, although some ships attempted to anchor in the lee of the South Foreland, while the rest followed tidal stream and wind back to the continent.[19] As the tide turned, say at around nine or ten o'clock that evening, and began to flow in the opposite direction to the wind, the wave pattern would have changed dramatically and a nasty sharp sea would have been kicked up by the wind-over-tide conditions. In such conditions the ships sheltering off the South Foreland would have found their berth untenable. After an unpleasant night at sea, possibly riding ahull, they too reached a haven in Gaul the following morning.

'Britain left behind to port'

If the storm of 55 BC can only be understood by assuming that Romans landed that year in East Kent, the evidence that they landed in East Kent the following year is less dramatic. Caesar reports that the fleet set sail around sunset with a gentle south-westerly. About midnight the wind failed and the fleet drifted with the tide. At daybreak Britain was sighted left behind on the port side. Most commentators take the straightforward view that Caesar's meaning is that the fleet had drifted offshore with the tide and that at daybreak

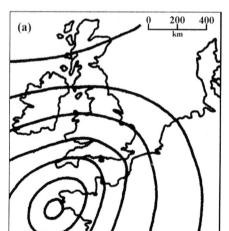
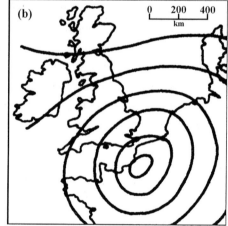

23 G.T. Meaden's weather chart showing the estimated position of the depression tracking south of the Channel at 0600 hours (a) and 1800 hours (b) on 30 August 55 BC. At 0600 hours the wind in the Dover Strait would be south light to moderate; at 1800 hours north-east gale. *Reproduced by kind permission of the Royal Meteorological Society*

the British coast was visible on the port quarter, i.e. as the fleet drifted north-eastwards from the South Foreland, the British coast was sighted on the port quarter – in the west. This, one might think, could only apply if the fleet were off the coast of East Kent at the time. However, supporters of a landing on the south coast have found other interpretations of Caesar's meaning. Airy, that master advocate of Pevensey as the landing place, has an idiosyncratic interpretation:

> I cannot conceive that the expression refers to any direction but to that of the drift; it asserts that, in reference to the direction of the tidal current, the coast was on the left hand. It is therefore indecisive as to place.[20]

Since Airy conceives that the fleet was drifting along the south coast, this construction no way accounts for the fact that, according to Caesar, Britain was 'left behind', i.e. that the tidal stream was taking the fleet offshore. That would not happen until the fleet passed the South Foreland and it is hardly likely that the fleet could have drifted that far from Pevensey before the tide turned. Ridgeway, who like Airy thinks that both expeditions landed at Pevensey, understands that the phrase 'left behind' must mean that the fleet was drifting offshore from the British coast. However, he realises that, starting from Pevensey, the fleet could not have drifted past the South Foreland. His interpretation only serves to show that he was not aware that along the south coast the tidal streams run broadly parallel with the shore. Francis Appach, who argued for a landing place on Romney Marsh, claimed that when the sun rose Caesar expected to see Britain to starboard. However, as the fleet drifted up channel, 'Britain could not have been in any other position', than on the left of the track of the drifting ships. This seems to be little more than a reformulation of Airy's argument.[21]

Among those who accepted that the incident can only be understood on the supposition that the expedition landed on the east coast of Kent, there appeared to be little unanimity about how far the fleet drifted. One literalist, Heller, took the expression 'left Britain behind' at face value, arguing that the fleet must have drifted to a point about 9 miles east of Ramsgate. Heller believed that Caesar would have had no means of knowing that the north coast of Kent was not the north coast of Britain. On this view Caesar thought that he was drifting northwards away from Britain. Dowker also has Caesar drifting on a course which took the fleet to the east of the Goodwin Sands 'beyond the North Foreland': with the turn of the tide, the legionaries took to their oars to pass north of the Goodwins to land near Richborough. Holmes also considers that the fleet was carried by the tide east of the Goodwins, but could scarcely have drifted further north than the latitude of Deal. Unlike others, Holmes arrives at his estimate by what is a standard navigational procedure, dead reckoning.[22] He enlisted the help of the Harbour Master at Dover and he invites his reader to check his estimate by reference to standard Admiralty publications. Yet it is not the navigational publications which are questionable; it is Holmes's assumptions about the heading and average speed attained by the fleet while the wind lasted. By an analysis of the correspondence between Quintus Cicero, serving on Caesar's staff, and his brother, Marcus Cicero, the orator, Holmes places Caesar's landing in Britain on 7 July. This was the day of the new moon, a day or two before springs. Holmes states quite correctly that, if the fleet had weighed between seven and eight o'clock,[23] it would have had 2 hours or so of foul tide to stem, before the tide turned to help them on their way. The Dover Harbour Master had advised Holmes that 'with a light south-westerly wind the ships could easily have sailed 6 knots an hour (*sic.*)'. Holmes combines this with the tidal data to suggest that over 5 hours, while still sailing, the fleet would have covered 25 nautical miles.[24] A further 3 hours drifting until the tide turned again at first light would add about 6 nautical miles to the ground track making 31 nautical miles in all, bringing the fleet to the latitude of Deal and east of the Goodwin Sands.[25]

I decided to accept Holmes's invitation and check out his estimate using modern charts and the *Dover Strait Tidal Stream Atlas*. A track made good from Boulogne of 25 nautical miles and a course over the ground of 345° true, would have brought the fleet to within 2 miles of the South Foreland. From that position, as it began to drift, the tide would have taken it inside, not outside, the Goodwin Sands. But it is not really possible to validate Holmes's estimate, because he does not state what he assumed as the course made good. Another estimate was published three quarters of a century later by McGrail. This had the fleet leaving around 2100 hours and making 5 knots over the ground for the first 3 hours to arrive at a position around 15 sea miles nor'-nor'-west of Boulogne. The fleet would then have drifted for some 4 hours with the north-east tidal stream going away from the shore of East Kent to arrive at sunrise at an estimated position of 6 sea miles east-south-east of the South Foreland (*24*).[26]

The problem is that we do not know from Caesar the average speed of the fleet while it was still sailing. It is a straightforward navigational exercise to reckon the distance that the fleet may have drifted from midnight, but, without information about the fleet's course and speed before midnight, any estimate of the fleet's position at daybreak must be treated with extreme caution. For the fleet to reach the positions proposed by Dowker and Heller north of the

Goodwins, it would have had to be already well east of the Goodwins at midnight when the wind failed. Even if the fleet had been sailing for the 5 hours that Holmes assumes, this would imply an unrealistic speed. McGrail's assumption of a speed of 5 knots is likely to be nearer the mark than Holmes's six. Even so, the fleet must have drifted at least as far as McGrail suggests; a position any further south would hardly have qualified as 'leaving Britain behind'. The position at first light might well have been further north, if the fleet had been sailing for longer than the 3 hours than McGrail allows. What we do know about the position the fleet reached at first light is that it took until midday for all of the fleet – under oars – to reach Caesar's chosen landing spot on the British coast, say about 7 hours. Again we have no data on the speed the legionaries could achieve rowing the transports. McGrail's suggestion of 1 knot over the ground – a not unreasonable one – is derived from the position he has estimated for the fleet at dawn and the distance to Walmer, which he takes as the landing site. Had he assumed a different landing place, this would have implied a higher, but not impossible speed. So while we may be confident that the landing in 54 BC was in East Kent, such navigational considerations lack the precision to determine exactly where on that coastline the landing may have been.

Did Caesar intend to land in 55 BC in Dover Harbour?

When Caesar questioned the Gallic merchants to gather intelligence about Britain, one of the points which clearly concerned him was that they were unable to give him any useful information about 'harbours suitable for a number of large ships'. We may reasonably suppose that, in briefing Volusenus before his departure to reconnoitre the British coast, Caesar would have ensured that he understood the paramount importance of identifying such harbours. In the secondary literature Gaius Volusenus Quadratus is usually mentioned as an officer of considerable experience, enjoying Caesar's high esteem. Sheppard Frere describes him as a 'trusted tribune'; for Peter Salway he was 'a military officer for whom he (Caesar) had a high regard'. Holmes sees him as 'a trained soldier who thoroughly understood his business', 'whom Caesar specially selected as a competent man'. Holmes expatiates further:

> Volusenus had distinguished himself in a campaign, conducted by one of
> Caesar's generals, against the mountaineers of the upper Rhône: he
> possessed, as his later history proved, not merely a keen eye for the features
> of a country, but daring of that kind which characterised the sons of
> Zeruiah; and how highly Caesar thought of him is evident from the fact

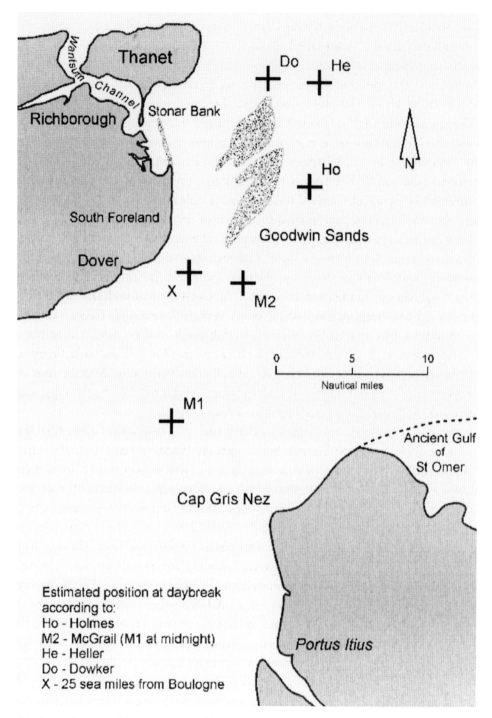

24 Approximate positions, as proposed by Holmes, McGrail and others, of the Roman fleet at daybreak on 7 July 54 BC after drifting since midnight. Holmes had reckoned that in the 5 hours from departure the fleet would have covered 25 sea miles over the ground. This combined with a course made good of 345° would have brought the fleet to within 2 sea miles of the South Foreland

that he was the only military tribune whose name is mentioned with honour in the *Commentaries*.[27]

Volusenus is mentioned seven times in the *Gallic War*. First is an account in Book III of the *Gallic War* of an assault by the Seduni and Veragri on the winter quarters of the Twelfth Legion under Servius Galba. Here Caesar describes him as 'a man of both sound judgment and great courage'. His part in the defence of the Roman camp was to go to his commander with the senior centurion of the legion to suggest to him that, with the legionaries running out of missiles after some 6 hours of fighting, their only hope was to go onto the offensive and make a sortie out of the camp. Galba responded to this by ordering the sortie, which resulted in the attackers being driven away.[28] Later, after the British campaigns Caesar records that Volusenus had been sent on ahead with a unit of cavalry to relieve a camp which had been under attack by the Germans. By the time he arrived the Germans had withdrawn, but the newly recruited legionaries would not accept his word that Caesar and his army were on their way. Lastly in the eighth book of the *Gallic War*, written by Caesar's continuator, Aulus Hirtius, he is involved in two botched attempts to assassinate Commius. All this may be sufficient perhaps to describe him as 'experienced' or even 'having Caesar's respect', but surely not much more and certainly not enough to justify Holmes's encomium.

The other three times we hear the name of Volusenus are all in Caesar's account of the expedition of 55 BC. Twice Caesar reports factually: that Volusenus has been sent to reconnoitre the British coast; and that Caesar advises his commanders – when anchored off the South Foreland – of the relevant part of Volusenus's report to him. The third mention – when Caesar allows himself a laconic comment on his report – is on the occasion of Volusenus's return from his reconnaissance. Volusenus, says Caesar, had 'observed all the country so far as was possible for an officer who did not dare to disembark and entrust himself to the rough natives'. This is hardly consistent with the image of the 'man of both sound judgment and great courage' recorded in the third book of the *Gallic War*. The clear implication is that Caesar had expected him to go ashore and that the fact that he did not made his report less comprehensive than Caesar would have wished. From offshore it is not always easy to make out the exact configuration of the shoreline, particularly when it is low-lying. As he moved north along the East Kent coast, Volusenus would have noted that the cliff line ended around the present site of Walmer to be replaced by an open shore backed by gently rising terrain (*colour plate 18*). If he did venture as far north as Thanet, his assessment of the value of the Wantsum as a sheltered natural harbour may well have been impaired by a failure to discern the entrance at the end of the Stonar Bank (*24*). However, we can be sure that Volusenus would have reported to Caesar on the possibility of landing on the open shore of East Kent from Walmer northwards. In addition he could scarcely have failed to have reported on the potential of Dover as a harbour, if it were anticipated that the landing would be unopposed. He had after all been instructed to report on adequate harbours.

It was while Volusenus was away on his mission that the ambassadors from a number of British tribes came to Gaul, promising both to give hostages and to submit to the protection of Rome. Caesar may well have thought that he now had every reason to suppose that when he arrived in Britain the landing of the legions would not be resisted. Caesar responded to this positively, sending Commius ahead to announce his imminent arrival and to urge as many tribes as possible to submit to Rome. When Volusenus presented his less than adequate report, Caesar would have settled on landing in Dover harbour. Two thousand years ago the estuary of the Dour would have formed a natural haven which would have offered protection to a significant fleet. The present artificial harbour works providing facilities for the very many cross-Channel services running between Dover and continental ports, which make it one of the busiest harbours in the world, are the end result of a centuries-old battle to preserve the viability of the harbour in the face of the steady silting up, which has choked so many of the other natural havens along the south and east coasts. Dover Museum displays models which demonstrate the evolution of the natural haven, sited where the centre of the town now is, into the present modern seaport relying entirely on artificial breakwaters for its protection (*colour plates 19* and *20*).

We may conclude then that, when Caesar eventually sailed, it was with the intention of landing at Dover. What clinches that conclusion is what happens when he arrives off Dover. He reports that, when he saw the cliff lined with British warriors, he decided that this is not the place to disembark. Why should he say that, if he had decided before sailing that he was not going to disembark beneath these cliffs overlooking Dover harbour? Perhaps, you might say, his plan was simply to treat landing at Dover as an option: if it proved in the event impossible to land in Dover harbour, he would move on to the open shore from Walmer northwards, which Volusenus had described in his report. If so, it is odd that Caesar did not share this plan with his commanders before they sailed. What happened is that, anchored off Dover, having decided that he could not land his legions there, he summoned his commanders to tell them what the new plan now was. Tellingly it is only now that Caesar reveals to his colleagues the intelligence he has had from Volusenus.

Why should he not have told them before? The only possible answer is that, because it concerned the existence of a possible landing place from Walmer northwards, which he had no intention of using, it was not relevant to the planned landing at Dover. It also seems to me significant that during this briefing off the South Foreland Caesar went out of his way to emphasise to his commanders the need for a rapid response to any order he might give. That suggests that he was about to lead his army into a situation which he had not thoroughly thought through, perhaps lacking adequate intelligence about the ground and faced with an enemy of whose tactics he was ignorant.

If we accept that Caesar's intention in 55 BC was to disembark in Dover harbour, that provides a clear indication as to where he actually did land. As the expedition moved along the East Kent coast, he would have been looking for the first possible landing place. That could only have been the open shore around Walmer, where the cliff line ends (*colour plate 18*).

'The best place for disembarkation'

If our reading of Caesar's account of the landing in 55 BC allows us to be reasonably certain that the expedition that year landed as soon as it reached the end of the cliff line around Walmer, such precision is denied about the landing place the following year. Caesar describes it as 'the best place for disembarkation' as he had learnt the previous year. We have already established that it can only have been on the coast of East Kent. If there continues to be doubt on that score, one can only say that, within the timescale of his first raid, Caesar would have found it impossible to send reconnaissance parties to report on the potential of landing places west of Dover. Indeed in the few days that they spent in Britain, the legions made no significant advance from their base camp. Where on the east coast of Kent the landing place was in 54 BC has to be inferred from the following information:

1. When marching forward in pursuit of the British forces immediately after landing, Caesar noted that he was easier in his mind about the place where he had left the fleet at anchor.
2. The fleet again suffered damage in a storm.
3. While the landing place of 55 BC was described by Caesar as 'even and open' (*aperto ac plano*), that chosen for the next year he describes as 'a soft and open shore' (*molli atque aperto*).
4. Holmes would add that the landing place had to be 12 (Roman) miles from the site of Caesar's engagement with the Britons, which he places on the Great Stour in the vicinity of Canterbury.

To take these pieces of information in order, Caesar can only have been easier in his mind about the anchorage of the ships, if the expedition had landed at a different point from 55 BC. The second point disposes of a landing place in the Wantsum, behind the shelter of the Stonar Bank. In spite of suggestions to the contrary, the Wantsum provided an extensive protected haven throughout the Roman and early medieval periods. I must admit to finding Dowker's suggestion of a landing at Richborough attractive, but it seems to me that he can only adequately account for the damage caused to the fleet by the unlikely supposition that it was left at anchor outside the Stonar Bank.

The adjectives applied by Caesar to his landing places have attracted a number of different and mutually exclusive interpretations. My instinctive understanding of 'open' (*apertus*), applied by Caesar to both landings, would be that of the sailor: open to the sea, not a sheltered beach within a harbour or natural haven. But Lewin argued that 'open' referred to the ground behind the shoreline. He argued that at Lympne the shore was 'open' because the hills to the north were at least a mile away. Guest denied that the shore here was 'open' because the hills were too near. Holmes argues that 'open' applies to the shore itself and means that it was free of obstructions. In the case of 'even' (*planus*), Lewin again argued that it described the land beyond the shoreline: 'between Walmer and Deal … the ground is uneven, and cannot be called flat'. Nor of course can the shore here, but it can be described as 'evenly shelving'. However, the most significant differences of interpretation concerned the word *mollis*. The normal translation would be soft. Edwards, the editor of the Loeb edition of Caesar's *Gallic War*, who knew his Holmes, translated it as 'sandy'. But sand is quite hard. So too is shingle, which was Lewin's preferred interpretation. 'The sea-beach (at Lympne) was also *molle* or soft… in the sailor's sense, i.e. it consisted of shingle, than which nothing can be more favourable to the security of vessels'. There is shingle, too, off the east coast of Kent, though how far it extended north from the cliff line in Roman times must be uncertain. Holmes translates Caesar's description of the landing place in 54 BC as 'a nice open shore'. He explains:

> *Mollis*, in the passage which we are considering, simply means that the shore was one where the anchorage was good, and where the ships if driven aground, would suffer comparatively little: it probably also implies that the shore was gently sloping.

One does have to say that to suggest that 'nice' adequately renders *mollis* is to do less than justice to Caesar's quite precise use of language. The meanings listed in the *Chambers Murray Latin-English Dictionary* do not include any which can be construed to mean 'nice'. While Holmes may well be right to say that it implied that the anchorage was good and that, if driven aground, the ships would be reasonably safe, such an interpretation does not say why. Moreover, it is an interpretation which is implicit in the context. Caesar was advancing an excuse for not having hauled his ships ashore and he would not have neglected to do that if he had not thought that they were safely anchored.[29]

In fact the only reasonable interpretation of *mollis* is that it means 'soft'. Caesar is describing the nature of the shore and the adjacent seabed and comparing it to that of the landing place the previous year. If sand and shingle can be hard, what will be soft is alluvial mud. A landing on a muddy shore would seem, therefore, to indicate a point north of the longshore shingle drift from Walmer, which at that time would not have extended as far north as it does today. In the last analysis there can be no certainty as to the precise location of the bridgehead of Caesar's second expedition. It is certainly on the east coast of Kent and would have been north of the place where he landed in 55 BC. Just how far north we cannot say.

'A damn' close run thing'

I was originally drawn to the study of Caesar's invasion passages about four years ago. I was researching my contribution to the debate about the bridgehead of the Claudian invasion and I believed that the very specific detail in Caesar's account could reveal much about how the Romans went about cross-Channel operations. At the time I accepted as a given the academic consensus that his fleets left Gaul from Boulogne and landed on the East Kent coast. Specifically my analysis of Caesar's account allowed me to formulate five hypotheses which may be taken to apply to Roman amphibious operations in northern Europe generally:

1. His warships were faster, and probably more manoeuvrable, than his transports and Romano-Celtic ships generally, at least when they were under oars; they certainly were less seaworthy.
2. His passages between Boulogne and East Kent were not particularly fast – at the most he seems to have achieved average speeds of no more than 3 knots through the water.
3. Of a total of seven recorded attempts at a cross-Channel passage by his fleet or parts of it, two were unsuccessful and did not arrive at their destination; in addition part of the fleet intended for both expeditions failed to arrive at the port of embarkation.

4. Caesar's preferred winds were not only favourable, but also very light, sometimes becoming a dead calm; he also seems to have preferred night crossings, possibly with a moon.
5. Caesar showed some understanding of the tidal streams in the Dover Strait and worked his tides.

In the light of the further work that I have done for this book, I believe that these hypotheses are still valid. I might now be less certain of Caesar's preference for a moon during his passages, but that is all.[30]

In that first study, I had not seen anything particularly significant in the fact that Caesar anchored off the South Foreland before catching a favourable tide to move on up the coast of East Kent. But if we are right to believe that in 55 BC Caesar did indeed intend to land beneath the cliffs in the natural harbour at Dover – without having a plan B which he had shared with his commanders, then much of his account of that first expedition acquires a new significance. Seen in this light the account of the campaign becomes a catalogue of misfortunes, near disasters and errors of judgment. The decision to land at Dover was based on a failure of diplomacy compounded by a failure of reconnaissance. Even though Caesar was in the event wrong to suppose that his arrival would not be resisted by the British tribes, all would not have been lost, had Volusenus identified the natural haven of the Wantsum. A landing here, even if opposed, would not have been out of the question, in the way that a landing at Dover turned out to be. The fact that Caesar did not know of the Wantsum meant that he could not consider it as an option, alongside Dover, for the landing place he originally intended; and that he could not shelter his ships here, when the planned landing at Dover proved impossible. Thus the storm damage to the fleet on the open coast of East Kent could be attributed to this combined failure of diplomacy and intelligence.

In fact when he moved off from the anchorage off Dover, Caesar had little option. In saying that he took advantage of a favourable wind and tide, he is asking his reader to believe that he is in control of events. Had the wind, if not the tide, been coming from the east, then the fleet could only have coasted westwards to seek a place to land, perhaps at Hythe or Lympne. The fact that both wind and tide were favourable for a run along the east coast of Kent must have been a happy fluke. The decision to divert the cavalry to the eighteen ships lying at Ambleteuse also proved to be a costly mistake. In the skirmishes with the British warriors, in particular, with their cavalry and their charioteers, Caesar's ability to respond was seriously impaired without his cavalry. The cavalry were not available to follow through the defeat of the Britons at the landing and he suspects that the absence of his cavalry was one factor which induced the Britons to renew hostilities after the storm. In the event, in the third attack on his camp he did what he could with the 30 cavalrymen who had come over initially with Commius.

But there is more yet. It is clear from Caesar's report that the legions on this first expedition were lightly equipped and, in particular, without supplies of food. No doubt on the basis of his advance diplomacy he had expected that the British tribes would keep the legions provided. Because this failed, the legionaries were sent out from the camp on a daily basis to collect corn and it was while they were out on this duty that the Seventh Legion was ambushed by the Britons. The soldiers had laid down their arms and were scattered across the field cutting corn. Only Caesar's arrival from the camp with reinforcements averted a serious outcome to this attack. In fact it is possible that the Seventh Legion was badly mauled. Caesar diverts attention from this by his boast that in neither year was any ship carrying soldiers lost. Caesar can have been in Britain for barely three weeks on this first raid. He had set out late, at the end of August if one accepts Holmes's chronology, largely because of the need to repel an invasion of Germans from across the Rhine before he left for Britain, and had returned before the equinox. In this time he had established a base camp near Walmer, had won three military encounters with the British tribes and received their submission twice.[31] He had adequately repaired his fleet, but apart from foraging and possibly reconnaissance parties, he does not seem to have left his base camp. Before leaving he doubled the number of hostages he had previously required, but left before they could be delivered; only two of the tribes sent the hostages demanded.

The art of political spin was not invented in the twentieth century. When Caesar's despatches reporting his raid reached Rome, the senate decreed twenty days' thanksgiving. But it had been 'a damn' close run thing'.[32]

6

CLAUDIUS:
AN OLD CONTROVERSY RENEWED

Evidence

Caesar had come, had seen, but had not conquered. In the words of the Roman historian Tacitus, he had 'revealed Britain to his successors, rather than handed it to them'. It would be very nearly a hundred years – AD 43 – before the conquest of Britain came to the top of the agenda of a Roman emperor. In that year an invasion force of four legions and associated auxiliary units left Gaul to invade Britain. This time the campaign would lead to the incorporation of the greater part of Britain into the Roman world until the end of the fourth century. It was in all probability the largest army ever to invade the British Isles, numbering perhaps as many as 40,000 men (*25*).

The documentary sources for the campaign give little detail and, in particular, do not say where the invasion fleet landed, or where it embarked. The principal ancient source for the campaign is Dio Cassius's *Roman History*, written in Greek. This is supplemented by a page in Suetonius's *Life of Claudius* and a brief comment in his *Life of Vespasian*. Archaeology provides evidence of very early Roman military activity in Britain, particularly at Richborough and in the Fishbourne/Chichester area, while excavations at Maiden Castle and Hod Hill in Dorset are testimony to assaults by the Romans on British hill forts in the south-west.[1]

According to Dio, the following are the main details of the invasion campaign. A certain Berikos (identified as Verica, king of the British Atrebates who had settled in a region focused on West Sussex, Hampshire and Wiltshire), who had recently been expelled from Britain, persuaded Claudius, newly raised to the purple, to undertake the invasion.[2] A senator named Aulus Plautius was put in charge of the invasion force and one of his legionary commanders was Vespasian, the future emperor. The soldiers were initially reluctant to embark, but, as we noted at the beginning of Chapter 2, were persuaded to do so when addressed by a senior member of Claudius's personal staff, the freedman Narcissus. The landing was unopposed and at first the invading forces failed to make contact with the Britons. After initial engagements in which the Britons were defeated, Plautius received the submission of a section of a tribe named as the Bodunni (commonly accepted to be the Dobunni settled in the Gloucestershire region). The invasion force next advanced to an unnamed river, which some take to have been the Medway, while others do not. After a two-day battle, in which the Britons were again defeated, the Romans crossed this river and advanced to the Thames. Here the Romans halted and consolidated their position. Plautius, says Dio, had become afraid of the strength of the British opposition. He had been instructed to send for Claudius from Rome if he encountered any particularly stubborn resistance and this he now did. Claudius arrived with extensive equipment, including elephants (*colour plate 21*), took over command of the troops and defeated the Britons opposing the crossing of the Thames. He advanced to capture Colchester and received the submission of numerous British tribes. He then handed command of the army back to Plautius, instructing him to pacify the remaining districts, and returned to Rome. Claudius had been away from Rome for six months, of which 16 days had been spent in Britain. Dio concludes his account with a description of the honours heaped on Claudius by the Senate. To this Suetonius adds that Claudius was motivated by a desire to achieve a military triumph and that the campaign was occasioned by the disturbances caused in Britain by the Romans' refusal to return certain refugees. In a brief paragraph in his *Life of Vespasian* he lists the activities of Vespasian in the south-west as including the fighting of 30 battles, the subjugation of two tribes and the capture of more than 20 *oppida*, no doubt hill forts, as well as the whole of the Isle of Wight.

In addition there is a brief reference by Tacitus in his biography of his father-in-law Agricola to the continuing loyalty to Rome of a King Cogidumnus to whom the Romans had handed over certain tribes and whose existence and royal rank in the Chichester region is corroborated under the name of Togidubnus by a dedication stone found in Chichester. Finally a comment by the fourth-century historian, Eutropius, associates a certain Cn. Sentius with Aulus Plautius in the conquest of Britain. This individual has been identified as Cn. Sentius Saturninus, a man from a distinguished family, who had been consul jointly with the former emperor Gaius in the early part of AD 41 and who had played a significant, if obscure, part in the events surrounding the accession of Claudius. There are only three details in the sources which might have a bearing on any interpretation of the Channel crossing itself. First Suetonius informs us that Claudius embarked from Boulogne. Secondly Dio states that the invasion force made the crossing in three divisions. Translations of the reason for this given in Dio's Greek text differ. Some translate it as: 'in order that they should not be hindered in landing – as might happen to a single force'. Other translations suggest that the

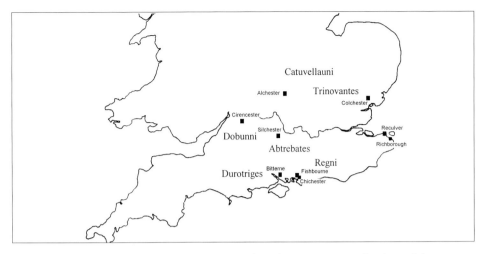

25 Approximate settlement areas of the tribes of south-east Britain at the time of the Claudian invasion, together with the principal sites mentioned in the text

division of the invasion force into three was to avoid an 'opposed' landing. Thirdly Dio reports that:

> In their voyage across they first became discouraged because they were driven back in their course, and then plucked up courage when a flash of light rising in the east shot across to the west, the direction in which they were sailing.

The sources documenting the invasion can only be described as scrappy and confusing. Far from having, as we do for Caesar's invasions, the contemporary account of the commander-in-chief and contemporary correspondence from an individual with a keen interest in the progress of the campaign, our chief source is the author of a general history of Rome running to 80 books, writing some two centuries after the event. Ernest Black describes Dio's method of working: after ten years collecting his material, he spent twelve more writing it up. In the process 'there must have been scope for misunderstanding his sources, either at the time he made his original notes or when he came to make sense of them later'.[3] Suetonius was closer to the event: he was born perhaps less than 30 years after the invasion and would have been writing early in the second century AD. As for Eutropius, who is the only authority to link Cn. Sentius with the campaign, his testimony dates to the fourth century AD. Moreover, these writers may well have had their own prejudices, conscious or unconscious. For example, we know from Suetonius of Vespasian's part in the invasion, but not of that of the other legionary commanders, not unnaturally because Vespasian, unlike them, went on to become emperor. But perhaps the major deficit in the written sources is the loss of that part of Tacitus's *Annals* which covered the year AD 43.

The archaeological evidence is scarcely more certain. Indeed, while there are clear indications of a very early Roman military presence at both Richborough and Fishbourne, and indeed elsewhere in southern England, it is often difficult to date the finds precisely and archaeologists can differ widely in their interpretations. Occasionally tree-ring dating can give a precise date and one such case is the Roman fortress at Alchester where a gate was built of timbers felled between October and December AD 44. Such precision is unusual and it simply is not possible to show that the earliest traces of the military activity, for example, at Richborough, date exactly to AD 43.[4]

Interpretations

It is not surprising, therefore, that there have been a number of widely varying proposals to identify the invasion landing site or sites and the Roman line of advance to Colchester. A matter which a number of them seek to address is to account for the capitulation of part of the Dobunni, settled as far west as Gloucestershire as they were, when the prime objective of the initial campaign appears to have been the taking of Colchester. A characteristically eccentric example is that of our friend, Sir George Airy. In 1860 he published in the *Athenaeum* a reconstruction which had the invasion force land in Essex, probably between the Crouch and the Colne and possibly at Maldon; on reprinting this paper in 1865 he included an addendum suggesting a landing site near Southend. After landing Airy had the Romans march to the Lea for the first river battle and then pursue the Britons across the Thames near London. At this point Plautius sent for the emperor. Led by Claudius, the Romans recrossed the Thames for the march on Colchester.[5]

Although now discounted, like his interpretation of the Caesarean invasions, Airy's approach had two merits. First he was alive to the need to reconcile any interpretation with the reality of the maritime environment. However, his argument that it would be possible to make the passage from Boulogne to Essex on one tack with a south-south-west wind and with a favourable tide falls because it is impossible to carry a favourable tide from Boulogne into the Thames estuary. Secondly he constructed a case for the strategic significance of Essex as an easily defended territory from which the Romans would have been able to consolidate the ultimate conquest of south-east Britain; in such a context Plautius's pursuit of the Britons across the Lea and then the Thames before marching on Colchester is a strategic nonsense.

Another nineteenth-century interpretation, one which attempts to account for the episode of the submission of the Dobunni, is that of Edwin Guest in his *Origines Celticae*. He has the invasion force land in East Kent – at Hythe, Dover and Richborough – and march westwards for engagements with the British at Silchester and Cirencester, after which the Dobunni surrendered, before returning east for the final assault on Colchester. On the other hand Emil Hübner took the view that the landing site could not be identified more precisely than as 'at one or more points between Dover and Southampton'. However, he toyed with the idea that one of these beachheads may have been on the Solent at *Clausentum* – modern Bitterne – seeing the origin of that place name in that of the empéror himself (★*Claudientum* from Claudius[†]). He then had the invaders march north-westwards to Winchester and Silchester where the submission of the Dobunni was received and a garrison was left at Gloucester. In Hübner's interpretation the first river battle was in the Bristol Channel region, possibly on the Avon. The Romans then turned east for the decisive battle before the capture of Colchester. Hübner rather spoilt his case for a beachhead as far west as the Solent by his belief that the predominant winds in the English Channel are from the south-east![6]

In contrast, with the twentieth century, academic opinion began to coalesce around the view that the invaders landed at three points in East Kent, for example Richborough, Dover and Lympne, with an advance to the Thames along the North Downs. This opinion was considerably strengthened by the excavations at Richborough and the identification of parallel defensive ditches dated to the Claudian period (*colour plate 22*). However, Verica and the Dobunni were not wholly forgotten. In 1952 the O'Neils sought to explain the context of eight apparently early Roman camps in the Cotswolds with the suggestion that they represented evidence of the activity of a Roman contingent that landed somewhere in Sussex to receive the submission of tribes such as the Dobunni. This idea was further developed by Christopher Hawkes, who suggested that a separate force under Sentius Saturninus landed in the Solent with the remit of restoring Verica or of installing Togidubnus. It would have been this expedition, rather than Plautius's main force, that advanced north-westwards into the territory of the Dobunni.[7] Even so a number of scholars have maintained the view that the invaders embarked at Boulogne and landed at or near Richborough. Malcolm Todd envisages the possibility of subsidiary landings at Reculver and elsewhere on the north Kent coast; otherwise these scholars explicitly or implicitly understand Dio's description of

---

[†]A word in an ancient language which is conjectured to exist, but which is not known from any extant text is by convention marked with an asterisk.

the organisation of the invasion army as a reference to a landing in three waves rather than at three points. Frere and Webster explain the capitulation of the Dobunni as the defection of part of the tribe from the British forces on or near the battle zone, perhaps somewhere in Kent, or shortly thereafter through the medium of envoys, rather than arising from a penetration of a Roman force into the far west.[8]

Nevertheless, the claim by Dio Cassius that Claudius was persuaded to order the expedition by Verica has kept alive the idea that the invasion force landed in three divisions at separate points and that one was in the Chichester area. This hypothesis has been associated with the Fishbourne Roman Palace and with the significant, if shadowy, figure of the British puppet king of the Atrebates, Cogidubnus, whom we have already noted and seemingly installed in Verica's place. It may be seen as drawing some force from the evidence for the campaign undertaken by the *Legio II Augusta* under the command of Vespasian in the south-west in the period immediately following the invasion.[9]

In 1989 John Hind introduced a new element into the academic debate by proposing that all three divisions of the expeditionary force landed near Chichester, arguing that this makes possible a more satisfactory interpretation of the record of subsequent events in the campaign, in particular the submission of the contingent from the Dobunni. He sees the initial skirmishes with the British forces as taking place in Hampshire with an excursion to the north-west by the Romans to receive the submission of the Dobunni. This, he suggests, could have been undertaken by a 'flying column' who would have established a protective garrison possibly at Cirencester. Strangely Hind's proposal did not attract much interest until the late nineties, when the Sussex Archaeological Society organised a conference at Chichester on the question whether the Claudian invasion bridgehead was in West Sussex or East Kent.[10]

David Bird more recently has also argued in support of Hind's hypothesis, although his interpretation of Plautius's line of advance differs from Hind's to allow for what he believes would have been the impossibility of advancing from the Chichester area towards the Thames across the Wealden clay. Also contributing to the hypothesis of a landing by the main invasion force on the Solent, Ernest Black has emphasised the need to interpret extant documentary sources with an understanding of the lost contemporary and near-contemporary sources which the extant writers would have used. Arguing that it is possible to assess the strengths and weaknesses and the political prejudices of both extant historians of Roman Britain and of their lost sources, he urges the exercise of extreme care when there is only one substantial extant source for a major event such as the Claudian invasion.[11]

Exploiting this approach, Black points out the similarities and differences between Dio's accounts of the two battles on the unnamed river and on the Thames; these can be accounted for, he suggests, by Dio's uncritical use of two separate sources for the same event. There would then be only one battle – on the Thames; this provides a solution to what Black sees as a weakness in the hypothesis of a landing on the Solent; namely, how to account for the first battle, if it did not take place on the Medway. Finally Black resurrects Sentius Saturninus as a major player in the invasion; while Plautius led the main invasion force to a bridgehead on the Solent, in this version of the hypothesis Sentius led a separate group to a landing at Richborough to secure a bridgehead there for Claudius's crossing from Boulogne. The failure of Dio to record the part played by Sentius can be understood, Black says, in the light of Dio's limitations as an historian, in writing about only one of the two separate forces involved.

In spite of the arguments now being mounted for a bridgehead in the Solent, the case for locating the invasion landing at Richborough has continued to find advocates. After the Chichester conference, personalities prominent in Kent archaeology, such as Nigel Nicolson and Brian Philp, responded vigorously, to defend the honour of Kent in letters to an archaeological newsletter, but perhaps lacked the space fully to set out the case.

In a more academic context Frere and Fulford restated the traditional arguments; they argued that a line of advance from the Solent via the territory of the Dobunni would have been a logistical impossibility and pointed to the risks involved in an invasion passage from Boulogne to the Solent, but otherwise added little that was significantly new. Since my contribution to the Chichester conference, I had been continuing my research into the naval aspects of the actual Channel crossing itself; this leads me to continue to believe on balance that the most likely scenario for the naval operation is a bridgehead at Richborough. On 1 April 2003 BBC2 ran a programme on the huge marble-clad monumental arch built at Richborough in the AD 80s and now reduced to its cross-shaped foundation. The central hypothesis advanced by the programme was that the monument was built by Domitian to mark the place where the legions landed in AD 43. This was not the first time that the monument had been advanced before in support of the Richborough hypothesis. However, in my view, it is not especially persuasive, certainly no more so than many of the other circumstantial arguments advanced to support both the Fishbourne and Richborough hypotheses (*26* and *colour plate 22*).[12]

More recently other contributors have highlighted the uncertainties of interpretation. In a critique of Frere and Fulford's paper, Eberhard Sauer stresses the dangers of too dogmatic an approach, while John Manley's reassessment of the archaeological, historical and other evidence does not conclude in favour of either hypothesis. Moreover, interest has begun to focus on the nature of the event in AD 43. Was it a military invasion or the culmination of a long process of the romanisation of southern Britain leading to political annexation – a process which had been going on since Caesar's departure a century earlier?

In a study of native coins circulating among the tribes of southern and eastern Britain, John Creighton discerns a significant shift in their imagery some time towards the end of the first century BC. The traditional native images are replaced by a range of images whose origin can be traced to the classical iconography employed by Augustus to impose and legitimise his authority as emperor. From now until the Claudian invasion this romanising imagery evolves on the coinage of southern and eastern Britain in the areas of the Catuvellauni/Trinovantes and of the Atrebates, drawing on new themes from classical sources to articulate political authority.[13] Creighton associates this use by British kings of images from the classical world to manipulate power with the ubiquity of hostage-taking by Romans. Such hostages would most often have been younger members of elite families, who would have been educated at a Roman centre such as Marseilles or Rome itself. In the course of an upbringing in such a Roman environment they must have been profoundly impressed by the way in which visual images and other displays were exploited to legitimise power in the Roman world. When they returned home to take over from their fathers, it would be to exercise power in the ways that they had seen exploited in Rome; the evidence for this can be seen in their coinage.

In support of the idea that Rome might well have been exercising effective political control over south-east Britain even before the Claudian invasion, Manley pointed to some enigmatic evidence from both Fishbourne and Colchester, which might just be explained by a Roman military presence in Britain before AD 43. With David Rudkin he has recently expanded on this, at least for Fishbourne. In an article in *Current Archaeology* which they acknowledge to be speculative, they address issues from their excavations at Fishbourne which have not been satisfactorily explained by the assumption of the arrival of the Roman military as late as AD 43. The chief of these is the presence at Fishbourne of sherds of Arretine pottery which are dated to the reigns of Augustus and Tiberius. The usual explanation that Vespasian's *Legio II Augusta* had been issued with out of date stock is scarcely adequate. Associated with these finds was a copper-alloy fitting which they consider was part of the scabbard of a Roman sword. This, together with other uncertain aspects of the Fishbourne excavations, leads them to speculate that they are best explained by a Roman military presence in support of the local client king even before AD 43.

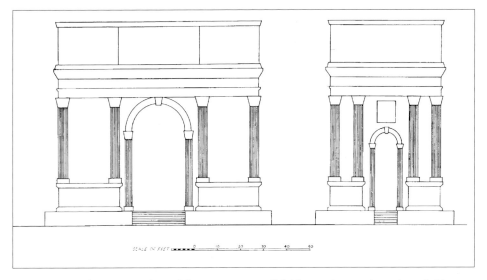

26 Conjectural reconstruction of the monument at Richborough, seen in main and side elevation as a quadrifrons. *From Cunliffe, B. (ed.), 1968,* Fifth Report on the Excavations at the Roman Fort at Richborough, Kent, *(58-9) by permission of the Society of Antiquaries*

Even so, whether his mission was to carry out a military conquest or to complete the political annexation of a territory, which already existed as a Roman province in all but name, Aulus Plautius arrived in AD 43 with a very considerable force and he must have landed somewhere. The balance of present academic thinking – even while accepting that there can be no certainty – seems to favour a bridgehead in the Solent, associated with Verica, sometime King of the British Atrebates. At the Chichester conference, which he chaired as President of the Sussex Archaeological Society, Barry Cunliffe closed the discussions with an invitation to those present to keep an open mind. However, even though in his earlier publications he had accepted that the landing had been at Richborough, by 1998 he had come to the view that 'a compelling case can be made for suggesting that the main landing took place in the harbours of the Solent with the Fishbourne/Chichester region as the focus'. Sauer, in his critique of Frere and Fulford, accepts that a landing at Richborough may be a possibility, but lists six counter-arguments – four of them related to the submission of the Dobunni – in favour of a landing 'far to the west of Kent'. In his report on the excavations at Alchester, where we have noted the tree-ring evidence for a date as early as AD 44, he argued for the possible identification of this fortress with that of the garrison left by Plautius with the Dobunni. This does not necessarily prove that the landing was in Sussex, since Alchester 'could have been quickly reached from either direction'. Nevertheless, he takes the view that the arguments for a landing in

Sussex are marginally stronger than those for Kent. As for John Manley, while he does not formally offer an opinion as to the location of the beachhead, he does appear to be keen to stress the links between Claudius and Verica and the rapid transformation of the Fishbourne/Chichester area with prestigious new buildings in the immediate aftermath of the invasion.[14]

The context of the naval operation

Of modern authors, only Frere and Fulford, and Sauer, as far as I am aware, have considered the naval context of Plautius's cross-Channel operation.[15] The former argue that an invasion passage from Boulogne to the Solent would have involved 'a lengthy passage past hazardous headlands at Dungeness and Beachy Head and along a harbourless coast against a contrary prevailing wind and a powerful contrary tide every twelve hours' and that for a fleet of 800 to 900 ships it amounted to 'a totally unjustified risk when a far less hazardous route was available' (*colour plate 23*). Sauer acknowledges that this is perhaps their strongest argument. His rebuttal is two-part: he cites a number of cases of Roman commanders deciding on risky campaign routes and he quotes Dio's statement that, at the time the legionaries saw the 'shooting star', their course was from east to west, which he finds 'hard to reconcile with the fairly straight south–north route from Boulogne to Richborough'.

Despite Sauer's refutation, the naval argument is worth setting out in some detail. Frere and Fulford outline the essence of it, but their brief summary scarcely does it justice. It involves not only the maritime environment, which we considered in Chapter 2 or the performance of the ships, particularly the transports, available to the Romans, which we looked at in Chapters 3 and 4; it also demands that we think about the conduct of fleet operations and what that means for the time required for the naval operation. We also need to think about the strategic context of the campaign, since the conduct of the naval operation must serve the overall campaign objective.

Was Boulogne the port of embarkation?

To a large degree the argument that an invasion passage to the Solent would have been too risky for Roman commanders to contemplate turns on the assumption that the invasion fleet embarked at Boulogne. As we shall see in the next Chapter, in the late third century AD a Roman invasion fleet would indeed land on the Solent, but it would sail from the Seine estuary. So what is the evidence that the Claudian fleet sailed from Boulogne? The only hint from the documentary sources is Suetonius's statement that Claudius himself, when summoned by Plautius, sailed from Boulogne. Boulogne was certainly to be a major base – possibly the headquarters – of the *Classis Britannica* and, as we have seen, was used by Caesar for both his expeditions. By contrast the evidence for a major naval base on the Seine estuary, certainly for the first century AD is scant, though Stephen Johnson does suggest the possibility of a Saxon Shore fort in the area of Le Havre.[16] Even so, we need not assume the pre-existence of a permanent naval base for the assembly of the invasion force; after all, there had been no pre-existent base at Boulogne when Caesar launched his two expeditions from there. All we can do is to ask ourselves whether it is a reasonable assumption that the emperor would have sailed from an embarkation harbour other than that used by the main invasion army.

Another way of considering the question is to ask whether, embarking at Boulogne, it would be reasonable to suppose that Claudius would land other than at the main invasion bridgehead. Whatever plans the naval staff adopted for the landing of the main force, they had to ensure that the beachhead where Claudius landed in Britain and his route thence to join Plautius was securely in Roman hands. Although he advocates Fishbourne for the landing of the main force, Hind accepts that Claudius may have landed at Richborough: 'If so, the journey would have been through an area cowed and submissive after Plautius' victories'. This scenario has been developed by Black with his proposal that Claudius landed in East Kent with a separate force led by Sentius Saturninus. On the other hand Bird, who also argues for the Fishbourne hypothesis, considers that the route through Kent 'might still be rather dangerous' and sees diplomatic advantages for Claudius in landing at Fishbourne to restore Verica (or install Togidubnus) in person.

If we accept the Fishbourne hypothesis as expounded by Hind, Black, Bird and others, we cannot identify from Dio's account any operation by the army which might have amounted to securing Richborough for Claudius's landing and the route he would have taken through Kent to join Plautius at the Thames. Indeed Black's proposal of a separate force under Sentius Saturninus escorting Claudius to a landing in East Kent is based on the hypothesis that Dio's sources covered the operations of only one of two forces involved in the invasion. Bird's hypothesis is that operations to secure this route might have been undertaken, 'from both directions', while Plautius was waiting for Claudius to arrive. If so, it would have been leaving things a little late and in the event Bird's proposal is that Claudius landed at Fishbourne. To put oneself in the position of the Roman commanders planning the operation, to have Claudius land other than at the main invasion bridgehead must have seemed to be a major complication requiring the input of significant additional effort and resources. Moreover, if the first task of the expedition was for

Claudius formally to reinstall Verica as King of Atrebates, it would be a little strange for him to arrive in East Kent when the main invasion force had landed at Fishbourne. The only rational choice was for Claudius to land at the main invasion beachhead. However, if the main force left the Seine to land on the Solent, it would seem utterly pointless for Claudius to have embarked at Boulogne for the much more difficult passage thence to the Solent.

A more difficult passage?

Let us look at some statistics. A study of attempts to invade Britain by Caesar, Claudius, Maximian and Constantius Chlorus, William the Conqueror, and the Spanish in the late sixteenth century and William of Orange shows that in total they involved sixteen cross-Channel fleet operations; of these, eight (50 per cent) failed to reach their destination. This study underlines the sheer unpredictability of passage making by fleets in the age of sail. The overall figures include seven cross-Channel passages by Caesar's fleet or parts of it, of which two (29 per cent) failed to reach their destination. The two failed attempts were the result of bad weather and adverse winds; arguably their commanders were under pressure from Caesar to make the crossing as soon as possible. If one disregards these two cases, the high success rate on the short Channel-crossing from Boulogne to the East Kent becomes impressive when compared with the low success rate of the other attempts taken together (33 per cent). Even if one excludes the ill-fated voyages of the three Spanish Armadas, the success rate of fleet passages on the other routes across the Channel is still as low as 50 per cent. These figures do not include a grotesque invasion attempt by the Normans in the 1030s. Duke Robert the Magnificent assembled a fleet which set sail for England from Fécamp. Caught in a storm, it was driven to Jersey.[17]

Other suggestive statistics come from Seán McGrail. For his study of prehistoric cross-Channel seamanship, he devised a method of assessing the relative reliability of the cross-Channel routes he described. This took account of the length of the passage, distance out of sight of land, the effect of tidal streams, the likelihood of favourable winds, and any unusual aspects of the passage. He calculated 'relative reliability factors' of 98 per cent for the passage from Boulogne to Walmer and of 71 per cent for that from the Seine to Spithead. What would this mean in reality? For a ship (or fleet) leaving the Seine for the Solent a favourable wind would be between due east and due south. However, modern data show that, during the summer months at Le Havre, such a wind would be blowing for only a quarter of the time (24 per cent). However, for nearly half the time (47 per cent) the wind is from the westerly quadrant. Moreover, if a southerly, or even a south-easterly wind is generated by an approaching Atlantic low, it may well, as we saw in Chapter 2, be followed by adverse windshifts which will bring the wind round to the west and even north-west, as the centre of the depression passes to the north. Such a sequence is quite possible within the likely timescale of the passage. This would have the effect of progressively bringing the wind forward until the point is reached when the ship (or fleet) would not be able to hold its course. By contrast at Boulogne modern data show the predominant winds to be from the south-west – 27 per cent of observations in summer months – while winds between south-west and south-east, favourable for a passage to East Kent, are recorded for 42 per cent of observations. The length of the passage would usually be sufficiently short not to incur adverse windshifts. Moreover, on the passage from Boulogne to East Kent a fleet could work the tides to considerable effect and there is evidence that Caesar endeavoured to do just that. On the other hand, as we saw in Chapter 2, on a passage from the Seine to the Solent the effect of the tides would be broadly neutral.[18]

There is a hint of just how difficult these factors might make an invasion passage from the Seine to the Solent in a panegyrist's account of the successful invasion of Britain in AD 296 under Constantius Chlorus:

> Indeed you (i.e. Constantius Chlorus) led the way in setting out from the coast at Gessoriacum despite the raging sea, and inspired in that army of yours which had sailed down the River Seine an unquenchable resolution, so much so that though your generals still hesitated, with sea and sky in wild disorder, of its own accord the army demanded the signal to sail, poured scorn on threatening portents to be seen, set sail midst rain, and since the wind was not behind, they tacked across it.[19]

It is not necessary to take the panegyrist's account of the weather conditions, and much else, at face value, but we may well believe that the fleet sailing from the Seine did not find a favourable wind. Ireland's translation of the last phrase 'tacked across it' suggests that the fleet had the wind, as yachtsmen would say, 'on the nose' and had to tack and tack again to make progress. However, we noted in Chapter 2 that the sailing ships available to the Romans would have been unlikely to be able to make progress over the ground against the wind and the Latin would allow us to understand that the fleet was sailing hard on the wind. If so, we may conjecture that the fleet sailed with what was initially a favourable wind, which veered during the passage until the fleet was close-hauled.[20]

The written sources are much more specific about the difficulties of another invasion launched from the vicinity of the Seine estuary. In the summer of 1066 Duke William of Normandy assembled his invasion fleet at Dives and in other natural harbours nearby. Here the fleet was delayed for some considerable time. William of Poitiers, who was a chaplain to Duke William, reports that they were waiting for a southerly wind. To this a contemporary Latin poem, *Song of the Battle of Hastings*, adds that during this period the weather was stormy with ceaseless rain. Although the *Song* speaks of easterly winds, its general description fits an unusually bad summer with depression after depression passing over with winds predominantly from the westerly quadrant. When the fleet did sail, both sources say that it was driven to St Valéry-sur-Somme, William of Poitiers specifying that this was before a westerly wind. It is quite clear from the sources that St Valéry was not William's intended destination, but it was from here that, with a change in the weather, he was able to make the passage to Pevensey a fortnight later.

Of course, there is nothing unusual about an invasion fleet being detained waiting for a favourable wind – after all Caesar was delayed for twenty-five days by a north-westerly wind before his second expedition. However, it seems unlikely that William would have sailed while the wind was still unfavourable for his destination in England. What seems to have happened is that the fleet left Dives with a favourable wind which, during the voyage, veered to the west, or even north-west, with the result that the fleet could not hold its course and was driven to the estuary of the Somme. Ultimately it is this possibility of adverse wind shifts linked to the fact that the distance involved is over twice as long (90 sea miles as against 40) that makes the passage from the Seine to the Solent more difficult than that from Boulogne to East Kent.

'*A lengthy passage… along a harbourless coast*'

But what of the passage from Boulogne to the Solent? To say that a passage from the Seine to the Solent would have presented a greater challenge than that from Boulogne to East Kent says nothing about the comparative difficulties of a passage along the South Coast from Boulogne to the Solent. There are three aspects to be considered: the predominant winds, the tides and, because this is a coastwise passage, the potential hazards and havens (*27*). A fleet on this coastal passage would need a wind from the easterly quadrant. Modern data shows that during the summer months the probability of such a wind would be about 1:4 – Boulogne 22 per cent; Newhaven 23 per cent; Thorney Island in Chichester Harbour 28 per cent. The figures for winds from the opposing, westerly quadrant for the same meteorological stations are: Boulogne 50 per cent; Newhaven 49 per cent; Thorney Island 48 per cent. The meteorological conditions which are likely to generate favourable winds for the passage down-Channel to the Solent would be those associated with a high pressure system. Such systems are more stable than Atlantic depressions and may last several days. Moreover, the winds may well be quite light. This could mean that once an easterly wind had set in, it might well be expected to blow for some time. However, there is no way that the single observer can predict how long such a wind would last and it may well fail before the end of the passage.

In a coastwise passage, such as that from Boulogne to the Solent, the tidal streams will run parallel to the coast, alternately favourable and adverse. If the fleet is not able to achieve a high speed, as seems likely if the winds are light, then the overall adverse effect of the tides will be particularly marked. This was shown in a study I undertook of the time likely to be required for a passage from a point off Boulogne to the Nab Tower at the eastern entrance to the Solent. The total distance involved is some 95 sea miles and I assumed two ships (or fleets), one making 5 knots through the water, the other three. The time required for the faster ship would have been 19 hours, while the slower would have taken 32 hours. Comparing the two ships it becomes clear that the slower the speed through the water, the more the time required for the passage is adversely affected by the changing tidal streams. For a reduction in boat speed of some 40 per cent the time required for the passage is nearly 70 per cent greater. This corresponds to the intuitive understanding of racing yachtsmen that slower yachts are more at a disadvantage from adverse tides. Moreover, off the Owers at the approach to the Solent, the tides can run very strongly; it was only because this tidal stream was running in its favour when it arrived off the Owers that the slower ship was able to complete the passage in the 32 hours estimated. Had she been delayed for any reason in her arrival off the Owers, she could have found the tide against her running at speeds approaching 3 knots.

Once they had arrived at the Nab, the ships would still have been an hour or more from the entrance to Chichester Harbour and perhaps 2 or even 3 hours from anchoring. Moreover, since we are estimating the passage time required from a point off Boulogne, we have made no allowance for the time required to leave the harbour. Allowances for these factors mean that the faster ship could not have completed the passage, anchorage to anchorage in less than 24 hours, or the slower in much less than 37 hours. In addition these estimates depend on a steady favourable wind. As we shall see, a fleet operation would have been affected by factors which would have made a fleet passage even longer.[21]

Frere and Fulford wrote of a passage 'past hazardous headlands at Dungeness and Beachy Head and along a harbourless coast'. While their

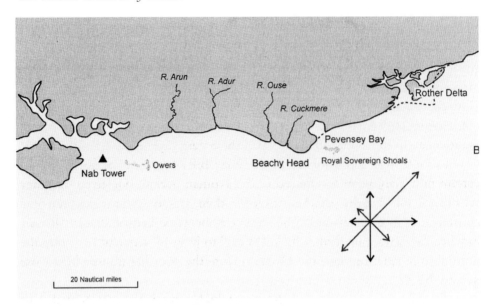

27 The south coast as it might have been in the Roman period. Dungeness would have been represented by the delta of the River Rother, Pevensey Bay would have been a fine natural haven, while shelter would also have been offered by the estuaries of the four Sussex rivers The length of the arrows shows the relative frequency of winds from various directions in the months April to September

summary of the argument from naval logistics is broadly accurate, they are wrong to describe the south coast as 'harbourless'. Moreover, during the Roman period there is unlikely to have been a headland at Dungeness, let alone a hazardous one. Inhospitable though much of the present coastline of Sussex appears, it seems probable that in the Roman period there were a number of substantial natural havens, which are now silted up or kept open by dredging. Pevensey Bay, the site of the Norman landing, in the lee of Beachy Head, is perhaps the best known. In addition there are the four river valleys penetrating the cliff line of West Sussex, the Cuckmere, now heavily silted, the Ouse, with the modern port of Newhaven at its mouth, the Adur, with the commercial harbour of Shoreham, both of them kept open by dredging, and Littlehampton on the Arun, which now is open only for some 6 hours in each tidal cycle. In the Roman period all may well have been large enough to serve as shelter for a substantial fleet (*colour plate 24*).

Along the South Coast there are two hazards to be considered. The first, some 7 miles eastward of Beachy Head, is the group of shoals centred on the Royal Sovereign Shoal. While, on the basis of modern charted depths, it is unlikely that the Roman fleet would go aground here, the chart is marked with overfalls here and the *Dover Strait Pilot* reports that the sea breaks heavily in bad weather. There are also overfalls close inshore of Beachy Head.

We cannot be sure that the charted depth over the shoals would not have been greater in the Roman period, but the Royal Sovereign Shoals are reported to be of rock and we may wonder whether, with the lower sea level of Roman times, they might not then have been more of a threat than today. The second and more serious hazard on this route is the foul ground and extensive rocky patches going under the collective name of the Owers. Standing across the apparent entrance to the Solent, they extend 3 miles south, 6 miles south-east and 4 miles east of Selsey Bill. Again we cannot know for certain how they were configured in the Roman period, but given that they are of rock and that the sea level was lower then, it is likely that they presented an even more serious hazard. The danger is increased because Selsey Bill is a low headland, not one from which it is easy to judge distance off, creating the possibility of running onto the Owers, before the pilot has realised how close inshore he is.

The danger here is essentially one which would have threatened craft coasting westwards, rather than completing a cross-Channel passage from, say, the Seine. The latter would have the high ground of the Isle of Wight on the port bow as a mark to guide them away from the Owers. The danger would be greater if the coasting craft is on the port tack, i.e. with a wind in the southerly quadrant because then Selsey Bill would be a lee shore. In fact the seafarer running close-hauled on the port tack westwards with the tide along the Sussex coast would face the same choice as the ninth-century Viking Egil did, as he coasted south along the Yorkshire coast towards the Humber. According to *Egil's Saga*, he saw breaking seas out to sea. With a favourable tide under him and an onshore wind, Egill could not tack to head offshore and pass outside the hazard. His choice was to go aground on the off-lying hazard or drive his ship ashore. He chose the latter. The less handy ships of the Romans would have been even less able to extricate themselves from such a danger. Moreover, the incident would have been even more exciting if it involved a whole fleet rather than a single ship.[22] The most obvious danger of a lee shore is that the wind may drive a ship ashore and that the pounding of the vessel, as it is lifted and dropped by the waves onto the ground, will break it up. Life will also be at risk if the crew cannot scramble safely ashore; the chalk cliffs along much of the coast from Beachy Head westward would make it impossible for crew members to reach safety. The less obvious danger of a lee shore would be that the wind could well hamper the vessel in trying to keep to windward of off-lying dangers, such as the Owers and the Royal Sovereign Shoals.

In the Roman period the configuration of Chichester Harbour would have been very different from today's. Even so, it would have provided a large body of sheltered water. Nowadays the entrance can be difficult, especially on the ebb with an onshore wind; local knowledge would have been necessary to make the entrance safely. By contrast on the route across the Dover Strait there is only one off-lying hazard and one which through the centuries has had an awesome reputation, the Goodwin Sands. Lying some 5 nautical miles off East Kent and drying at low water, they offer a formidable threat to any ship that goes aground on them. A matter for some doubt seems to be whether or in what form the Goodwins existed in Roman times. There appears to have been a popular tradition which associates the Goodwin Sands with Earl Godwine, father of King Harold, dating their origin to the eleventh century. According to this tradition the Sands were once part of mainland Kent and formed an estate belonging to the earl which was submerged in an eleventh-century storm following the robbing of stones from its protecting sea wall. An alternative, and maybe more likely, explanation is that the Sands existed until the eleventh century as the remnants of an offshore island. I have previously tended to the view that the development of the Goodwins was associated with the silting up of the Wantsum Channel, which certainly would have had an impact on the tidal currents in the immediate locality. However, that view is not really tenable. When Trinity House was taking soundings on the Goodwins for a lighthouse in 1871, these showed 15 feet of sand resting on blue clay. Dowker took the view that the Goodwins are the remnant of an island represented by that blue clay. The fact remains that we are not able to assess to what extent the Goodwins would have been a hazard in Roman times. But a fleet from Boulogne which made a landfall at the South Foreland and then followed the coastline northwards should have been able to give them ample clearance.[23]

'A fleet of 800 to 900 ships'

In his *Epitome of Military Science,* the fourth-century writer Vegetius makes a revealing point about the concerns of naval commanders for the security of their fleets. In describing the weeks immediately before the opening of the sailing season, he says:

> It is still perilous to venture upon the sea right up to the Ides of May[24] by reason of very many stars and the season of the year itself – not that the activities of merchants cease, but greater caution should be shown when an army takes to the sea in warships than when the enterprising are in a hurry for their profits.[25]

1 The cliffs of the South Foreland. In a letter to his friend Atticus, the Roman orator Cicero wrote: 'It is notorious that the approach to the island is defended by astonishing masses of rock'. Even without warriors on the cliff top, Caesar could not have landed here. To the right is the route northwards towards Caesar's landing place in the vicinity of Deal

2 The eastern entrance to the Wantsum as it is today, seen from Thanet. Now heavily silted, the sand spit beyond the present River Stour would not have existed in the Roman period

3 Dover Castle overlooking the eastern bank of the estuary of the Dour. It would have been here, rather than on the heights of the South Foreland, that Julius Caesar saw the massed ranks of the British warriors opposing his landing in 55 BC, when he decided that this would be no place to land

4 The high cirrus cloud and the low cumulus portend an approaching depression; if it has not already done so the wind will shortly back to the south-west, south or even south-east. *Photograph by Chris Tibbs*

5 Mist and low featureless cloud typical of the warm sector; the wind will have veered to the west, as the warm front passed over. *Photograph by Chris Tibbs*

6 The cold front has now passed over some time ago; the likely wind direction is from the north-west. *Photograph by Chris Tibbs*

7 Above left Gold medallion struck to commemorate the arrival of Constantius Chlorus in London in AD 296. *Photograph by Ken Elks of an electrotype in his collection*

8 Above right Silver denarius of Carausius showing a warship, possibly celebrating his success in repulsing the attempted invasion of Maximian of AD 289. *Copyright The British Museum*

9 Above left Billon quinarius of Allectus depicting a warship. It is difficult to identify a naval victory that it might represent. Perhaps it was simply a show of naval defiance in the light of Constantius's threatened invasion. *Photograph by Ken Elks of a coin in his collection*

10 Above right Carausius and his brethren. Carausian coin showing the heads of Diocletian and Maximian, alongside his own. *Copyright The British Museum*

11 Reconstruction of one of the new-style warships found in Mainz in 1981-2 on display in the Museum für Antike Seefahrt, Mainz. *Photograph reproduced by permission of the Museum Director, Dr Barbara Pferdehirt*

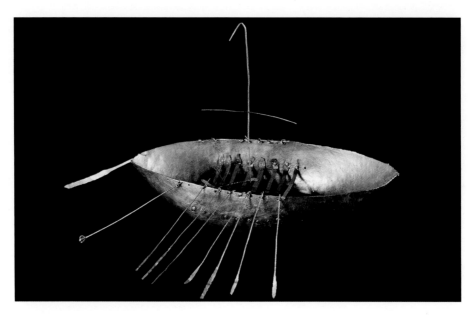

12 The gold model boat from Broighter, Co. Derry, Ireland, dated to the first century BC. *National Museum of Ireland*

13 *Asterix*: this model reconstruction of St Peter Port 1, on display at Castle Cornet, Guernsey, was named *Asterix* after a competition among the schoolchildren of Guernsey. The detail of the superstructure, including the deckhouse is, although conjectural, based on evidence found on site. *Reproduced by permission of the States of Guernsey Heritage Committee*

14 Model reconstruction of the floor timbers and planking recovered from St Peter Port 1, on display at Castle Cornet, Guernsey. The darker pieces represent components actually found. They clearly demonstrate the characteristic massive framing of the Romano-Celtic tradition. The bows are to the right and the mast step may be discerned in the middle of the group of three darker timbers about one third back from the bows. *Reproduced by permission of the States of Guernsey Heritage Committee*

15 A 1:10 scale model of the Barland's Farm boat as reconstructed by McGrail and Roberts. *Courtesy of Newport City Council Museums and Heritage Service*

16 Above Third-century AD mosaic floor from Bad Kreuznach, Rheinland-Pfalz, Germany; excavated in 1966. *Photograph reproduced by permission of Dr Angela Nestler-Zapp of the Schloßparkmuseum und Römerhalle, Bad Kreuznach*

17 Opposite The present-day Humber keel *Comrade* hard on the wind. Although certainly not linked in evolution to the sea-going ships of the Romano-Celtic tradition, modern Humber keels share with them many features of design and function, including the forward-located mast. *Photograph supplied by the Humber Keel and Sloop Preservation Society*

North ⟹

18 The end of the cliff line northwards from Dover. The cliffs, which can be seen in the middle of the photograph behind the modern shingle beach, would in Caesar's day have been on the shoreline. The first practicable landing point would have been just a little further to the north around the site of Walmer Castle

19 The natural haven of the estuary of the river Dour as it was in the Roman period (AD *c*.200). *Photograph of model in Dover Museum*

20 The modern harbour at Dover in 1990. *Photograph of model in Dover Museum*

21 Claudius arrives in Britain in state. He would have brought his elephants as a display of his imperial status. They would certainly have been in evidence at the submission of the British kings at Colchester. Did they also appear in West Sussex? If Claudius also went there to install Cogidumnus in place of Verica, they would have been a necessary part of the imperial display. *Photograph of model in Dover Museum*

22 Richborough from the air. The two parallel ditches to the right of the photograph are dated to the earliest period of the Roman occupation. The cross-shaped feature in the centre of the photograph is the foundation of the monumental arch. *English Heritage Photo Library © Skyscan Balloon Photography*

23 'A lengthy passage…along a harbourless coast.' The cliffs of East Sussex looking west from Birling Gap. Behind the line of cliffs in the foreground is the entrance to Cuckmere Haven

24 Cuckmere Haven. This heavily silted and managed estuary would in the Roman period have been a significant haven

25 The seventh-century chapel of St Peter ad Murum at Bradwell, standing on the west gate of the fort at *Othona*

26 'Twin Towers Reculver'. The ruins of the medieval church stand above the vestige of the west wall of the Roman fort in lower right of the photograph

27 The remains of the south-east corner of the walls of the fort at Reculver

28 The northern entrance to the Wantsum as it is today, looking from Reculver towards Thanet. From this perspective any garrison at Reculver would have been able to control the passage of ships, not only through the Wantsum, but also along the north coast of Kent

29 The south-east corner of the walls of the Roman fort at Pevensey

30 Wide views from Bradwell across the estuary of the Blackwater towards the Colne

Frere and Fulford refer to 'a fleet of 800 to 900 ships'. This is broadly in line with other estimates of the size of the Claudian invasion fleet. John Peddie, who brought personal experience of military logistics to bear, calculated a total requirement for 933 ships to carry the men, cavalry horses, baggage animals, heavy equipment and rations, adding that the final figure was probably nearer 1,000. My estimate, extrapolating forward from the data Caesar gives for his expedition of 54 BC, is that the fleet would have numbered between 725 and 1,040 vessels. In fairness to Peddie, he does speak of 'the high percentage error in calculating such logistical detail without firm information about Roman custom in these matters'. In reality the only assessment we can make is to state an order of figures within which it is likely that the size of the fleet was bracketed. For those who require precision, Frere and Fulford's figure of 800 to 900 will do; those who can live with greater uncertainty will go for a figure between 725 and 1,040.[26]

However, this is to assume that the whole invasion force sailed at the same time. If Dio's reference to the fleet sailing in three divisions is taken to mean that the invasion force crossed to Britain in three waves, this would reduce the shipping requirement to a third, say between 250 and 350 ships. Either way we have to consider the way in which the conduct of fleet operations would have impacted on the invasion passage.

The most significant of the factors affecting fleet operations is that a fleet will travel more slowly than would a single ship in comparable conditions of wind and weather. One can detail a number of reasons for this, but it is the inevitable result of the determination of the commander-in-chief to keep the fleet together in good formation. To do so, he will sail his flagship at less than the maximum possible speed to ensure that the individual ships can maintain strict formation with him. Of course it may be that a strict formation is not maintained. This seems to have been the case with Caesar's first expedition when he anchored off Dover to wait for stragglers. Even so, the fleet will progress only at the speed of the slowest. Drawing on data from Casson and a suggestion from McGrail, Neumann offered for his study of the Norman invasion passage guesstimates of the ratio of 'fleet-speed-to-single-ship-speed' in the range of half and seven tenths. However, none of the factors involved is susceptible to mathematical analysis and it is just not possible to calculate a precise figure which would fit all circumstances.[27]

Also significant for the time required for a fleet passage is the time required to leave harbour and take up formation at the start of the voyage and to enter harbour at the destination. A fleet numbering hundreds of vessels cannot all leave harbour at the same time. Clearly the operation will take a period of time running into hours. This will be especially true when the fleet is constrained by the configuration of the harbour to leave in single file. Sir John Dalrymple recorded the length of the fleet of William of Orange approaching the Channel from the north as formed up in 'a line of twenty miles in extent'. The wind direction at the time from the east would have dictated a line-ahead formation. If the fleet was making 5-6 knots, a likely speed in the very windy conditions at the time of the voyage, it would have taken three to 4 hours in line ahead to leave its embarkation harbour in the Maas estuary.[28]

The case of the Spanish Armada of 1588 was extreme. The fleet started to move down river to the mouth of the Tagus on 9 May 1588, but was prevented by adverse weather from putting to sea until the end of the month. It then took two days to get the whole fleet out to the open sea. In this case the operation was hampered by the inability of the more unwieldy ships to weather the shoals to the south of the estuary. Similar considerations would apply to entering harbour at the destination. Whether we have in mind Chichester Harbour or the Wantsum as the destination of the Claudian invasion fleet, both would have had restricted entrances. Any attempt to enter either in other than good order would lead, to put it mildly, to some excitement. As with the ratio of fleet-speed-to-single-ship-speed, it would be futile to attempt to put a precise measure on the time that would be required for a fleet to leave harbour and form up or to enter harbour at the end of the voyage; much would depend on the prevailing conditions and the size of the fleet. The two days spent by the Spanish Armada clearing the Tagus were clearly unusual. Excluding that case, all we can say is that leaving harbour and forming up or entering harbour at the end of the passage might take several hours.

Earlier I have suggested that a single-ship passage from Boulogne to Chichester Harbour at an average speed through the water approaching 3 knots could not have been made in under 37 hours. If one then adds to that the constraints under which a fleet operation would have been conducted, it is probable that a fleet passage could not have been made in much less than two or 2½ days, perhaps more. This immediately raises the question whether it would be possible for the fleet to stay at sea for that long without coming ashore at night. In Chapter 3, we saw that ancient warships had to put ashore at night for their crews to be fed and to sleep. The cavalry horses and draught animals of the invasion force also had to be fed and watered. In 1123 a Venetian fleet transporting horses direct to the Levant is reported to have needed to land every day to water the horses. If this applied to the invasion force of AD 43, it would have meant that the passage to the Solent could scarcely have been completed within a week. It would in fact have been sufficient to rule it out as an option.

Dio and the strange episode of the Dobunni

Sauer was right to base his main criticism of Frere and Fulford's paper on Dio's account of the submission of part of the Dobunni tribe; for if we understand it as Sauer (and others) do – and accept that Dio is accurate in this part of his narrative – then it is impossible to reconcile it with the hypothesis of the Roman landing at Richborough. But Sauer's interpretation and, for example, Hind's, turns on a single word in the Greek text which some understand to mean 'there' and those of the contrary view to mean 'thereupon' or 'next'. The text in question is:

> After the flight of these kings he gained by capitulation a part of the Bodunni, who were ruled by a tribe of the Catuellani; and leaving a garrison there, he advanced further and came to a river.

The incident occurs very soon after the landing, after initial skirmishes with the Britons and before Plautius's advance to the river, which some take to be the Medway. 'He' is Plautius; the 'Bodunni' are of course the Dobunni. The Greek word is '*κανταυθα*'. This is equally an adverb of place: 'and there'; and of time and sequence: 'and then'; 'thereupon'. The Dobunni were, as we have noted, settled in the Gloucestershire area and, for those who follow Hind, the submission of the section of the Dobunni occurred when a detachment of the Roman forces arrived in their territory. On this view the Romans left a garrison 'there' to protect their new allies from their former masters, the overweening Catuvellauni. Other commentators argue that the surrender and the establishment of the garrison are unrelated, but consecutive, events in Dio's narrative. According to them, the submission of 'part' of the Dobunni follows on quite naturally from the defeat of the British tribes in the initial skirmishes and the submission was offered either on the battlefield or by an embassy sent from the homeland of the Dobunni in Gloucestershire, in either case in the context of the defeat of the Britons in the initial skirmishes. The possibility of such remote submissions is well documented, including the cross-Channel submissions of British tribes before Caesar's first invasion. Those who support this interpretation see the establishment of the garrison as just the next thing in Dio's narrative, having nothing to do with the submission of the Dobunni.

Hind argues that the more natural translation is 'there' and I have to say that I agree with him. After all the question is not so much how far modern scholars can manipulate the meaning of the text to support their version of the campaign; rather it is how would Dio's contemporary readers have understood him and what did he intend that they should understand. On this basis it must be accepted that Hind's view carries considerable weight. However, this does beg the question as to what Dio's source or sources may have intended to convey and whether Dio understood them aright. Black's study of Roman-period historians of first-century Britain proposes the identification for Dio's account of the invasion of at least two, if not three, contemporary or near-contemporary sources, one with little grasp of military matters, none of them now extant. We need to be aware that Dio – or his source – may well not have realised the strategic significance of what he was saying. After all, Dio, or at least his manuscripts, confused the name of the Dobunni. It is perfectly conceivable that he did not know where they were settled. A statement by him which can be read as implying that a garrison was established in the territory of the Dobunni may have amounted to no more than an attempt to make sense of a source whose meaning was no longer entirely clear, when he came to write up his notes several years after making them. Black suggests that in Dio's method of working there must have been room for misunderstanding his sources and gives us two possible examples: the first being the interpretation of two accounts in different sources of a battle on the Thames as accounts of two separate river battles; the second the complete omission of any reference to Sentius Saturninus as one of two overall commanders of the expedition. Now we cannot say, of course, that Dio did on this occasion misunderstand his source, nor can we assume that his source was unreliable. Nevertheless these considerations may well undermine the confidence we have in the accuracy of Dio's account of the episode of the Dobunni.

The unidentified flying object

In the light of such doubts about Dio's shortcomings as a historian, his account of the 'flash of light' which heartened the invasion force during their crossing may also be viewed with some uncertainty. Its significance is that the object is described as going in the same direction as the fleet i.e. 'from east to west' and it is argued that this westward heading is hard to reconcile with a course from Boulogne to East Kent; but rather that it squares with a course from Boulogne to the Solent. Such omens are not unusual in ancient sources. In his evaluation of the ancient historians of first-century Britain, Black reviews the omens listed by both Tacitus and Dio in their accounts of the Boudican rebellion. Some at least of these omens, for example the ocean between Britain and Gaul growing blood-red on the flood tide, must be reckoned to be invented. Of course there is nothing improbable about seeing a shooting star, if that is what Dio meant, particularly in an age before the night skies were obscured by light pollution. Even so, it may well have been invented, if not by Dio, then by one of his sources. What is significant, however, is not the factual accuracy of the story, but Dio's belief that the fleet was sailing from east to west.

One might argue that such a belief should not be taken as inconsistent with a passage from Boulogne to Richborough.[29] At the time they saw the shooting star, the invaders were being 'driven back in their course'. On the passage from Boulogne to Richborough, this could mean that a combination of a north-west wind (or a failing wind) and a north-east going tide was taking the fleet rapidly offshore; eastwards from Kent and the Isle of Thanet. Their intended course might then indeed lie east to west. We have seen that this happened to Caesar on his second expedition when the wind failed and the tide took his fleet offshore; it was at sunrise that the Romans realised what had happened and took to their oars. In such a context the light which inspired Dio's story might even have been the sunrise itself, an event which certainly would have raised the spirits of men who had spent an uncertain night at sea, as anyone who has done so can confirm.

But, you may argue, that is no more than fanciful equivocation. The central point is that Dio believed that the fleet was sailing 'from east to west', and we may take it that his contemporary readers would have assumed that this applied to the whole voyage. We must face up to the fact that at face value the argument from naval logistics does not stack up with Dio's evidence. So the question must be what weight we can put on what Dio says in this instance. We do not know the source for his belief. It seems unlikely that he ever visited north-west Europe and he would not have had first-hand knowledge of the coasts of the English Channel. He does not tell us where the port of embarkation or the bridgehead was and may not have known. On the other hand he may have known from Suetonius's *Life of Claudius* that the emperor embarked at Boulogne, but been unable to place Boulogne in relation either to the British coast or even to the coast of Gaul. Of course we cannot know, but given the significance of the naval argument, we should take care in the reliance we place on this single phrase in Dio.

Chronology of the invasion

An Alexandrian coin, a diobol, dated to the third year of Claudius's reign, has been noted with the inscription '*ΒΡΕΤΑΝΝΙΚΟΣ ΚΑΙΣΑΡ*'. Since the Alexandrian mint began its year on 29 August, the latest possible date for its minting is considered to be 28 August AD 43. The title 'Britannicus' was conferred on Claudius – and on his son – by the Senate after they had learnt of his success at Colchester, the news of which Claudius had sent ahead of his own return to Rome. Anthony Barrett considers that this indicates that at the very latest

Claudius achieved the submission of the British kings shortly before mid-August, with his arrival in Britain no later than 'the closing days of July'. However, he has added in an email to me that his suggested *terminus ante quem* of mid-August for the surrender of the British kings is 'an absolute metaphysical terminus' and that a reasonable terminus would set 'at the very least a month between the surrender and the coin's appearance', perhaps two. The evidence of this coin cannot be reconciled with the account of the campaign given by Dio.[30]

According to Dio, Claudius was away from Rome for a total of six months. The dates that this implies for his absence from Rome may be deduced from the names of men given by Dio as holding the office of consul at the time he left and when he returned. Dio reports that he returned to Rome when Gaius Crispus and Titus Stabilius were consuls. Since these men are known to have been in office during the first half of AD 44, it would follow from Dio's account that Claudius cannot have left Rome before the end of June AD 43. Further confirmation of this might be found in Dio's earlier statement that 'Claudius entrusted affairs at home…to his colleague, Lucius Vitellius, whom he had caused to remain in office like himself for a whole half year'. If Dio means by this that Claudius had completed six months as consul with Vitellius, before leaving Rome, it must also imply that Claudius did not leave Rome before the beginning of July AD 43 at the earliest. However, there must be some doubt whether Claudius and Vitellius held six-month consulates in AD 43. According to Suetonius, the consulates held by Claudius were all for two months, except the last – for six months – in AD 51. Moreover, it appears from a comment by the elder Pliny that the suffect consuls for AD 43, L. Pedanius Secundus and Sex. Palpellius Hister, took office by the end of February of that year. What Pliny says is that during their consulate the shrine of the Capitol was desecrated by the entry of an owl and that the ritual purification of the city took place on 7 March. This would square with Claudius and Vitellius holding office as consuls for two months only from 1 January AD 43.[31]

It is hard to credit that Claudius could have left Rome no earlier than the beginning of July, made his way by sea and land through Gaul, crossed to Britain and achieved the submission of the British kings, in time for the news of it to have reached Alexandria via Rome by the end of August. A detailed examination of the events of the campaign suggests, if we are to take Dio at face value, that the submission of the British kings could not have happened much before early to mid-August. As we have noted, the Romans would not have committed a fleet to sea during the winter months; according to Vegetius, it would not have been safe to do so until 27 May. Allowing Vegetius to be ultra-cautious, we might conceive of the fleet being ready to sail around the middle of March. However, the legions mutinied and, because the commander-in-chief, Plautius, was said to be unable to enforce his authority, Claudius's freedman, Narcissus was summoned; though Dio did not say so, the usual assumption from what Dio says is that Narcissus had to come from Rome. Certainly Dio did say that the need to involve Narcissus caused the expedition to be delayed. Persuaded by Narcissus, the legionaries returned to their duty and the invasion force sailed. After initial skirmishes and perhaps one major battle, the campaign stalled on the banks of the Thames. Plautius sent for Claudius and the army settled down to wait for him. Claudius arrived – Dio was explicit that he had been summoned from Rome – and led the army to Colchester. This sequence of events involved two return journeys to Rome, which can scarcely have taken less than two months each, as well as the campaign which took the legions across the Channel and thence to the Thames, which might well have taken up to a month. Even allowing for some saving of time on this schedule, this would scarcely bring Claudius to join the legions in Britain before the beginning of August.

For the news of Claudius's success at Colchester then to have reached Egypt in time for a commemorative coin to have been minted before the end of August would have involved yet another (single) journey this time to Alexandria with a stopover in Rome. Barrett's suggestion that this last journey might have taken as little as a fortnight or so is based on a statement by Suetonius that Caesar was capable of completing journeys of 100 miles a day and another by Pliny the Elder citing 'nine days for a fast journey by sea from Puteoli to Alexandria'. The possibility of completing a voyage from Italy to Egypt in nine days, which implies an average of just over 5 knots, is validated by a number of other similar voyages recorded in antiquity. Even so a revealing study by Richard Duncan-Jones of the speed of communication between Italy and Egypt suggests that for official news from Rome to reach Egypt in nine days would be unprecedented. As for Caesar's journeys of 100 miles a day, it seems clear that this was outside normal experience, both because Suetonius saw fit to mention it and because he says that Caesar often arrived before the messengers sent to announce his approach! Butler and Cary, who edited Suetonius's *Life of Julius*, claim that 'there is no other record of such a distance being covered in a day by Caesar or any other Roman before the institution of the Imperial post'. According to Holmes, Caesar's despatches from Gaul were taking up to a month to reach Rome. On the other hand, with the establishment by Augustus of the imperial post, a system of posting stations along strategic routes, there is evidence for the achievement of considerable speeds in the transmission of the urgent messages. The news of the refusal of the legions in Upper Germany to swear allegiance to Galba in January 69 reached Rome within nine days. Seen in this light of course, it might well have been possible for news of the submission of the British kings to have reached Rome within the fortnight suggested by Barrett. However, speeds of this order seem to be a specific response to a major crisis, quite unlike the transmission of the type of official news analyzed by Duncan-Jones, such as the death and accession of emperors and, one might say, news of an imperial victory. Taken all in all, if we accept the evidence of the Alexandrian diobol, Dio's account sets out an impossibly tight schedule for the transmission of what was after all routine news.[32]

A striking feature of Dio's account is that Claudius spent only 16 days in Britain. This would have been long enough for him to arrive at Colchester for the appropriate display of imperial status at the formal submission of the British kings and to return. However, it is in stark contrast to the relatively leisurely progress through Gaul and Italy implied by the six months he was said to have been away from Rome during which we might suppose that on his return he dallied to receive the homage of the many Gallic and Italian cities he passed to celebrate his victory over Oceanus. Do we need then some reason for the brevity of his stay in Britain? If so, Black sees it in the imminence of the autumn equinox. In his proposal for the timing of the events of AD 43, Black accepts that the invasion may well have happened late in the year. The optimum time for the invasion would, he says, be just before the harvest, say about mid-June. An original intention to invade in June would not only mean that any defending forces might be occupied with the harvest, but would also allow the invaders to live off the land. However, the mutiny would have delayed the invasion until late July or early August with Claudius arriving to embark at Boulogne for Britain late in August or early in September. The expectation of deteriorating sailing conditions with the approaching autumn equinox would have necessarily curtailed his stay in Britain.[33]

Black's chronology is in line with Dio's account, including Claudius's departure after holding a six-month consulate and his return to Rome in AD 44. But it does not square with the Alexandrian coin as evidence of a *terminus ante quem* for the surrender of the British kings and Black recognises this. It is the only known specimen of the coin and it may, he suggests, have been struck in anticipation of an honour not yet awarded. However, apart from the problem of reconciling Dio's account with the Alexandrian diobol, there are two details in it which frankly verge on the unbelievable: that the mutiny should have been allowed to fester for the weeks which would have been necessary for Narcissus to arrive from Rome; and that Plautius should have waited at the Thames for the two months or so which it must have taken

Claudius to respond to Plautius's summons, if he received it at Rome. Scholars have expressed disbelief at the reason given by Dio for summoning Claudius; is it really credible that he should have instructed Plautius to send for him – from Rome – if he met with 'any particularly stubborn resistance'? Dio's account becomes more credible if one assumes that Narcissus was already at Boulogne when the mutiny occurred. If so, it would be entirely natural that, as the emperor's personal representative, he should address the troops. In like vein, it is not unreasonable to assume that when Plautius sent for Claudius, not to strengthen his resolve against difficult opposition, but to receive the submission of a new province that was virtually ready to surrender, Claudius was waiting in the wings at Boulogne. If Claudius intended all along to lead the legions into Colchester, I personally cannot see him waiting in Rome for a summons to do so.

A chronology constructed on this basis would allow an early invasion, one planned to be launched as soon as weather conditions allowed, but it would give us no reason for the brevity of the emperor's stay in Britain. Perhaps we don't need one. But if we do, Ernest Black has suggested to me one possibility, which, although there is no direct evidence for it, does fit with known facts. Claudius was born on 1 August 10 BC in Lyons and it was there that on the same date his father dedicated the Altar of Rome and of Augustus. In celebrating his victory in Britain, Claudius would have every incentive to join the annual gathering in Lyons on that date of the representatives of the Gallic tribes. This would square with an early invasion, as soon as the weather allowed, a relatively rapid campaign by Plautius and a six-month absence by Claudius from Rome from late spring to early autumn AD 43. In the last analysis, whether we follow Black in assuming an invasion planned to coincide with the harvest or my suggestion that the Roman commanders would have been anxious to launch the invasion as early in the season as possible, we are faced with errors in Dio's account and a direct conflict of evidence between it and the Alexandrian coin. While there may be ways of explaining away the evidence of the coin, we know that Dio was wrong about Claudius's consulate in AD 43. We cannot ignore the possibility that Dio may have been mistaken about the details of the part played by Narcissus in the legionaries' mutiny, the dates for Claudius's absence from Rome and the near certainty that he was wrong about the reason why Plautius summoned his emperor to Britain.

An opposed landing?

Dio gives the reason for the crossing of the invasion force in three divisions in a phrase which is usually understood as meaning that this would ensure that the invaders were 'not hindered in landing – as might happen to a single force'. However, some scholars offer an alternative: 'to avoid having an opposed landing, which might hold up a single force'. If this were a valid translation, it would actually give strength to the case for three landing points, rather than the one at Fishbourne that Hind has advocated.[34]

Dictionary research suggests that Dio's contemporary readers would probably have understood him to mean 'hindered', since that is the normal meaning of the word he used.[35] To infer from Dio's text a reference to the possibility of an opposed landing is stretching interpretation to the extreme. It is hard to see how splitting one's army would avoid the landing being opposed. On the other hand, if we think of the practicalities of bringing a thousand ships into either the Wantsum or Chichester Harbour at the same time, we can only describe the resultant confusion as being likely to cause some excitement. What Dio is saying, is that too many troops arriving at the bridgehead together would create a traffic jam and that the commanders wished to avoid this by staggering the landing. There is no need to postulate three separate bridgeheads to account for Dio's Greek.

Dio and the Claudian invasion

Dio is not a primary source for the Claudian invasion. Nor are any of the other extant writers of the classical period who provide us with information about it. Black has identified a 'stratigraphy' of writers of the first century who may have been used by Dio, Tacitus, Suetonius and others as their sources for their accounts of first-century Britain. These include Fabius Rusticus, Pliny the Elder and Cluvius Rufus, who are known to have written on Roman Britain. Black explores the possibility that among their eyewitnesses were two governors of Britain, Tacitus's father-in-law, Agricola, and Suetonius Paulinus, who was governor at the time of the Boudican revolt. On the basis of what is known of these earlier writers, their experience and the political context in which they were writing, Black argues that it is possible to infer the particular biases and expertise (or lack of it), which each might have contributed to the accounts which have come down to us. Black had earlier proposed that Dio's accounts of the battle on the unnamed river and the battle on the Thames reflected two separate sources giving different accounts of the same battle. Now he offers possible identifications for these two sources. The account of the first battle is short on topographical detail, but highlights the role of Vespasian and two other senior officers. Black suggests that the source for this account might have been Cluvius Rufus, a man 'without experience of warfare', but whose background suggests a strong interest in personalities. On the other hand the battle on the Thames is 'a straightforward account of the engagement without naming or elaborating on the roles of individuals'. Black asks if this could have been taken from Fabius Rusticus, a writer whose sympathies might be expected to make him unwilling to praise Vespasian. Black's conclusion is that there are dangers in trusting Dio's account, as there are in trusting that of Tacitus. Unlike Tacitus, who would reshape what he took from his sources to create 'a homogeneous narrative', Dio juxtaposes the information which he gets from his sources 'with little attempt at integration'. Black notes in particular the licence which Cluvius Rufus would take in inventing material to enhance the rhetorical appeal of his story. Tacitus preferred to avoid Cluvius; as a result his work is of greater value to modern historians. It is, therefore, a considerable loss to students of the Claudian invasion that the relevant books of Tacitus's *Annals* have not survived.

By and large, Black's approach is one of textual analysis. However, given the deficiencies that this has revealed, we are entitled to go further. We are entitled to test what Dio says against the evidence of other disciplines, numismatics, archaeology, maritime studies and even common sense; what we are not entitled to do is to reject the evidence of these other disciplines, simply because it does not fit with what Dio tells us. This must be particularly so when our understanding of Dio turns on a single word or phrase, as it does in the case of the meteor shooting 'east to west' or of the Dobunni. This is a process which calls for the exercise of judgement. Seeing the Alexandrian diobol as being minted in anticipation of the honour which would be bestowed on Claudius, if, and only if, his British enterprise was successful, without asking ourselves how convincing we find the preposterous reason offered by Dio for the summons sent to Claudius is not to exercise judgement.

This may not increase the confidence with which we can embrace any particular interpretation of the events of the invasion. Even so, after entering all the caveats and weighing Dio's text against an assessment of the naval aspects of the campaign, I would tend to favour an interpretation of the cross-Channel operation on the following lines:

1. A first wave, of perhaps a single legion and supporting units, would cross as soon as the sailing season opened to secure a beachhead at Richborough and fortify it as a supply base.
2. As soon as this had been achieved, a second and a third wave would cross and move through the now fortified beachhead of Richborough to secure the route to the Thames and to deal with British resistance.

3. The fleet would be available to ensure secure, swift communications and logistics between Boulogne and Richborough throughout the campaign and beyond.
4. Claudius would travel to Boulogne in time to cross as soon as he heard from Plautius that he was ready to march on Colchester and formally take possession of the new province as emperor.

7

CARAUSIUS AND THE SAXON SHORE

Forts of the Saxon Shore

Among the most striking of the architectural remains of Roman Britain is the series of fortresses along the east and south coasts of Britain, which are today known as the forts of the Saxon Shore. They are generally thought to have been part of a defensive system against the sea-borne raids of Germanic tribes. In the late third century they played a significant role in the secession of Britain – and of part of northern Gaul – from the Roman Empire under the pseudo-*Augustus*, Carausius, and in their reintegration into the empire by the *Caesar*, Constantius Chlorus, a decade later.

The name 'Saxon Shore' comes from a remarkable document, known as the *Notitia Dignitatum* and dated to the end of the fourth century/beginning of the fifth century. This sets out military and civil commands throughout the empire. Among the senior officers named is the Count of the Saxon Shore in Britain (*comes litoris Saxonici per Britanniam*). In the late empire the Latin words, *comes* (companion) and *dux* (leader), came to designate senior ranks. By the end of the reign of Constantine the Great (306-337) virtually all frontier forces had been transferred from the control of the provincial governors, who until then had exercised military as well as civil authority in their provinces, to the new *duces*. In a number of cases the command of the individual *dux* might span more than one civil province. At the same time Constantine created a new order of nobility whose members were given the title of *comes*. The title itself was not specifically military, nor did possession of it imply that the owner held a specific post. However, if he was appointed to a specific post his official title became *comes et…* ('Count and…') Thus the more important frontier forces came under the control of *comites*. The implication is that the Count of the Saxon Shore held one of the more important frontier commands.

The coastal garrisons listed in the *Notitia* under the command of the Count of the Saxon Shore were stationed at *Othona* (Bradwell), *Dubrae* (Dover), *Lemannis* (Lympne), *Branodunum* (Brancaster), *Gariannonum* (Burgh Castle or Caister-on-Sea), *Regulbium* (Reculver), *Rutupiae* (Richborough), *Anderida* (Pevensey) and *Portus Adurni* (*28* and *29*). In most cases the modern

28 Left The insignia of the Count of the Saxon Shore from a fifteenth-century manuscript of the *Notitia Dignitatum*, showing the forts under the Count's control. *Reproduced by permission of the Bodleian Library, University of Oxford, MS Canon. Misc. 378, fol. 153v*

29 Below The Forts of the Saxon Shore, together with fortified coastal sites in Gaul

identifications are secure. *Gariannonum* seems clearly associated with the river *Gariennus* listed by Ptolemy, which would be the modern Yare in Norfolk. On that basis *Gariannonum* has usually been identified as Burgh Castle, where there are significant remains of a Roman fort on the banks of a tributary of the Yare. However, the nature of the Roman site at nearby Caister-on-Sea was reassessed in 1993, with the conclusion that it might have been a military installation, rather than a civilian settlement. In this light either Burgh Castle or Caister-on-Sea could be *Gariannonum*. In the case of Portus Adurni, competing proposals have been made that it may have been located at Portchester in Portsmouth Harbour or at Walton Castle in Suffolk. Stephen Johnson argued in favour of Walton Castle since his review of the dating evidence led him to conclude that from the late fourth century, Portchester was no longer occupied and would not have been actively part of the system around 395 when the British section of the Notitia would have been drawn up. Cunliffe, on the other hand, whose excavations extended the coin list at Portchester after the previously accepted date of 369, believed that Portchester could reasonably be identified as *Portus Adurni*. Be that as it may, it does seem possible that the command of the Count of the Saxon Shore may have originally been more extensive than it is recorded in the Notitia and it may well at one stage have encompassed coastal forts and perhaps signal stations, from Portchester in the west to Brough-on-Humber in the north.[1]

In some cases little remains of the forts. Walton Castle, for example, stood on a cliff near Felixstowe, Suffolk, which succumbed to coastal erosion in the eighteenth century and is now known only from antiquarian drawings. The Saxon Shore fort at Dover, like the two bases of the *Classis Britannica* (the 'British fleet') which preceded it, now lies under the town centre of Dover and is known only from rescue archaeology. Brancaster is known only from crop marks. Little has survived at Bradwell and the walls have largely been destroyed. It is now best known for the Saxon Chapel of St Peter, built around 652 of material robbed from the wall of the fort (*colour plate 25*). Reculver is well known to mariners plying the Thames Estuary as 'Twin Towers Reculver', being recorded as such on Admiralty Charts, leading from the Four Fathoms Channel into Margate Road. The twin towers belong to a twelfth-century church, now disused and ruined, standing within the site of the Saxon Shore fort. Of the fort walls, all that remains is a 'sorry, overgrown, ruin', just the core of the original wall.[2] When the Tudor scholar, John Leland, visited the site in the 1530s, he appears not to have noticed the fort, concentrating on the antiquities of the church. There has been much coastal erosion here; a map dated 1685 shows the walls of the fort apparently intact close to the shore; half of the fort has since been washed away and the church stands right on the sea wall (*colour plates 26, 27* and *28*). At Stutfall Castle, the Roman fort at Lympne, the walls survive in fragmentary form, in many cases displaced by landslips from their original locations. Elsewhere, at Burgh Castle, Richborough, Pevensey and Portchester, a significant proportion of the stone-built walls remain. The circuit of the walls is complete at Portchester and was maintained in medieval times; within the circuit at Pevensey, where the southern wall is now missing, is a Norman castle (*colour plate 29*).[3]

The forts are striking in their location. All of them were close to the sea and associated with estuaries or coastal waterways, even if now some, like Richborough and Pevensey, are far from the sea. The sites are on low ground close to sea level and in all cases were most probably associated with a natural harbour. Certainly that is true of Portchester, Pevensey, Lympne, Dover, Richborough, Burgh Castle and Brancaster. In many cases the sites afforded a strategic view of a considerable stretch of coastline. At places like Dover and Lympne the view, perhaps restricted at sea level, is supplemented by what can be seen from the nearby heights.

The Saxon Shore on the British side of the Channel is complemented by two references in the *Notitia* to the Saxon Shore on the coast of Gaul. It lists, under the command of the Duke of the Armorican and the Nervian regions and that of the Duke of *Belgica Secunda*, a parallel chain of garrisons along the coast of Gaul and two of them, one in each command, are stated to be 'on the Saxon Shore' (*29*). They are stationed at *Grannona* and *Marcae* respectively. There is neither archaeological nor firm place name evidence to locate *Grannona*. The other sites under the command of the Duke of the Armorican and the Nervian regions can be identified with greater certainty, on the Cherbourg peninsula (Avranches and Coutances) and along the Brittany coast (St Malo, Nantes, Vannes, Blaye and Brest). All these sites lie to the west of the Duke's command, leaving a gap between it and *Belgica Secunda*. On these grounds it would be possible to suppose that *Grannona* was somewhere in Normandy.

Marcae is one of three places listed in the *Notitia* garrisoned by units commanded by the Duke of *Belgica Secunda*. The identification of all three is more problematic than that of the forts on the British Saxon Shore or of the fortified sites in Armorica. Archaeological evidence is much scarcer and the place names given in the *Notitia* are less than helpful. Even so, taking account of archaeological evidence, it is perhaps possible to discern the vestiges of a chain of fortifications along the coast of Flanders and Picardy as far west as the Somme, where the Prefect of the Fleet of the Somme (*Classis Sambrica*) was stationed.[4] Etymology suggests that *Marcae* itself might be one of three villages near Calais, Marquise, Mardyck or Marck, with the latter being the most favoured candidate. The question arises whether *Grannona* and *Marcae* were the only sites on the coast of Gaul to be properly described as being situated 'on the Saxon Shore', or whether the designation extended originally to cover other Gallic coastal fortifications. Associated with that is another question. Did 'Saxon Shore' mean the shore 'attacked by Saxons' or 'settled by Saxons'? Donald A. White, for whom this was a question with major significance for Saxon Shore studies, concluded that on both sides of the Channel the term meant 'shore settled by Saxons'. Taking *Grannona* as located in the Bessin in lower Normandy, possibly at Port-en-Bessin, and *Marcae* in the Boulonnais, he argues that both were areas of Saxon settlement in the late Roman period. Thus their designation among the Gallic garrisons as being 'on the Saxon Shore' was unique to them and would not have applied to any of the others. It is certainly true that it is possible to discern, in both districts, archaeological and documentary evidence for Germanic settlement, but whether such settlement can be traced back as far as the fourth century or earlier is a matter of disagreement.[5]

Johnson, who was persuaded that 'Saxon Shore' meant 'shore attacked by Saxons', argued for the wider application of the term along the coast of Gaul. For him, the forts of the Gallic Saxon Shore would have been located on the stretch of coast opposite that defended by their counterparts on the British coast. He suggests, therefore, that all three units commanded by the Duke of *Belgica Secunda* would have been part of the system. To this he adds *Grannona* from the command of the Duke of the Armorican and the Nervian regions as the westernmost component of the original Saxon Shore system on the Gallic coast. Largely on the not unreasonable grounds that it would be surprising if there were no fort at the mouth of the Seine, he tentatively proposes that *Grannona* would have been somewhere near the site of Le Havre. This would correspond to the positions of Pevensey and Portchester on the opposite side of the Channel. Thus defined, for Johnson, the Saxon Shore was a single defensive system based on both sides of the Channel.

Johnson does not see the other garrisons in Brittany as part of this system, partly because they do not figure in the way he sees it operating and partly because there are significant differences in the topography of their location from that of the known forts of the Saxon Shore. For example, the defensive walls at Avranches and Coutances are set high above the sea, too high to be associated with the defence of harbour installations. These two sites, as well as others listed under the Duke's command are not forts as such, but rather walled cities. The garrisons stationed here were no doubt intended to protect these cities against raids by Germanic tribes, but would not, Johnson suggests, have been part of the coordinated system of the Saxon Shore. Nevertheless, there does seem to be one indication that in the late third century all these fortifications along the

Brittany coast were linked with the Saxon Shore system under one unified command. When, in around 285 Carausius was commissioned to clear the sea of Saxon and Frankish pirates, his command was described as covering the coast of *Belgica* and Armorica. It is perhaps possible that it also included the units stationed at the British forts. If so, Carausius's command extended not only over the coastal units later assigned to the Dukes of the Armorican and the Nervian region and of *Belgica Secunda*, but also over those later commanded by the Count of the Saxon Shore in Britain.

Carausius, the pseudo-Augustus

Soon after he became emperor in 284, Diocletian began to introduce significant innovations in the top management of the Empire. In 285, he took one of his senior officers, Maximian, as his deputy with the title of *Caesar*. Maximian's responsibility was the defence of the west and he was particularly concerned with the suppression of disturbances in Gaul caused by the *Bagaudae*, a little understood group apparently made up of rootless peasants and veterans. The following year Diocletian promoted Maximian to share with him the rank of *Augustus* and to continue to be responsible for the West. In 293 he introduced the Tetrarchy: each of the two *Augusti* was to have a deputy, styled *Caesar*. Maximian's *Caesar* was Constantius Chlorus, father of Constantine the Great. This is the background against which the ten-year secession of Britain under Carausius and his successor as pseudo-*Augustus*, Allectus, took place.

    The source material includes coins, accounts by two near-contemporary historians and eulogies by contemporary panegyrists; the latter have necessarily to be treated with some caution. The two historians, Aurelius Victor and Eutropius, were high-ranking imperial servants, who came to prominence in the second half of the fourth century; Aurelius publishing his *Book on the Emperors* (*de Caesaribus*) shortly after 360, while Eutropius followed with his *Concise History of Rome* (*Breviarium*) a decade later. Both were born a generation or so after the events of the Carausian rebellion and appear to have relied on a single lost source for their accounts, the so-called *Kaisergeschichte*.[6] Even this scarcely ranks as a primary source for the late third century, if, as has been suggested, it was published as late as 358.[7] Yet there is no reason to question the overall thrust of the brief accounts that Aurelius Victor and Eutropius give of the Carausian episode. It is as follows:

> Carausius was a Menapian – native of a region within modern Belgium –
> who had achieved an outstanding reputation in the course of a number of

military campaigns, including that against the *Bagaudae*. Because of this and because of his experience as a mariner, a profession he had followed as a young man, he was given the task of clearing the coast of Armorica and *Belgica* of Frankish and Saxon pirates. In this he achieved considerable success, but returned the pirates' booty neither to its original owners nor to the imperial treasury. It was alleged that he was letting the pirates in deliberately so as to take the opportunity to enrich himself by intercepting them and expropriating their booty, as they returned. Maximian, therefore, ordered his execution. When he learnt this, Carausius seized the British provinces. Given the problems elsewhere in the Empire, Diocletian and Maximian acquiesced in Carausius's secession. Eutropius says that, because of his military competence, war was ineffective against him, while Aurelius Victor's spin is that he was judged competent to defend the inhabitants 'against warlike tribes'. After six years (Aurelius Victor) or seven years (Eutropius), Carausius was killed by Allectus, his finance chief, who took his place as pseudo-*Augustus*. Three years later Constantius's praetorian prefect, Asclepiodotus was despatched with a detachment from the fleet and the legions and succeeded in overthrowing Allectus.

The account is short on detail, neither Maximian nor Constantius are credited with any active part in it and the reason given for the imperial acquiescence in Carausius's rebellion can only be described as economical with the *actualité*. For all their faults the panegyrics give more details. The first is a speech in praise of Maximian, delivered in 289. Although it gives little specific but much adulatory detail, it affirms that Maximian's forces have reached Oceanus victorious and that a fleet has been made ready for an assault on Britain. The speech was apparently delivered before the invasion fleet sailed, because no mention is made of the outcome. Quite what happened to this invasion attempt is unclear. But its failure must have been the reason for the emperors' temporary acquiescence in Carausius's rebellion. One may infer from the reference to the success of the army in reaching the Oceanus that Carausius was in a position to deny the legitimate imperial authorities access to the Channel coast of Gaul. It seems probable that Maximian's fleet had been made ready on the Rhine and that it was from there the invasion of Britain was to be launched. If so, then the reference to the arrival of Maximian's army at Oceanus would mean that they had assembled for embarkation somewhere on the Rhine estuary.

The second panegyric, delivered in praise of Constantius Chlorus in 297, is more specific. The key details are as follows:

1. Constantius's first step was to take Boulogne by building a mole which closed off the harbour.
2. Constantius delayed the invasion to allow for the construction of ships.
3. The panegyrist claims that Carausius's troops had boasted that the reason that an invasion had not been launched lay in the fear that they inspired, rather than in the rough seas which had caused the invasion to be put off as a 'matter of policy'.
4. As a preliminary to the invasion Maximian undertook the pacification of the barbarian tribes on the Rhine frontier, while Constantius focused on building and equipping his fleets.
5. The fleet was organised in two groups, one under Constantius sailing from Boulogne, the other under Asclepiodotus from the Seine.
6. In response to the ardent resolution of the troops, both fleets sailed in extreme conditions of wind and rain and, not having a favourable wind, sailed close-hauled.
7. Allectus's fleet was on station at the Isle of Wight, but failed to see the arrival of that of Asclepiodotus because of fog.
8. Because Asclepiodotus's fleet is said to have bypassed that of Allectus in the fog, it is assumed, not unreasonably, that it landed in the Solent area. They burned their ships after they landed.
9. There is no clear indication from the panegyrist where the fleet from Boulogne landed, or even if it landed at all. Allectus is said to have fled from the sight of it towards Asclepiodotus who defeated him and his Germanic mercenaries. There is a reference to some of Constantius's troops being separated from the rest in fog (another fog?) and finding their way to London, which they successfully defended against Allectus's Germanic mercenaries.

These points merit a number of observations. First, those who know the present layout of Boulogne harbour with its breakwaters encompassing the whole of the estuary of the Liane will perhaps think the claim that Constantius had the harbour blocked off by a mole rather far-fetched; after all if Constantius's mole had attempted to close off the harbour across the present harbour entrance, it would have meant damming the flow of a major river (*30*). It is much more likely that the harbour which Constantius had cut off was a bay on the north bank of the Liane just below the height on which the medieval fortified town still stands; its walls follow those of the Roman fort and there is evidence that a fortified harbour in this bay was linked to the fort. Though the panegyrist makes much of this feat and its implication that this denied the inhabitants access to the sea, it would in fact have been essential to

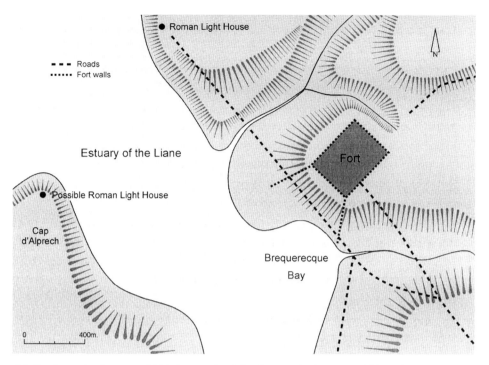

30 Boulogne in the second/third centuries. The Roman harbour would have been in Brequerecque Bay. *After Seillier, 1996*

cut off the harbour if the place was to be effectively besieged; Caesar had noted the impregnability of the strongholds of the Veneti because, situated as they were at the end of promontories, it was impossible to deny them access to the sea.[8]

Even considering this, the taking of Boulogne must have been the strategically critical achievement in the reconquest of the British provinces. It would have meant that Constantius's forces now had broken through to the Channel and in the process had loosened Carausius's grip on the coastal region of northern Gaul. Any new invasion attempt would not come from the Rhine and, therefore, would not have to contend with the defensive strength of Saxon Shore. When it came, the invasion to be launched by Constantius from Boulogne and by Asclepiodotus from the Seine would simply bypass the system. Some have seen in the rebels' boast that the invasion had been cancelled because the government troops were afraid of them and the panegyrist's counter-claim that the invasion had simply been delayed by bad weather a reference to the failure of Maximian's attempt at invasion. It is, however, difficult to accept that either delay due to bad weather or fear of the enemy would be a plausible reason for abandoning such an expedition. Moreover, the context of the panegyrist's comment does not require us to assume that he has Maximian's expedition in mind. He may well have simply been referring to the fact that the eventual invasion was long delayed. The fact of the matter is that we have no clear documentary evidence to tell us why Maximian's invasion failed; but we may assume that Maximian's invasion attempt was probably launched from the Rhine. If so, it would necessarily have been directed at the very centre of the Saxon Shore chain.

What the panegyrist says about the weather seems questionable. It is not credible that the expedition could have been delayed for the years that it was, simply because of the weather. A delay of this duration can only plausibly be accounted for by the need to build and equip a fleet and to pacify the barbarians on the Rhine. As for the panegyrist's description of the conditions prevailing during the eventual crossing in 296, one might well think that a commander who has waited several years to prepare his invasion forces is not going to risk the successful outcome of his campaign by sailing in bad weather and with adverse winds, however enthusiastic his troops are. We know that for his invasion crossings Caesar had preferred favourable winds and fair weather. It is of course possible that Constantius, like William the Conqueror and later William of Orange, felt compelled to set sail in marginal conditions because the season was getting late and the prospect of favourable conditions that year was diminishing by the day. For both the Williams it was critical to seize the moment; for William the Conqueror, both the politics and the logistics would have prevented the reassembly the following year of his invasion force, while for William of Orange the politics of Court and Parliament, and, in particular, the birth of a son to James II meant that his bid for the English throne could not long be delayed. Constantius, on the other hand, was playing it long.[9]

However, there could be some basis of truth in the panegyrist's statement that the fleets were 'sailing close-hauled'. This might be understood to mean that the fleets set sail with a south-westerly, which, for the fleet sailing from the Seine, would have meant a beam reach. It would seem quite unlikely that the fleet from Boulogne would have sailed with anything other than a wind in the southerly quarter. For the fleet sailing from the Seine, if such a wind veered during the passage to the Solent, this fleet would have found it increasingly difficult to maintain its course. A further point which merits comment is the panegyrist's report that, once they had landed, Asclepiodotus's men 'set fire to all their ships'. Salway describes this as 'the traditional gesture of confidence' and certainly this is what the panegyrist says.[10] However, there seems little in the act that is traditional. The traditional thing seems rather to prepare a fortified base for the protection of the fleet. This seems to have been done by Caesar, is what the archaeological record shows was done at Richborough in

AD 43 and was certainly done by William the Conqueror. The only tactical reason for burning one's boats must be to deny them to the enemy, but this not only cuts off one's own retreat, but also denies the possibility of communication with one's base and reinforcements of both men and supplies. Frankly the gesture is incomprehensible and, if it is to be credited, can only mean that Asclepiodotus's force was lightly equipped, fast moving and not large enough to spare a garrison to protect the ships. The intention would have been to achieve a swift victory and, in the meantime, to live off the land.

Quite what the fleet sailing from Boulogne did is not clear. The panegyrist does speak of Allectus preferring to take his chance with Constantius's commanders, rather than to face Constantius himself, and in this context reports that Allectus deserted his fleet and harbour when he saw Constantius's sails bearing down on him. Even so, it would seem that a frontal assault from the sea on the fortified coast of East Kent was not to be contemplated and there is no evidence that Constantius attempted it, though he may have made a show of force off the East Kent coast. Haywood opines that Constantius simply sailed for London and Frere that Constantius 'contented himself with a demonstration which was perhaps diversionary in intent', while Salway concurs in the possibility 'that Constantius' own use of the short crossing was a deliberate feint, particularly sensible if a substantial part of the Second Legion was now garrisoning the new fortress at Richborough'.[11]

Carausius and his brethren

Carausian coinage merits study in its own right.[12] From an analysis of mint marks, legends and images scholars have perceived, even if 'through a glass darkly', the extent of the territory that Carausius controlled in Gaul, identified the legions which may have been loyal to him and, as we saw in an earlier Chapter, endeavoured to discern modifications to warship design. The use of the images and legends on the coins as propaganda also allows us an insight into the developing politics of the Carausian secession. Among the early coins was a series of silver denarii showing Britannia clasping hands with Carausius, with the legend *EXPECTATE VENI*, 'Come, long have we looked for you'. This is a slight misquotation of a phrase from Book II of Virgil's *Aeneid* which would have been well known to people of the time.[13] This is not to say that the legend was aimed only at those who were well versed in their Virgil; it would have evoked a response in those for whom it was no more than a vaguely remembered phrase. One may imagine the impact by thinking of the response, had British coins been issued during the Second World War with the legend 'Once more into the breach'. Many would have responded to its familiar martial ring without realizing that it comes from the speech Shakespeare puts into Henry V's mouth before Harfleur. Of course at the time of the Second World War the medium was radio and Churchill had a rhetoric of his own. In Carausius's case the legend on the coin would have invoked comparison between the expectations placed on him and those which Aeneas was to fulfil as the ancestor of the founder of Rome; this would have reinforced the message on other contemporary coins whose legends made the message more explicit: *PAX BRITANNIAE* or *RESTITUTOR BRITANNIAE*, claiming in effect that Carausius would bring peace and recovery to Britain.

The silver denarii issued by Carausius a little later with the image of a warship and the legend *FELICITAS* ('good fortune') may commemorate a naval victory, just possibly one which aborted the first invasion attempt by Maximian (*colour plate 8*). When, after this failure, the imperial authorities acquiesced in Carausius's secession, he began to issue coins with legends designed to legitimise his authority alongside that of Diocletian and Maximian. These carried the heads of the three emperors with legends such as *PAX AUGGG*, 'Peace of the three Emperors'.[14] One series which one can only describe as barefaced in its arrogance and which must have caused enormous irritation in legitimate imperial circles showed images of the three emperors with the inscription *CARAUSIUS ET FRATRES SUI*, 'Carausius and his brethren' (*colour plate 10*).

The end was also recorded by an image and a legend, not on a coin, but on the Arras gold medallion, struck to commemorate the arrival of Constantius in London after the defeat of Allectus. Bearing the inscription *REDDITOR LUCIS AETERNAE*, 'restorer of the eternal light', it shows Constantius on horseback receiving the homage of a kneeling figure representing London. The significance of the navy in his victory is invoked by the inclusion of a warship in the image (*colour plate 7*).

When were the forts built?

The dating of the construction of the individual forts depends in part on coin finds and in part on typology. The rounded corners and absence of bastions might place Reculver, Caister-on-Sea and Brancaster early in the third century; Burgh Castle has been seen as displaying transitional characteristics: its bastions are not bonded to the lower part of the wall and the corner bastions are rendered ineffective by its rounded walls.[15] The Saxon Shore fort at Richborough has been dated to the 270s, but numerous coins of Carausius found in the lowest occupation levels of the new fort suggest that it may have been constructed at any time up to the beginning of his reign. Dover might be dated to 275-280, while for Lympne a date in the 270s or a little later might be plausible. Bradwell is not closely dated, but would appear on coin evidence to have been built in the late third century. The dating evidence for the construction of Portchester, in particular a coin of Carausius, points to a *terminus post quem* for its construction in the mid 280s and makes it credible that Carausius can be credited with its construction. A coin find at Pevensey has in the past been taken as evidence that it may have been a late addition to the group in the 340s or later. This, a coin of the latter part of Constantine's reign, was found in a hole in a wall left to support a timber beam and so ought to have been deposited when the wall was being constructed. However, recent work at Pevensey now dates it firmly to the reign of Allectus, AD 293 or shortly thereafter.[16]

Although the design of the forts is by no means standardised, they have characteristics in common with many of the new city walls, which were being built in Gaul in the late third century, as a response to the barbarian invasions of the third century and in particular that of 276. They are quite different from trends in contemporary British architecture, for example in forts being constructed in the north of Britain. To Johnson, this was significant evidence that the British Saxon Shore forts are to be seen as part of a unified defensive system designed to protect Gaul as much as Britain. While the new city defences may have been instigated by local magnates, no doubt in cooperation with the military, the construction of the new coordinated chain of Saxon Shore forts would have had its origin in an imperial initiative. According to Johnson, this would have seen most of the forts, with the exceptions noted above, being built between 276 and 285, perhaps under Probus.[17] The forts already in existence – at Brancaster, Caister-on-Sea and Reculver – would have been integrated into the system. Such a dating would mean that, whilst he might not have been its designer, Carausius could well have been its first operational commander.[18] On the other hand, White, writing some 40 years ago before recent reassessments of the dating evidence, argued that there was nothing in the archaeology to contradict his view that the forts were built during the reign of Carausius. White's dating can no longer be maintained at least in its entirety, but he advanced it in support of a hypothesis about the original purpose of the system which still merits discussion.

What were the Saxon Shore forts for?

Until White published his study in 1961, the traditional view was that the purpose of the Saxon Shore forts was to defend the coast of south-east Britain from attacks by Germanic pirates. White argued that the forts were far more massively built than would have been necessary for this purpose. In his view 'a palisaded camp was all that would have been necessary' to deal with 'a few boatloads of Germans motivated solely by thoughts of plunder'.[19] At the same time White did not discern any evidence, whether documentary or archaeological, that the Saxon piracy was a serious threat to Britain in the late third century. If that was so and if, as White argued, the forts of the Saxon Shore in Britain were built by Carausius, they could have had only one credible purpose: to defend Britain against invasion by the legitimate imperial authorities. However, in the second half of the fourth century, when there was evidence of serious Saxon raiding on the coasts of Britain, the system would have been reactivated to counter that.[20]

That the Saxon Shore system was exploited and perhaps expanded by Carausius and Allectus, for example by the addition of Portchester and Pevensey, to defend Britain against Maximian and Constantius Chlorus, seems very likely. However, White's argument that it was built by them for that purpose has not received a lot of support among academics. With his study, originally published in 1976, Stephen Johnson returned to the traditional view. Setting the origin of the system in the context of the Germanic invasions of Gaul in the late third century, particularly of those of 276, he did not accept White's point that there was no evidence for Saxon raids on Britain in the late third century. He wrote: 'Contemporary sources graphically describe the Franks and Saxons, both seafaring tribes, infesting the seas and posing a dangerous double threat to the shores of Britain and of Gaul'.[21] For Johnson the function of the forts was threefold. They served as fortified naval bases for flotillas, whose job was to intercept the raiding pirates; they accommodated units of land forces which could be rapidly deployed to counter the pirates as they landed; sited as they were on the estuaries of the major rivers, they were a deterrent to the penetration inland of raiding parties. From the vantage point of Bradwell one can fully appreciate the validity of at least the first and last of these points. The site encompasses an unparalleled view of the entrances to the Blackwater and the Colne, the latter leading to the important town of Colchester (*31* and *colour plate 30*). It is not difficult to imagine the relative ease with which raiding fleets could be observed as soon as they entered one of the estuaries, to be intercepted, at least when they returned from their business ashore. Less easy to imagine is the possibility of the effective deployment of land troops, at least if the destination of the pirates was the Colne or the north shore of the Blackwater. Much the same would have applied to Walton Castle, which commanded views of the Stour, Orwell and Deben, but where the effective deployment of land forces would have been restricted to the north shore of the

Orwell and the west shore of the Deben. At Caister-on-Sea the fort would have been situated on an island, while Burgh Castle was on a peninsula, with significant limits on the deployment of land troops in each case.[22]

Johnson saw the genius of the forts of the Saxon Shore in the fact that they provided an integrated system of defence. Linked together by signal stations, they offered defence in depth facing north-east, the direction from which the raiding pirates would come. As the pirates approached from the area of the Rhine, they would run the gauntlet of the forts and their watching flotillas until they reached what Johnson terms the 'natural interception point' of the Dover Strait. The chances of interception would be high, given that in all likelihood the pirates would have followed the ancient pilotage practice of following the coast. Even so, they would have kept a respectable distance offshore, precisely to reduce the risk of interception, and it should not be taken for granted that raiding fleets would always be observed as they passed south-westwards through the Strait. Here, too, the probability of interception would have been much greater on the way back.

Johnson's hypothesis is not without its difficulties. The evidence of third-century raids on the south-east coasts of Britain is less than compelling. The 'graphic description' of late third-century Franks and Saxons 'posing a dangerous double threat to the shores of Britain and of Gaul' is the statement

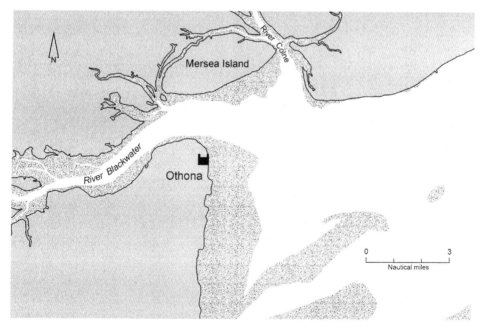

31 Othona, the Saxon Shore fort at Bradwell with its commanding views over the river systems of the Colne and Blackwater

by Eutropius that Carausius was commissioned to 'clear the sea along the coast of *Belgica* and Armorica which the Franks and Saxons were infesting' and this does not mention Britain. The only documentary evidence in the *Notitia* of fleets being attached to British Saxon Shore is the reference to the Pevensey fleet (*Classis Anderetianorum*) which, by the time the *Notitia* was compiled, was stationed at Paris. The evidence for signal stations in south-east Britain, certainly in the late third century, is slight. One site at Shadwell, Stepney, which appears to have been in use in the late third century, is a possibility, but how it would have served the chain of forts many miles downstream on the Thames estuary and beyond, must be uncertain. Others, which have been mentioned as possible signal stations, include Hadleigh, Essex, Corton, Suffolk, and Thurnham, Norfolk. Johnson admits that Hadleigh could have been 'a small native farm enclosure'.[23] The case for the hypothesis of an integrated command which encompassed bases along the Gallic coast depends in essence on the fact that two of the Gallic bases listed in the *Notitia* are said to be 'on the Saxon Shore'. As we have seen, that phrase can be interpreted in two ways.

In an article published in 1993 John Cotterill launched an all-out assault on Johnson's hypothesis. The following were the main elements in his argument:

1. Drawing on work done by Charles Green, he asserted that 'it would have been physically impossible for the Germanic seafarers to have raided the coasts of Britain in the late Roman period'.[24]
2. There is no documentary or other evidence for Germanic raids on Britain until the Saxon incursions of the fifth century.
3. The naval tactics implied in Johnson's model are unworkable.
4. The size of the garrisons required to maintain adequate fleets at each base cannot be reconciled with the archaeological evidence for the level of occupancy at the forts.[25]

Of these arguments the first will not do. Green made a distinction, which Cotterill apparently does not appreciate, between the all-male crews of ships engaged in piracy in the late Roman Empire and family parties making their voyages in what he calls the 'true Migration Period'. According to Green, the former might have involved a crew of between 60 and 80 men in a 30-oared open rowing ship of the Nydam type able to relieve one another at the oars. The latter in the same type of ship might have amounted to 30 oarsmen, together with women and children, as well as bulky personal possessions. Green's assumption, that the women would not have been expected to take to the oars to relieve the men, limits the time under oars each day to 6 hours or so. While he makes a detailed assessment of the progress which might have been made by such a family party on a coastal passage from Esbjerg in south-west Jutland to East Anglia, he makes no attempt to estimate the time that might be required for a similar passage by a pirate crew. Cotterill fails to make it clear that his quotation from Green to the effect that for these passages 'the minimum allowance of two months or more is fully justified' applies to family parties on migration, not to pirate crews.

Moreover, there is now a body of opinion among maritime historians and archaeologists prepared to question the traditional view that, among Germanic and Scandinavian tribes, the use of sail was not adopted until the seventh century. In his study of Frankish and Anglo-Saxon sea power, John Haywood argued that there was a strong circumstantial case for the use of sail by these Germanic tribes by the fourth century and possibly as early as around 250, although the feasibility of this remains questionable. What is noteworthy is that an assessment of what Cotterill calls 'the low level of vessel technology' of the raiding Saxons which does not address the possibility that they were using sailing ships must be open to question.[26] Cotterill's criticism that the naval tactics implied in Johnson's model are unworkable may be more sustainable, particularly when taken with his point about the discrepancy between the manpower required for the fleets and the archaeological evidence for the occupancy levels at the forts. But it would seem that he has not quite understood how Johnson saw his model working. For example, Cotterill writes of the need for the individual fleets attached to each fort to provide a defensive screen at sea and therefore he envisages a requirement for three vessels for every one at sea, the second being on standby and the third being 'needed to allow for repairs, or rest and recreation'. However, while Johnson allows that the effectiveness of the system would be increased by the use of regular patrols, he is explicit in saying that the commander did not need to mount constant patrols over the whole of the Channel. All he had to do was to wait for the pirates to sail into the trap set for them.[27]

Cotterill asks whether the fleets would have patrolled within sight of land or whether the defensive screen was maintained in deep water. This raises the question of the near impossibility of interception of hostile ships on the high seas in the Roman period and through the first millennium to the end of the Viking Age. In fact we can be virtually certain that such patrols as may have been mounted would not have been out of sight of land. Throughout the first millennium the pursuit and interception of fleets or individual ships on the open sea was not a practical proposition and when naval battles did occur they took place in coastal waters when the possibilities of manoeuvre and escape were limited by the configuration of shoreline and shallows. A case in point is that of the new ships which Alfred the Great commissioned in 896 to counter the Viking raids. The *Anglo-Saxon Chronicle* records that in their first outing nine of the new ships achieved a hard fought victory over six Danish ships which they were able to bottle up in a river on the Solent. It is in fact an argument in favour of Johnson's model that the location of the forts would in most cases effectively exploit this factor.

Cotterill envisages that the forts of the Saxon Shore and others were developed as a chain of fortified ports running from the Wash around the south and the west coasts to the Solway Firth. As well as providing in this way a secure coastal supply route to the north, the ports, situated as they were in most cases with good communication by river with their hinterland, would act as trans-shipment centres for state supplies being conveyed to and from the interior, much in the same way as Ostia did for Rome. The example of Ostia is, however, not apposite. This trans-shipment centre at the mouth of the Tiber, which is well documented, was necessary because the mega grain-freighters, which we discussed in Chapter 4, were too large to go upstream from Ostia as far as Rome. Such ships have not been detected outside the Mediterranean and there is no reason to suppose that the ships for which there is archaeological evidence in the north, such as St Peter Port 1 or Blackfriars 1, could not have made their way upstream beyond such places as Bradwell, Walton Castle, Burgh Castle and Caister-on-Sea. Moreover, while one might appreciate the need for the fortification of the trans-shipment centres which Cotterill envisages on the west coast where they were open to attack from Ireland and Scotland, the need is less apparent along the coast of south-east Britain, unless there was indeed a threat from Germanic pirates.

In 1995, with the publication of new dating evidence from Pevensey, the debate came full circle. Fulford and Tyers reported on excavations of the medieval castle in the south-east corner of the Roman fort. These revealed a section of the Roman foundations beneath which were found an array of oak piles. Associated with the foundations were found a coin of Carausius and one of Allectus. Together with the dendrochronological dating of the piles, which gave a probable range of 280 to 300, the Allectan coin establishes what Fulford and Tyers describe as an unequivocal *terminus post quem* of 293 for the construction of the fort and a high probability that it was built in the reign of Allectus. The best context, they suggest, for the construction of Pevensey and the near contemporary Portchester and the modernisation of other coastal forts in south-east Britain was the usurpation of Carausius and Allectus. The dating of Pevensey to the reign of Allectus makes it possible that he rather than Carausius was responsible for the development of these defences, given that the fall of Boulogne in 293 would have left Britain much more vulnerable to invasion by the legitimate authorities.[28]

Conclusions

I have always had a certain sneaking admiration for Carausius, if only because at least in part the charge, that he deliberately let the Saxon pirates in, so as to take them on their way out when they were laden with booty, seems to be a serious misunderstanding of the nature of interception at sea in Roman times and for centuries afterwards. In his study of Frankish and Anglo-Saxon naval power, Haywood stressed that naval warfare in the modern sense was very rare. The main function of naval fleets in this period was the sea-borne transport of armies and raiding parties, not interception at sea. If a naval defence strategy was to have any chance of success, it had to exploit the potential of the configuration of shoreline to intercept the intruders. Whatever the deficiencies in Johnson's model of the Saxon Shore as an integrated defence system, it has the merit that it combined the defensive potential of the north-eastern approaches of the Dover Strait with Roman military technology to produce a system of defence in depth. Even so, whether a pirate ship sneaked into a river estuary north-east of the Strait or a pirate fleet made it through the Strait to plunder rich villas further west, the likelihood that it would be taken would have been much greater on the way out than on the way in, before the Romans could deploy their naval forces. It could not be otherwise and, whatever the strategy adopted by Carausius, he would have had greater success intercepting pirates as they returned.[29]

It would be wrong in the present state of our understanding of the evidence to opt for any of the competing interpretations of the origin of the Saxon Shore. All have their deficiencies. White's idea, that the forts were built by Carausius as a defence against a Roman invasion from Gaul, is not supported by the latest dating for the construction of most of them. Johnson's model is undermined by the deficiencies in the evidence for Saxon raids on the coasts of south-east Britain in the late third century and by the less than persuasive evidence that the forts were linked at that stage by signal stations. Setting aside the manifest mistakes in Cotterill's critique of Johnson, his proposal that the forts were intended to serve as fortified ports and trans-shipment centres in a chain linking south-east Britain with the west coast, depends on indirect evidence and does not explain the need for the massively over-engineered fortifications of the forts on the south-east coast. The latest dating from Pevensey does, however, allow us to be reasonably confident that the forts, whatever their origin, were updated and extended by Carausius and in particular Allectus, to defend their regime against invasion from Gaul. They were, therefore, an important strategic factor in the events which culminated in the reintegration of Britain into the Roman world.

The story of Carausius and of Constantius's successful reconquest of the British provinces, contrasted with the invasions of Julius Caesar and Claudius, provides an instructive case-study in strategy. If our interpretation of the limited evidence is correct, it points up the significant influence that strategic considerations would have had on the conduct of sea-borne invasions. Though the details of Maximian's initial invasion attempt are vague, we may suspect that its failure had its cause in the likelihood that it was launched from the Rhine against a defensive system designed to cope with invaders from that direction. The success of the eventual invasion in 296 depended on bypassing the Saxon Shore system and it is that which would have dictated a main invasion passage west of the Dover Strait and a main landing somewhere on the Solent allied, as it happened, with a pincer movement further east, whether this was a display of force off East Kent or a landing on the Thames close to London. An invasion plan which involved a straightforward passage to East Kent, which met the strategic requirements of Caesar's invasions and, I would say, of Claudius's, would have been out of the question in 296.

8

CONCLUSIONS

In his book *The Great Invasion* written not so long after the Second World War, Leonard Cottrell thought that some of his readers would find comparisons between their wartime experiences and those of the Roman legionaries:

> Among the readers of this book may be some who have known what it is to wade on to an enemy beach under heavy fire. Others may have commanded troops in such an action, and experienced that nerve-racking moment when all hangs in the balance, when the defenders have the advantage of protected positions, and the attackers have not had time to establish their fighting formations; a moment like this.[1]

Cottrell then quotes Caesar's detailed narrative of the landing under fire of his legionaries near Walmer in 55 BC and suggests that his account 'could almost describe an attack on the Normandy beaches, or on a Japanese-held island in the Pacific'. It is remarkable that, of the invasions which we have discussed in this book, only Caesar's first raid was opposed on the beach. In fact, during the age of sail, it would seem to have been unusual for an invasion army to find resistance as it landed. Apart from the invasions launched by the Romans, we may cite the landings of Harald Hardrada and William of Normandy in 1066 and that of William of Orange in 1688, all of whom were able to disembark their armies without encountering opposition.

Even so, in many ways all sea-borne invasions are alike. They always involve the logistical business of mustering men and supplies at a harbour (or harbours) of embarkation, of building or requisitioning transport ships to convey personnel and materiel and warships to protect the convoy, and, in most cases, making adequate arrangements to establish lines of communications and resupply with the base from which the operation is to be launched. They also involve strategic issues. The commander-in-chief will have a clearly defined strategic objective. The way in which the campaign, including the invasion passage, is planned and conducted will be subordinated to that objective. In his treatise on warfare the late Roman writer, Vegetius, tells us that the commander-in-chief will evaluate the intelligence available to him, not only about the enemy's order of battle, but also about the layout of the country over which the campaign is to be waged. He will assess the relative risks and difficulties of the various sea routes available. There will also be preliminary stages before the main operation can be launched.

This is most clearly demonstrated in the campaign by Constantius and Maximian to depose Carausius and, after him, Allectus. Before the invasion was launched it was necessary to pacify the Germanic tribes on the Rhine, in all likelihood in alliance with Carausius, and to break his control of the fortified north coast of Gaul, by taking the strategically important base at Boulogne. The failure of Maximian's first invasion attempt from the Rhine points up the crucial importance of these initial steps. Once Constantius and Maximian had secured the base from which they would launch their invasion, they had to consider where the invasion force would land, and where it would embark. A frontal assault on the coast of East Kent, defended by the garrisons of Reculver, Richborough, Dover and Lympne, was not to be contemplated. It would be necessary to bypass the coordinated strength of the Saxon Shore with a pincer movement: one fleet would sail from the Seine to land in the Solent to the west of the Saxon Shore; the other would sail from Boulogne and offer a diversion off East Kent and in all probability make for London. It seems reasonably likely that the force under the command of Asclepiodotus was relatively small and lightly equipped. I can think of no other reason why they should have burnt their ships. But this must imply that once they had landed the imperial forces did not expect to encounter heavy resistance or to have to wage a prolonged campaign. As it turned out, Allectus was swiftly defeated and seems to have been able to rely on the loyalty only of his German mercenaries.

It is rather harder to assess the strategic objective of Caesar's British adventures. Partly this is because the picture is complicated by Caesar's own political objectives; the *Gallic War* was certainly a work of political propaganda, composed, it has been suggested, in the winter of 52/51 BC to promote his candidature at the consular elections of 50 BC. One important strand in the spin in Caesar's account is that he must be seen throughout to have the initiative. Stevens identifies two significant episodes in the *Gallic War* when Caesar's account conceals the fact that he had lost the initiative. One is the invasion of Britain, when Caesar's plans went astray.[2] We have seen that behind the cool narrative of his first raid, designed to show that he was in control throughout, we can discern moments, such as that when the armed British forces appeared on the heights over Dover, when things went badly wrong. In fact, as we saw, the campaign in 55 BC was a near disaster in which the strategic planning had been undermined by faulty intelligence.

Stevens notes that Strabo, but not Caesar, records that the revolt of the Veneti in 56 BC was occasioned by their concern to prevent an invasion of Britain, because they thought that this would damage their trade with the island – Caesar has a story about the detention of Roman emissaries as blackmail for the return of hostages. Among other things which he claims he did in response to the revolt, Caesar ordered the construction of warships on the Loire and the requisitioning of ships from the 'pacified regions'. Picking up on inconsistencies in Caesar's account, Stevens argues that these regions lay along the north coast of Gaul as far east as the territory of the Morini and the Menapii, who were among the tribes who joined the Veneti in their revolt, and that the ships were requisitioned not to suppress the revolt, but for an invasion of Britain in 56 BC. Stevens sees as possible that what was planned for that year was a double invasion using the 'age-old prehistoric sea-route to south-west Britain', as well as the short crossing of the Dover Strait (7; McGrail's routes 3 and 8). But for the revolt, the western invasion force, says Stevens, would have been transported by the Venetic ships.

Stevens's hypothesis is not without its attractions. It is certainly true that it resolves some of the undoubted difficulties of interpretation presented by Caesar's account of the Venetic revolt and its suppression. But the double invasion would have been a strategic nightmare. Not only would the western force have been committed to the most demanding of the Channel crossings with vastly extended lines of communication and resupply, but also communications with the eastern force would have been non-existent. The commanders would not have had clear intelligence about the terrain which separated them once they had landed and Caesar's eight legions would have had to be divided between the two invasion forces and a force left behind in Gaul to maintain control. But what for me puts Stevens's hypothesis out of court is that it is difficult to see what strategic objective could have been served by such a double invasion. We may suspect with Stevens that Caesar's strategic objective in 54 BC was the conquest of a new British province, even if we don't go as far as he does in saying that Caesar 'intended to conquer not only the whole of Britain but Ireland as well in the five campaigning seasons' left to him before his command expired.[3] But nowhere does Caesar say this. The closest he gets to saying why he invaded is his statement that in most of his campaigns in Gaul the enemy had received support from Britain. There is a hint that in 54 BC Caesar had intended to over-winter in Britain. He gives as his reason for returning to the continent the troubles which had suddenly broken out among the Gallic tribes. Moreover, Stevens had earlier pointed out that the dispositions left by Caesar – the legal terms for the submission of the British tribes and for the tribute imposed – amounted to the establishment of a 'provisional' Roman province of *Britannia*.

These provisional arrangements lapsed only because of the failure of the Romans to follow them up during the lifetime of the British kings involved.[4]

Whether Caesar's objective was the conquest of a new province or simply making a show of force which would deter further interventions from Britain in his Gallic campaigns, the strategic context was one which would have commended the short Channel crossing which Caesar used on both occasions. This would have guaranteed effective lines of communication and resupply which we know that Caesar exploited. It would have minimised the disadvantage of his lack of intelligence. There was no need to bypass an established system of coastal defence, as there would be three centuries later. Like Constantius and Maximian, Caesar had to prepare the ground for his invasions. In his account he gives a uniquely detailed account of the ships he had built and requisitioned, even if we may consider, with Stevens, that some aspects of it are exaggerated. He had to secure his base in Gaul and he tells us that he did this by obtaining the submission of the Morini, from whose territory he was to sail. He also undertook campaigns against the Germanic tribes in the Rhineland in both years before the invasion forces left Gaul and there are those who see the campaign against the Veneti as a necessary preliminary.[5]

When we come to look at the Claudian invasion, our understanding is clouded by the fact that the renewed debate about the location of his bridgehead, focusing as it does on the claimed imperial intention to restore Verica, has the effect of putting in doubt the strategic objective of the first year's campaign. Without Verica, we might reasonably believe that that objective was to defeat the Catuvellauni and take their power base at Colchester. This after all is what Dio tells us was achieved and, although he does tell us of Verica's intervention in persuading Claudius to undertake the invasion, he gives no hint that an intention to restore Verica was either formed or realised. If that happened or if the Romans' first step was to install Cogidumnus in his place, it is strange that Dio should tell us of the relatively unimportant episode of the submission of the Dobunni, while failing to report the achievement of what would have been a significant objective.

But that is to stray from the point. Advocates of the Fishbourne hypothesis have claimed that, if a Roman invasion force landed on the Solent in 296, a Roman invasion force could have done so in AD 43. Some have claimed that a landing in the territory of the British Atrebates would have ensured a ready welcome from the friendly inhabitants. But, whether the campaign objective was to restore Verica or not, the strategic context of AD 43 was entirely different from that of 296, at least from the naval point of view. There was no co-ordinated defensive system, such as the Saxon Shore, to bypass. East Kent was wide open and strategically speaking a landing there was perfectly feasible.

An invasion passage to East Kent from Boulogne would have been relatively undemanding, compared with one from Boulogne to the Solent, and supply lines across the Channel would have been easily maintained. Richborough on its island or peninsula would have provided a very suitable and easily defended bridgehead. As for a friendly reception from the inhabitants, some in the Roman high command might well have recalled that in 55 BC Caesar had expected a friendly reception at Dover. All in all, from the naval point of view, an invasion passage from Boulogne to the Solent is a strategic nonsense.

However, I have to accept that this may well be an over-simplistic view. It sees the invasion of AD 43 as a straightforward military operation, launched from a single embarkation harbour with a straightforward strategic objective. Hind did propose the possibility that invasion fleets sailed, not only from Boulogne, but also from the Canche, the Somme and the Seine and there is clear evidence that the Seine/Solent route was a well established trading route in the late first millennium BC. Moreover, it is easy to underestimate the extent of Roman influence in British political affairs before AD 43. John Manley has suggested that some of the enigmatic archaeological and numismatic evidence might well be understood in terms of a deepening romanisation of at least the south and the east, which might have seen an increasing number of Roman military units stationed in Britain even before the invasion. This could lead to an interpretation of what happened in AD 43 as a political annexation of an already romanised province, rather than a military invasion. Manley is careful to stress that he does not wish to advance this as a new orthodoxy, but it remains a possible interpretation, which does emphasise that neither the traditional view of an invasion through East Kent nor the new orthodoxy of a landing on the Solent accounts adequately for all the evidence.[6]

The problem is in our sources. Even taken on its own, Dio's account comes across as garbled and confused. When read in conjunction with the other sources, it becomes clear that there are significant omissions. In this the sources for AD 43 offer an interesting contrast with those for the Carausian adventure. The two panegyrists, together with the near identical reports of Eutropius and Aurelius Victor, present a consistent, albeit brief, account of the events of the decade 286-296 from which it is possible, with the support of the archaeological evidence, to draw out the principal strategic thrust of those events. It is also important to recognise that for all the high blown prose of their adulatory style the panegyrists were contemporary sources and that Eutropius and Aurelius Victor, while not primary sources, were writing within eighty years of the Carausian secession. Only Suetonius and Tacitus were writing close to the events of AD 43 and what they have to tell us amounts to no more than additional, even if important, detail.

So we come back to Dio, writing some two centuries after the event, and there can be no doubt that what he wrote was an account of a military campaign, not a political annexation. So much of the detail is concerned with such operational issues as the seeking out of the enemy, battles, the death of enemy leaders and the surrender of enemy forces. (One might add that the same is true of Suetonius's description of Vespasian's campaign in the south-west). Ernest Black was right to draw out the need to evaluate Dio's account in the light of what we may infer to have been the bias of his sources and to take account of the deficiencies in his methods. But I would go further. We are entitled to test what Dio tells us against other evidence, whether archaeological, environmental, numismatic, what Manley calls 'contemporary evidence' or sheer common sense.[7] It is such a test which leads me to assert that the hypothesis of an invasion passage from Boulogne to the Solent makes little sense when viewed in the light of what we can learn from maritime archaeology and the contemporary experience of seafaring under sail in the eastern Channel. To reject such experience and such lessons on the grounds of Dio's belief that the invasion fleet was sailing in a westerly direction is to give undue primacy to a throwaway remark by someone who was writing of the event at least at third hand and perhaps was not too certain in his grasp of the geography of north-west Europe.

Even so I have to accept that the evidence is not conclusive. When I first published my research on the Claudian invasion, I concluded:

> I have to say that, in my view, the weight of the maritime argument is so strong, that the landing in AD 43 must have been at Richborough... For my part, only the discovery of Tacitus's lost *Annals* confirming a landing elsewhere than at Richborough could provide the basis for a different view.[8]

Perhaps I would now be less certain, but not much. It is not that the maritime argument is any less strong in the context of a major invasion campaign, such as Dio describes – an invasion passage from Boulogne to the Solent with perhaps 40,000 men remains no less a strategic nonsense. Rather it is that recent study, such as that outlined by Manley, does at least raise the possibility that what happened in AD 43 was the culmination of the political and military infiltration of the tribes of south-east Britain over a number of years, involving a number of minor operations with different harbours of embarkation and different landing points. However, that is absolutely not the campaign which Dio describes. To accept such an interpretation is to place even more questions on his reliability as a source for the Claudian invasion.

GLOSSARY

Ahull: A sailing ship is said to be lying ahull, when she is drifting without sails set, a tactic adopted in storm conditions; she might alternatively be described as 'under bare poles'

Apparent wind: Wind as observed and measured from a moving vessel, the movement of which alters the speed and direction of the wind as it affects the vessel

Artemon: In Graeco-Roman ships, fore sail or the mast on which it is hoisted

Aplustre: In Graeco-Roman ships, the curved decorated stern

Augustus: Roman imperial title; under Diocletian's reforms in the late third century it designated the two senior members of the Tetrarchy

Azimuth: True horizontal bearing of a heavenly body; one of two elements defining the apparent position of the body relative to the observer, the other being its altitude above the horizon

Back: Of the wind, to shift anti-clockwise, against the sun. The opposite of veer (*q.v.*)

Beaufort scale: Scale devised by Admiral Beaufort to denote the strength of the wind in numbered stages from Force 0 (calm) to Force 12 (hurricane). Originally defined in terms of observed criteria (sea state or the point at which frigates reefed their topsails), it is now defined in terms of ranges of wind speeds measured in knots

Billon: Alloy of gold and silver with a large proportion of copper or other base metal, used in coinage

Caesar: Roman imperial title; under Diocletian's reforms in the late third century it designated the two junior members of the Tetrarchy, deputies to the *Augusti*

Carvel-built: Built with the hull planks flush or edge to edge (see Clinker-built)

Caulk: To render a hull leak proof by inserting a suitable sealing material between the planks of the hull. A wide range of organic materials were used in antiquity, including moss, animal hair and twisted fibres

Centre of Effort (CE): Point on an aerofoil, for example a sail, through which the total aerodynamic force is considered to act

Centre of Lateral Resistance (CLR): Point on the fore-and-aft cross-section of the underwater body of a vessel, through which the total hydrodynamic force is considered to act

Clinker-built: Built with planks or strakes overlapping; method used, in particular, in north-west Europe in ships built in the Nordic tradition

Cog: Single-masted, flat-bottomed, straight-stemmed cargo vessel used in Frisia and Scandinavia from the beginning of the second millennium AD

Course made good: The course of a vessel measured by reference to its progress over the ground (or seabed). It takes into account the effects of leeway (*q.v.*) and tidal streams

Dead reckoning: A method of estimating a ship's position at sea by laying off on the chart the course steered and the distance run. Tides are allowed for by laying off the 'set' and 'drift', i.e. the direction of the tidal stream and the distance that it has run. All the data used are estimates and the position marked on the chart is the estimated position

Denarius: A Roman coin, worth a quarter of a sestersius

Dendrochronology: A method of dating archaeological finds by analysis of the tree rings in wooden components and comparing them with established sequences; it can be remarkably accurate, especially if the bark and sap rings survive, since this makes it possible to establish when the tree was felled

Distance covered over the ground: The distance a vessel travels measured by reference to its progress over the ground (or seabed). It takes into account the effects of leeway (*q.v.*) and tidal streams

Drift: See Set and Drift

Equinox: The two days each year (in March and September) when day and night are of equal length. Astronomically speaking this is when the sun crosses the celestial equator. Tradition has it that the autumn equinox is associated with particularly stormy weather

Force: see Beaufort Scale

Fore-and-aft rig: A type of sailing rig in which the sails and spars are rigged along the fore-and-aft centre line of the hull

Freeboard: Vertical distance from the waterline to the gunwale when the hull is upright

Front: Boundary in the atmosphere between warm and cold air masses; a characteristic feature of Atlantic depressions, defined by Lamb (1988, 266) as 'essentially a line or narrow zone of discontinuity in the horizontal distribution of temperature, with an associated discontinuity in the barometric pressure and wind fields'. An advancing front in which cold air is displaced by warm is called a warm front; it will be followed by a cold front marking the advance of cold air displacing the warm air behind the warm front. The mass of warm air between the fronts is known as the warm sector

Humber keel: Traditional inshore cargo carriers, plying the waters centred on the Humber estuary until the twentieth century and characterised by a single-masted rig with two square sails, a main and a top sail

Knot: Speed of one nautical mile an hour; the term derives from counting the number of knots in the log line passing over the stern of the ship in a specified time; the log was a triangular piece of wood weighted so as to float vertically in the water and attached to the end of the log line which unwound from a reel held aloft; the time was measured by the turn of a sand glass; all in all a cumbersome three-man operation

Legate: In the Roman military structure designates either a legionary commander or a staff officer advising the commander-in-chief. Both Quintus Cicero and Vespasian were legates, the first on the staff of Julius Caesar, the second as the commander of the Second Legion under Plautius

Lee: Downwind; the side of the ship opposite the direction from which the wind is blowing; protection from the wind

Lee helm: The tendency of a sailing ship to turn downwind when the helm is released; the opposite of weather helm (*q.v.*)

Lee shore: Shore towards which the wind is blowing

Leeway: Sideways movement of a vessel under the influence of the wind; measured as the difference in degrees between the ship's track through the water and her heading

Marine transgression: Flooding of low-lying coastal areas arising from a rise in sea level

Mortice: Slot cut in the edge of a plank to allow the insertion of a tenon (*q.v.*) to hold it flush to an adjoining plank; mortice-and-tenon joints were used in Greek and Roman shipbuilding in antiquity to create the flush-laid shell of the hull

Nautical mile: Distance equivalent to the length of one degree of latitude on the surface of the earth; the average length approximates to 6,080 feet, but varies slightly with latitude; divides into 10 cables of about 200 yards

Neap tides: Tides with the least range between high and low water in each fortnightly period; occur twice a month a day or two after half moon. At neaps tidal streams are at their weakest

Overfalls: Turbulence caused in the water flow when it is disturbed by irregularities in the sea bed. They often occur close to land, off a promontory, for example, and can be dangerous

Polar diagram: Circular graph plotting ship speed for a particular wind speed against wind direction relative to the ship's bow

Quadrifrons: Of a monument, having four faces

Quinarius: A Roman coin, worth half a sestersius ot two denarii

Revet: To support a steep or vertical bank or the side of a ditch with a wall or fence to prevent it slipping

Set and drift: Set indicates the direction of a tidal stream; drift the distance it has moved in a given period of time

Shear Forces: Forces bearing sideways on a joint, as opposed to tensile forces tending to pull it apart and compressive forces tending to force it together

Spring tides: Tides with the greatest range between high and low water in each fortnightly period, occurring a day or two after new and full moon. At springs tidal streams are at their strongest

Spritsail: A type of fore-and-aft (*q.v.*) sail in which the after top corner is supported by a spar running down to the foot of the mast

Square rig: A type of sailing rig in which the sails and spars are rigged transversely across the hull

Storm surge: An abnormally high tide, significantly above the predicted level, generated by meteorological conditions

Suffect consul: Consul elected to a vacancy in the office occurring during year. Under the Empire, when the office became honorific, it became usual for consuls to stand down after less than the full year so as to allow others to share in the honour

Tack: The forward lower corner of a sail. As a verb to tack means to alter course when sailing so that the bow passes through the eye of the wind. A sailing ship is said to be on the port (or starboard) tack if the wind is blowing from her port (or starboard) side

Tenon: Tongue to be inserted into a mortice (*q.v.*) to create a mortice-and-tenon joint; it is secured in its slot by a peg or treenail

Terminus ante quem: the date before which an archaeological event happened

Terminus post quem: the date after which an archaeological event happened

Tidal diamond: Position, marked on a chart, for which hourly tidal data are given;

conventionally marked with a diamond

Tribune: In the Roman army officer ranking after the legionary commander.

True wind: Wind as observed and measured at a fixed point on the surface of the earth

Under bare poles: See ahull

Veer: Of the wind, to shift clockwise, in the same direction as the sun. The opposite of back (*q.v.*)

Weather helm: The tendency of a sailing ship to turn into the wind when the helm is released; the opposite of lee helm (*q.v.*)

NOTES AND REFERENCES

CHAPTER 1 INTRODUCING CAESAR, CLAUDIUS AND CONSTANTIUS

1 Cunliffe 1971, 22; 1998, 21.
2 Accounts of both conferences can be found on the Sussex Archaeological Society website at www.sussexpast.co.uk.
3 McGrail 1983, 330-4.

CHAPTER 2 THE ENGLISH CHANNEL IN MYTH AND REALITY

1 Frere 1987, 44; Peddie 1997, 20; Salway 1998, 60-1. Martin Henig (2002, 37) offers an unusual, not to say unique, interpretation of the mutiny of Plautius's legionaries: the incident took place during the Roman midwinter festival of 42/43, when Plautius's legionaries re-enacted the events of 40. After consuming a 'booty' of shellfish, they staged a mock mutiny, which was 'put down' by Narcissus in a humorous speech much appreciated by the troops and greeted with cries of '*Io Saturnalia!*'.
2 Braund 1996, 4; 12-23.
3 The translation is my own, following the Latin text published by Courtney (1993, 315-6). I have somewhat simplified Pedo's convoluted sentence structure, which makes the original even more 'puffed up' than my translation.
4 A point well illustrated by the sixtieth anniversary passage of the Dunkirk Little Ships in May 2000. The Little Ships were unable to make their anniversary passage on the intended date because of high winds.
5 Hawkes 1982, 65; Pirazzoli 1991, 64-5; Lamb 1995, 163.
6 Briquet 1930, 199-202; 355-9; Devoy 1990, 17; Pirazzoli 1991, 62-9; 77-8; 83-8.
7 Keys 1982, 146-7.
8 Dowker 1876, 63-4; Guest 1883, 348-52; 365-6; Holmes 1907, 605-6.
9 Airy 1865, 11; Burrows 1888, 8.
10 Darwin in a personal communication to Holmes (1907, 606).
11 Guest 1883, 366.
12 Devoy 1982, 85.
13 Taylor 1956, 121.
14 Riley 1976A, 50-79; McGrail 1983, 299-337.
15 Grainge and Grainge 1993, 270.
16 Lindgrén and Neumann 1985, 639-40.
17 Lamb 1995, 152-9; 165.
18 Riley 1976B, 114-5.
19 Hiscock 1965, 265; Shewan 1996, 37.
20 Boulogne, Dover, Manston, Newhaven, Thorney Island, Le Havre.
21 NP 28 1977, 39; 41-2; 46; NP 27 1977, 50; 57; Grainge 2002, 70-1; 134-9.

CHAPTER 3 THE ANCIENT WARSHIP

1   Casson 1994, 51-8; Morrison with Coates 1996, 122; 130; 260-1; 268-77.

2   Morrison with Coates 1996, 122; 257. T. Rice Holmes, author of the major study of Caesar's invasions which we discuss in Chapter 5, adopted a variant reading (*maiorem navium multitudinem*) 'a largish number of ships' (Holmes 1907, 596). The authority for this reading is based on one manuscript. Whether Holmes would have altered his view, had he known of Morrison's interpretation, must be for each reader to decide.

3   Morrison with Coates 1996, 265.

4   Morrison with Coates 1996, 248-53; 264.

5   The Cheops ship was found in a pit alongside the Great Pyramid at Giza. It had been dismantled, virtually a kit of parts.

6   McGrail 2001A, 26-8; 133-8; 145-8. See also Kahanov and Pomey (2004) for further discussion, including the suggestion that mortice-and-tenon joinery might have spread westward with the Phoenicians.

7   See Glossary.

8   Marsden 1994, 109-29; Tyers 1994, 202; 205.

9   Morrison with Coates 1996, 316-18.

10 Marsden 1964, 260; 1972, 115-6; Dove 1971, 15-20.

11 Höckmann 1986, 389-97; 1993, 125-35.

12 The Mainz ships have striking similarities with a well identified local shipbuilding tradition which has been designated Romano-Celtic. Höckmann doubts, however, whether they can be assigned to this tradition. The planking of the Mainz ships is much thinner than that typical of firmly identified Romano-Celtic ships. He considers that it was the need for lightness of construction which led the builders of the Mainz ships to abandon mortice-and-tenon joinery, which could not be accommodated within the thickness of the planks. While the use of clenched iron nails is characteristic of the Romano-Celtic tradition, it has also been found in two wrecks from Sicily and Israel dated to *c*.500 BC. Höckmann considers, therefore, that the Mainz ships represent the continuation of a special Mediterranean tradition, ultimately linked to Phoenician or Italic practice. However, in these Mediterranean wrecks the clenched nails are not used to fasten the planking to the framing, as in the Mainz ships and in the Romano-Celtic tradition, but the framing to the planking; the influence of contemporary local practice in the construction of the Mainz ships cannot reasonably be denied.

13 Haywood 1991, 47-9. Vegetius distinguishes two types of fleet: those made up of liburnians and those of *lusoriae*. The function of the fleets, he says, is to hold 'the seas and the rivers'. The implication is that liburnians are sea-going and *lusoriae* river craft.

14 In a computer-based hydrostatic study of Höckmann's reconstruction of one of the Mainz warships, Marsden (1993, 140) concluded that 'beyond 6-7 knots it would be difficult to go faster'. He also concluded that 10 knots was 'effectively the maximum speed of the boat'. Although these assessments suggest a speed potential higher than Höckmann's, they do not invalidate his general conclusion that the Mainz ships would have been slower than liburnians, since 'effective maximum speed' depends on the waterline length of the hull.

15 Marsden 1993, 138-41. McGrail lists the freeboard of a number of ancient vessels (1987, 200). Of sea-going vessels listed only the ninth/tenth-century boat from the Graveney marshes, Kent, has a freeboard less than Marsden's study suggests for the Mainz ships (0.35m as compared with 0.48m). Unlike the Graveney boat, the Mainz ships were oared ships which would have required a certain minimum freeboard for efficient rowing at sea. It is important in a seaway, particularly when the ship is rolling, that the oar blade should be able to clear the wave crests on the forward stroke and this would point to a minimum height for the freeboard.

16 The dating is by dendrochronology. Analysis of the oak used to build the hull suggests felling dates of AD 90 ± 10 years and AD 102 ± 10 years. No doubt because they still retained their sap rings, the oak piles are more precisely dated to being felled in AD 118.

17 de Weerd 1988, 180-94.

18 Morrison *et al.* 2000, 102-6.

19 Morrison *et al.* 2000, 81-3; 97-8; 104-5.

20 Morrison *et al.* 2000, 106.

21 Coates *et al.* 1990, 33-6; Morrison *et al.* 2000, 231-75.

22 Casson 1971, 302-9; Morrison with Coates 1996, 271; 349-50; Morrison *et al.* 2000, 107-18.

23 Casson 1971, 310-14.

24 This does depend on your choice of translation. According to the Loeb translation (Edwards 1917, 148-9), the rowers were 'drafted from the Province' (*institui ex provincia*). However, the meanings of *institui* listed in the Chambers Murray Latin-English Dictionary (Smith and Lockwood 1976, *s.v. instituo*) include 'to be trained'; 'drafted' sits less well among the alternative meanings offered.

25 Morrison with Coates 1996, 355-6; Morrison *et al.* 2000, 151-3.

CHAPTER 4 SUPPLY SHIPS – TROOP SHIPS

1 One detail the translator, Jackson (1962 390-3), seems to have got wrong: if rudders were fitted 'at each end', this would be a highly unusual configuration, not otherwise attested in ancient seafaring as far as I am aware. The word Tacitus uses (*utrimque*) is normally understood to mean 'on each side'. It would appear that Tacitus is describing two side rudders fitted to the port and starboard quarters, an arrangement which would have been normal at this time.

2 Marsden gives a list of such excavations (1994 168). It includes the few mortice-and-tenon joined hulls found in northern Europe.

3 Casson 1971, 171-2; 186; 1996, 46. Casson compared the dimensions of the *Isis* with those of the USS *Constitution* (53.3 x 13.25 x 4.3m) and the HMS *Victory* (56.7 x 15.7 x 6.6m).

4 Some time in the sixth century AD, St Brendan undertook with 17 monks an extended voyage into the Atlantic, which some have seen as the first ever transatlantic crossing. To judge by the number of surviving manuscripts, the story was hugely popular in the Middle Ages.

5 McGrail 1987, 173-87; 2001A, 181-3.

6 The *umiak* (or 'women's boat') is an open hide boat which served mainly as a people-carrier off the coasts of Greenland. In it the women of the family took the oars, while the men accompanied it in their lighter decked kayaks. *Baidara* is the term for the equivalent craft used in Siberia.

7 Severin 1978, 236-43.

8 Severin 1978, 289-90.

9 For St Peter Port 1, see Rule and Monaghan 1993; for Blackfrairs 1 see Marsden 1994, 33-95; for Barlands Farm see Nayling, Maynard and McGrail 1994; McGrail and Roberts 1999; McGrail 2001B, 117-32. For the Romano-Celtic tradition generally see Marsden 1994, 166-8; McGrail 1995; 2001A, 196-206; Ellmers 1996.

10 Ellmers 1996, 66.

11 Arnold 1999, 40-42. The Dover boat, recovered in a rescue excavation in 1992 and dated to the fourteenth century BC, is on display in Dover Museum. The Ferriby boats, found in 1937 and 1946 on the foreshore of the Humber estuary, are dated to the fourteenth century to twelfth century BC (North Ferriby 1) and to the fifteenth to fourteenth century BC (North Ferriby 2). These craft typify the use of stitching and of transverse timbers through mortised cleats.

12 The Bruges boat was found during the construction of a canal at Bruges. Although two witnesses were able to make a quick record of the wreck and of the geological context in which it lay, the contractors almost immediately had the wreck destroyed by a mechanical digger. Marsden's assessment, like those of earlier scholars, was made on the basis of the eyewitness records, of contemporary drawings and of the few surviving timbers in the National Scheepvaartmuseum in Antwerp (Marsden 1976).

13 McGrail 2001B, 130-1.

14 Andersen 1986, 209; Godal 1986, 201-4. For Centre of Effort and Centre of Lateral Resistance see Glossary.

15 de Weerd 1988, 143-5; Grainge 2002, 32-44. The use of the mast as a derrick was still practised centuries later in modern-day Humber keels.

16 Ellmers 1969; 1996, 61-2.

17 Grainge 2002, 45-51.

CHAPTER 5 CAESAR: AN OLD CONTROVERSY REVIEWED

1 Ptolemy lists *Cantium* as a promontory.

2 Caesar gives the times in terms of the Roman hours of the day (*horae*) and watches of the night (*vigiliae*). These divide the day into 12 hours and the night into four watches and measure the time respectively from sunrise and sunset. Therefore, the actual time depends on the season.

3 A Roman mile is 1,000 double paces; 1,480m or 0.9 statute miles.

4 Caesar was referring to spring tides, which in point of fact occur a day or two after full and new moon.

5 *Leni Africo*. The translation is approximate. *Africus* denoted a wind blowing from west by ⅓ south. Corus, the wind which delayed the fleet for 25 days, blew from

west by ⅓ north (*9*).

6   Henry 1810; Lewin 1862; Airy 1865; Napoleon III 1865-6; Dowker 1876; Guest 1864; 1883; Ridgeway 1891.

7   Holmes's stricture is less than fair. Airy did not use the word 'valueless'; his comment addressed the issue of estimating the distance across the Dover Strait, which he described as a 'fair and an insoluble question' before the advent of modern triangulation methods.

8   Holmes 1907, 552-666.

9   Ptolemy measures latitude northward from the Equator. Longitude is measured eastward from a prime meridian somewhere in the Atlantic, effectively further west than any point he catalogues. The coordinates for individual locations appear in many cases to be based on estimates of distance, rather than measurements of latitude, which results in a number of accumulating errors. Boulogne's latitude is in fact 50° 44′ N.

10 Strabo uses the adjective 'Itian' without a noun. The grammatical gender of the adjective suggests that word agrees with the Greek noun used by Ptolemy for promontory.

11 According to this website the text given is based on a translation published by New York Public Library (Stevenson 1991). This also gives the latitude of the Itian Promontory as 52° 30′. The address of the website is: http://penelope.uchicago.edu/Thayer/E/Gazetteer/Periods/Roman/_Texts/Ptolemy/2/8*.html

12 Guest 1864, 227-8.

13 24.25 nautical miles. The actual distance is 25 nautical miles.

14 A point is a thirty-second part of the old compass rose, equivalent to 11.25°.

15 In his argument, Holmes neglected the difference between true and apparent wind. The apparent wind is the wind as observed on the moving vessel and it is to this wind that the ship sails. The phenomenon will have two effects. First it moves the apparent wind forward; thus the crew of the transports supposedly lying five points of the wind, will believe that they are lying much closer to the wind than this. Second, if the true wind is forward of the beam, the apparent wind will be stronger than the true wind, thus making the storm more violent. These two effects would have strengthened Holmes's argument.

16 The account in Chapter 27 of *The Acts of the Apostles* of the storm in which St Paul was shipwrecked is relevant here. In verse 15 we read that, when the ship was caught in the storm, she 'could not bear up into the wind'; so 'we let her drive'; 'drive' here means 'drift' and what we are being told is that the ship was left to drift downwind under bare poles.

17 NP 28 1977, 23.

18 Meaden 1976; 1986.

19 Shelter from a north-easterly would have had to be rather further along the south coast than the South Foreland.

20 Airy 1865, 33.

21 Appach 1868, 102.

22 See Glossary.

23 Greenwich Mean Time.

24 Holmes does not make it clear, but it would appear from the logic of his argument that his estimate is of distance covered over the ground.

25 Heller 1865, 124; Dowker 1876, 67-8; 70; Holmes 1907, 576; 658.

26 McGrail 1983, 328-9.

27 Holmes 1907, 308; 627; 639; Frere 1987, 19; Salway 1998, 26. Zeruiah was the sister of King David and mother of Abishai, Joab and Asahel (I Chronicles, 2, 16); accounts of the exploits of her sons are given in the Old Testament books of Samuel, Kings and Chronicles.

28 I find it hard to resist the thought that Caesar's overt praise of Volusenus is covert criticism of Galba for the latter's failure adequately to assess the tactical situation.

29 Smith and Lockwood 1976, *s.v. mollis.*

30 If Holmes is right in placing Caesar's passage to Britain in 54 BC on the night of 6/7 July, this would have been the night of the new moon.

31 Three times, if one counts the ambassadors sent to him before he set out from Gaul.

32 Wellington on Waterloo.

CHAPTER 6 CLAUDIUS: AN OLD CONTROVERSY RENEWED

1 For Richborough see Bushe-Fox 1932, 10-13; 1949, 11-36 and Cunliffe 1968, 231-7; for the Fishbourne/Chichester area see Down 1988, 7-16, Cunliffe 1998, 25-32, Manley 2002, 111-28 and Manley and Rudkin 2003; for Maiden Castle see Wheeler 1943, 61-8 and for Hod Hill see Richmond 1962, 31-3.

2 The coinage evidence suggests that after the Gallic Wars the Commius we met in Chapter 5 became king of the British Atrebates; Verica is one of three subsequent kings of the Atrebates to claim descent from him.

3 Black 2000, 6.

4 Sauer 2002, 355.

5 Airy 1865, 55-61.

6 Guest 1883, 396-401; Hübner 1881, 16-21; 1890, 520; 527-30.

7 O'Neil and O'Neil 1952, 29-33; Hawkes 1961, 64-65.

8 For example, Frere 1987, 48-50; Peddie 1997, 47-65; Todd 1997, 58-60; Webster 1999, 95-7.

9 Salway 1998, 82-3.

10 Hind 1989.

11 Bird 2000; Black 1998; 2000; 2001.

12 Nicolson 2000; Philp 2000; Frere and Fulford 2001; Grainge 2002. The television programme was *Britain's Lost Roman Wonder*. One might take the cynical view that the programme amounted to an hour's free advertising for English Heritage who control the site at Richborough. It was presented by Simon Thurley, the Chief Executive of English Heritage.

13 Creighton 2000; Manley 2002; Sauer 2002.

14 Cunliffe 1998, 21; Sauer 2000, 39-41.

15 I exclude authors, such as Hind (1989, 14) and Bird (2000, 92), who assert that, because Asclepiodotus landed in the Solent in AD 296 or the commanders of the

Spanish Armada in 1588 had considered taking the Isle of Wight, a landing here was a feasible option in AD 43.

16 Johnson 1979, 94.

17 Apart from the celebrated Enterprise of England in 1588, the Spanish made two further attempts to invade in 1596 and 1597. Both were scattered by Atlantic gales before they could reach their destination.

18 McGrail, 1983. It should be emphasised that McGrail's figures are relative, a figure of 100 per cent being assigned to the easiest passage (Wissant to Walmer). This does not imply that 100 per cent of passages from Wissant to Walmer would succeed. The wind data quoted here and elsewhere are tabulated in Grainge (2002, 134-9).

19 Ireland 1986, 133.

20 The Latin phrase (*ventum quia derectus non erat captaret obliquum*) might better be translated 'because the wind was not directly behind them, they sailed close-hauled'.

21 Grainge 2002, 127-30.

22 Binns 1968, 111-116.

23 Dowker 1876, 60-1.

24 15 May.

25 In a note to this passage in his translation, Milner notes that 'the greed which makes merchants brave the high seas was a commonplace' (1996, 146-7).

26 Peddie 1997, 37-41; Grainge 2002, 45-51.

27 Casson 1971, 271-8; 292-6, Neumann 1989, 232-3; Grainge 2002, 55-9.

28 Dalrymple 1771, 158.

29 I can recall one occasion, when sailing to Ramsgate from France, when the last leg of the passage into Ramsgate was due west. We had passed north of the Goodwin Sands.

30 Barrett 1998.

31 Barrett 1980. For suffect consul see Glossary.

32 Butler and Cary 1927, 123; Duncan-Jones 1990, 7-29; Wells 1992, 138-41.

33 Black, 2001, 425.

34 Cary 1924, 417; Ireland 1986, 45; Cunliffe 1971, 22; 1998, 21; Hind 1989, 6.

35 The key word in Dio's text is κωλυθωσι. According to Liddell and Scott (1997, *s.v.* κωλυω), the normal meaning to be ascribed to this word is 'hinder'.

CHAPTER 7 CARAUSIUS AND THE SAXON SHORE

1 Cunliffe 1977, 3; Johnson 1979, 68-71; Pearson 2002, 130.

2 Philp 1996, 5.

3 Johnson 1979, 34-63; Pearson 2002, 11-38.

4 Johnson 1979, 90-3. This identification depends on assuming a scribal error in recording *Samarica* as *Sambrica*. The alternative is to see this fleet as a river flotilla stationed on the Sambre, a tributary of the Meuse (White 1961, 61).

5 White 1961, 68-82.

6 *History of the Emperors.*

7   Bird 1993, xlvii–xlix; 1994, xii–xiii.
8   Seillier 1996, 215-18.
9   Lindgrén and Neumann 1985, 640-2; Grainge and Grainge 1993, 268.
10 Salway 1998, 308.
11 Frere 1987, 330; Haywood 1991, 40; Salway 1998, 308.
12 I found a useful source of information on the coinage of Carausius and Allectus on a web page published by Ken Elks (www.users.globalnet.co.uk/~kenelks/carausius.htm).
13 *Quibus, Hector, ab oris, expectate, venis*. 'What shores do you come from, Hector? Long have we looked for you'. The translation is by C. Day Lewis (1966, 170).
14 The number three is indicated by the tripling of the letter G.
15 The rounded corners had the effect of restricting the angle of fire from the corner bastions.
16 Cunliffe 1977, 3; Johnson 1979, 96-115; Pearson 2002, 54-62.
17 Emperor from 276 to 282.
18 Johnson 1977, 68-9.
19 White 1961, 40.
20 White 1961, 19-54.
21 Johnson 1979, 7.
22 Johnson 1979, 126-31; Pearson 2002, 107-8.
23 Johnson 1979, 125-6; Pearson 2002, 48; 62; 168.
24 Green 1963, 103-14.
25 Cotterill 1993.
26 Haywood 1991, 68-75; Greenhill with Morrison 1995, 182.
27 Johnson 1979, 130; Cotterill 1993, 232.
28 Fulford and Tyers 1995.
29 Haywood 1991, 4.

CHAPTER 8 CONCLUSIONS

1   Cottrell 1961, 9.
2   The other is the campaign of 52 BC against Vercingetorix (Stevens 1952, 3-5; 8-18).
3   Stevens 1952, 14.
4   Stevens 1947, 7-8.
5   Frere 1987, 17.
6   Hind 1989, 14; Manley 2002, 143-6.
7   Manley uses the term 'contemporary evidence' to designate the evidence of modern experience of such activities as seafaring, soldiering and building (2002, 28-30). Manley urges caution in the use of such evidence – and indeed of common sense – on the grounds that we cannot know whether the Romans 'were like us'.
8   Grainge 2002, 108.

BIBLIOGRAPHY

ANCIENT SOURCES

In the text I have not given detailed references to ancient sources. However, the main ancient sources for the Roman invasions of Britain are as follows:

For Julius Caesar's raids, Caesar's own *Gallic War*, Books III (7-16), IV (20-36), V (1-23), is the principal source, but it needs reading with care, given the political purpose for which it was written.

For the Claudian invasion, the main source, Dio Cassius's *Roman History*, Book LX (19-22), suffers from the fact that it is not a primary source and appears to be a confused and garbled synthesis of sources, which are not themselves primary. Suetonius's *Lives of the Caesars* provides supplementary information, particularly for the part in the invasion played by the future emperor Vespasian.

Most of these texts, as well as of others which I have cited, are available in the editions of the Loeb Library, with the Latin (or Greek) text and the English translation on facing pages.

Brief and very similar accounts of the career of Carausius and the invasion mounted by Constantius Chlorus are given by Aurelius Victor in his *Book on the Emperors* (*de Caesaribus*), (39) and by Eutropius in his *Concise History of Rome* (*Breviarium*), Book IX, (21-2). A fuller picture may be derived from the panegyrics delivered in praise of Maximian and Constantius Chlorus, but one must allow for the eulogising intentions of the panegyrist. These are available in a Latin text, known as *XII Latin Panegyrics* (*XII Panegyrici Latini*), edited by R.A.B. Mynors (1964, Clarendon Press, Oxford), but as far as I know there is no translation available of the complete text into English. Translations of extracts have been published by Ireland (1986). The panegyrics I have quoted are X(II), (11-12) and VIII(V), (6-7; 12- 20).

For Roman military affairs I have found Vegetius's *Epitome of Military Science* a useful source, especially for the conduct of naval operations (Book IV, 31-45). I have used the translated edition by Milner (1996). I found the text for the extract from the poem by Albinovanus Pedo in Courtney's *Fragmentary Latin Poets*.

There are a few internet sites devoted to publishing both original texts and translations, which I have found useful. One site where I have found a lot of material is the Lacus Curtius site at: http://penelope.uchicago.edu/Thayer/E/Roman/home.html. These sites can be found quite rapidly with a search engine, such as my favourite, Google.

I have not in the text given references for translations that I have quoted. They come, in a few cases with minor amendments, from the following editions:

Bird, H.W., 1993, *The Breviarium ab Urbe Condita of Eutropius*, Liverpool: Liverpool University Press.

Bird, H.W., 1994, *Aurelius Victor: De Caesaribus*, Liverpool: Liverpool University Press.

Butler, H.E., and Cary, M.A., 1927, *C. Svetoni Tranquilli Divvs Ivlivs*, Oxford: Clarendon Press.

Courtney, E., 1993, *The Fragmentary Latin Poets*, Oxford: Clarendon Press.

Day Lewis, C., 1966, *The Eclogues, Georgics and Aeneid of Virgil*, Oxford: Oxford University Press.

Edwards, H.J., 1917, *Caesar: The Gallic War*, Cambridge, Massachusetts and London: Loeb Classical Library.

Ireland, S., 1986, *Roman Britain: A Sourcebook*, London and New York: Routledge.

Jackson, J., 1962, 'The Annals', in *Tacitus*, vol. II, Cambridge, Massachusetts, and London: Loeb Classical Library.

Milner, N.P., 1996, *Vegetius: Epitome of Military Science (Second Edition)*, Liverpool: Liverpool University Press.

Stevenson, E.L., 1991, *The Geography: Claudius Ptolemy*, New York: Dover, London: Constable.

Webb, J.F., 1983, 'The Voyage of St Brendan', in Farmer, D.H. (ed.), *The Age of Bede*, Harmondsworth: Penguin Classics, 211-45.

MODERN WORKS

For the study of the ancient Mediterranean warship, I found a mine of detailed information in the books by John Morrison and John Coates, in particular their *Greek and Roman Oared Warships*, and by Lionel Casson, in particular his *Ships and Seamanship in the Ancient World*. For the Romano-Celtic shipbuilding tradition, Peter Marsden's *Ships of The Port of London* and Margaret Rule and Jonathan Monaghan's *A Gallo-Roman Trading Vessel from Guernsey* give detailed accounts of two significant type finds.

For Julius Caesar's invasions the ground-breaking work is T. Rice Holmes's 1907 *Ancient Britain and the Invasions of Julius Caesar*. For the Claudian invasion the most up to date assessment of the totality of the evidence is John Manley's *The Roman Invasion of Britain: a reassessment*. Apart from this, much of the recent work has been published in academic journals such as *Britannia* and the *Oxford Journal of Archaeology*. It was the former that in 1989 carried John Hind's paper, 'The Invasion of Britain in AD43 – An Alternative Strategy for Aulus Plautius', which renewed the current debate on the landing place of the invasion force.

Donald A. White in his *Litus Saxonicum* and Stephen Johnson in his *The Roman forts of the Saxon Shore* advanced hypotheses about the function of the Saxon Shore forts as a defensive system and, in Johnson's case, sought to explain how it worked in practice. These books predate much recent research, especially on the dating and the type of occupation of the individual forts. Andrew Pearson's *The Roman shore forts* has the merit of drawing on such recent work and points to recent papers which have seen the Saxon shore sites as fortified ports and trans-shipment centres. In doing so, his book serves as a counterbalance to the views of White and Johnson, but, at least in my view, does not wholly invalidate them.

The detailed references in the notes are to the following bibliography:

Airy, G.B., 1865, *Essays on the Invasion of Britain by Julius Caesar; the Invasion of Britain by Plautius and Claudius Caesar; the Early Military Policy of the Romans in Britain; the Battle of Hastings, collected and printed for private distribution*, London: Nichols and Sons.

Andersen, E., 1986, 'Steering Experience with Square-Rigged Vessels', in Crumlin-Pedersen, O., and Vinner, M. (eds), *Sailing into the Past*, Roskilde: Viking Ship Museum, 208-219.

Appach, F.H., 1868, *Caius Julius Cæsar's British Expeditions from Boulogne to the Bay of Apuldore, and the subsequent formation geologically of Romney Marsh*, London: Smith.

Arnold, B., 1999, 'Some Remarks on Romano-Celtic Boat Construction and Bronze Age Wood Technology', *International Journal of Nautical Archaeology*, 28,1, 34-44.

Barrett, A.A., 1980, 'Chronological Errors in Dio's Account of the Claudian Invasion', *Britannia*, 11, 31-3.

Barrett, A.A., 1998, 'The Date of Claudius' British Campaign and the Mint of Alexandria', *Classical Quarterly*, XLVIII, 2, 574-7.

Binns, A.L., 1968, 'The Navigation of Viking Ships round the British Isles in Old English and Old Norse Sources', in Niclasen, B. (ed.), *The Fifth Viking Congress Tórshavn, July 1965*, Tórshavn: Føroya Landsstýri, 103-117.

Bird, D.G., 2000, 'The Claudian Invasion Campaign reconsidered', *Oxford Journal of Archaeology*, 19, 1, 91-104.

Black, E.W., 1998, 'How Many Rivers to Cross', *Britannia*, 29, 306-7.

Black, E.W., 2000, 'Sentius Saturninus and the Roman Invasion of Britain', *Britannia*, 31, 1-10.

Black, E.W., 2001, 'The First Century Historians of Roman Britain', *Oxford Journal of Archaeology*, 20(4), 415-28.

Braund, D., 1996, *Ruling Roman Britain: Kings, Queens, Governors and Emperors from Julius Caesar to Agricola*, London and New York: Routledge.

Briquet, A., 1930, *Le littoral du nord de la France et son évolution morphologique*, Paris: Librairie Armand Colin.

Burrows, R.M., 1888, *The Cinque Ports*, London: Longmans.

Bushe-Fox, J.P., 1932, *Excavations at the Roman Fort at Richborough, Third Report*, London: Society of Antiquaries.

Bushe-Fox, J.P., 1949, *Excavations at the Roman Fort at Richborough, Fourth Report*, London: Society of Antiquaries.

Casson, L., 1971, *Ships and Seamanship in the Ancient World*, Princeton, New Jersey: Princeton University Press.

Casson, L., 1994, *Ships and Seafaring in Ancient Times*, London: British Museum Press.

Casson, L., 1996, 'Sailing Ships of the Ancient Mediterranean', in Christensen, A.E. (ed.), *The Earliest Ships: The Evolution of Boats into Ships*, London: Conway Maritime Press, 39-51.

Coates, J.F., Platis, S.K., and Shaw, J.T., 1990, *The Trireme Trials 1988: Report on the Anglo-Hellenic Sea Trials of Olympias*, Oxford: Oxbow Books.

Cotterill, J., 1993, 'Saxon Raiding and the Role of the Late Roman Coastal Forts of Britain', *Britannia*, 24, 227-239.

Cottrell, L., 1961, *The Great Invasion*, London: Pan Books.

Cunliffe, B. (ed.), 1968, *Fifth Report on the Excavations at the Roman Fort at Richborough, Kent*, Oxford, Society of Antiquaries.

Cunliffe, B., 1971, *Fishbourne: A Roman Palace and its Garden*, London: Thames and Hudson.

Cunliffe, B., 1977, 'The Saxon Shore – some problems and misconceptions', in Johnstone, D.E. (ed.), *The Saxon Shore*, London: C.B.A. Research Report No. 18, 1-6.

Cunliffe, B., 1998, *Fishbourne Roman Palace*, Stroud: Tempus.

Creighton, J., 2000, *Coins and Power in Late Iron Age Britain*, Cambridge: Cambridge University Press.

Dalrymple, J., 1771, *Memoirs of Great Britain and Ireland. From the Dissolution of the Last Parliament of Charles II until the Sea-Battle off La Hogue*, vol. I, London, Edinburgh and Dublin.

Devoy, R.J., 1982, 'Analysis of the geological evidence for Holocene sea level movements in S.E. England', *Proceedings of the Geologists' Association*, 93, 65-90.

Devoy, R.J.N., 1990, 'Controls on Coastal and Sea-Level Changes and the Application of Archaeological-Historical Records to Understanding Recent Patterns of Sea-Level Movement', in McGrail, S. (ed.), *Maritime Celts, Frisians and Saxons*, London: CBA Research Report 71, 17-26.

de Weerd, M.D., 1988, *Schepen voor Zwammerdam*, Amsterdam.

Dove, C.E., 1971, 'The first British Navy', *Antiquity*, XLV, 15-20.

Dowker, G., 1876, 'Caesar's landing Place in Britain', *Archaeological Journal*, xxxiii, 56-71.

Down, A., 1988, *Roman Chichester*, Chichester: Phillimore.

Duncan-Jones, R., 1990, *Structure and Scale in the Roman Economy*, Cambridge: Cambridge University Press.

Ellmers, D., 1969, 'Keltischer Schiffbau', *Jahrbuch des Römisch-Germanischen Zentralmuseums Mainz*, 16, 73-122.

Ellmers, D., 1996, 'Celtic Plank Boats and Ships, 500 BC – AD 1000', in Christensen, A.E. (ed.), *The Earliest Ships: The Evolution of Boats into Ships*, London: Conway Maritime Press, 52-71.

Frere, S., 1987, *Britannia: A History of Roman Britain, (3rd edition)*, London: Pimlico.

Frere, S. and Fulford, M., 2001, 'The Roman Invasion of AD 43', *Britannia*, 32, 45-55.

Fulford, M. and Tyers, I., 1995, 'The date of Pevensey and the defence of an *Imperium Britanniarum*', *Antiquity*, 69, 1009-14.

Godal, J., 1986, 'Recording Living Traditions of Square-Sail Rigged Norwegian Boats', in Crumlin-Pedersen, O. and Vinner, M. (eds), *Sailing into the Past*, Roskilde: The Viking Ship Museum, 194-219.

Grainge, C.P. and Grainge, G., 1993, 'The Pevensey Expedition: Brilliantly Executed Plan or Near Disaster?', *Mariner's Mirror*, 79, 261-273.

Grainge, G., 2002, *The Roman Channel Crossing of AD 43: The constraints on Claudius's naval strategy*, Oxford: BAR British Series 332.

Green, C., 1963, *Sutton Hoo: the Excavation of a Royal Ship-Burial*, London: The Merlin Press.

Greenhill, B. with Morrison, J., 1995, *The Archaeology of Boats and Ships: An Introduction*, London: Conway Maritime Press.

Guest, E, 1864, 'Julius Caesar's Invasion of Britain', *Archaeological Journal*, xxi, 220-42.

Guest, E., 1883, *Origines Celticae (a Fragment) and other contributions to the History of Britain*, vol. II, London: Macmillan.

Hawkes, S.C., 1982, 'Anglo-Saxon Kent *c*.425-725' in Leach, P.E. (ed.), *Archaeology in Kent to AD 1500 in memory of Stuart Eborall Rigold*, CBA Research Report 48, 64-78.

Haywood, J., 1991, *Dark Age Naval Power: A Re-assessment of Frankish and Anglo-Saxon Seafaring Activity*, London and New York: Routledge.

Henig, M., 2002, *The Heirs of King Verica*, Stroud: Tempus.

Henry, J.F., 1810, *Essai historique, topographique et statistique sur l'Arrondissement Communal de Boulogne-sur-Mer*, Boulogne.

Hind, J.G.F., 1989, 'The Invasion of Britain in AD 43 – An Alternative Strategy for Aulus Plautius', *Britannia*, 20, 1-21.

Hiscock, E.C., 1965, *Cruising under Sail (2nd edition)*, London, New York and Toronto: Oxford University Press.

Höckmann, O., 1986, 'Römische Schiffsverbände auf dem Ober- und Mittelrhein und die Verteidigung der Rheingrenze in der Spätantike', *Jahrbuch des Romanisch-Germanischen Zentral Museums Mainz*, 33, 369-415.

Höckmann, O., 1993, 'Late Roman Rhine vessels from Mainz, Germany', *International Journal of Nautical Archaeology*, 22.2, 125-135.

Holmes, T.R.E. 1907, *Ancient Britain and the Invasions of Julius Caesar*, Oxford: Clarendon Press.

Hübner, E, 1881, 'Das Römische Heer in Britannien', *Hermes*, xvi, 513-84.

Hübner, E, 1890, *Römische Heerschaft in Westeuropa*, Berlin: Verlag von Wilhelm Hertz.

Hydrographer of the Navy (NP 233), 1963, *Dover Strait: Tidal Stream Atlas*, Taunton.

Hydrographer of the Navy (NP 250), 1973, *Tidal Stream Atlas: The English and Bristol Channels*, Taunton.

Hydrographer of the Navy (NP 27), 1977, *Channel Pilot (2nd edition – revised 1984)*, Taunton.

Hydrographer of the Navy (NP 28), 1977, *Dover Strait Pilot (4th edition)*, Taunton.

Johnson, S., 1979, *The Roman forts of the Saxon Shore (2nd edition)*, London: Elek

Kahanov, Y. and Pomey, P., 2004, 'The Greek sewn shipbuilding tradition and the Ma'agan Mikhael ship: a comparison with Mediterranean parallels from the sixth to the fourth centuries BC', *Mariner's Mirror*, 90, 6-28.

Keys, G., 1982, *Practical Navigation by Calculator*, London: Stanford Maritime.

Lamb, H.H., 1988, *Weather, Climate & Human Affairs: A Book of Essays and Other Papers*, London and New York: Routledge.

Lamb, H.H., 1995, *Climate, History and the Modern World (2nd edition)*, London and New York: Routledge.

Lewin, T., 1862, *The Invasion of Britain by Julius Caesar (2nd edition): With replies to the Remarks of the Astronomer-Royal [G. B. Airy] and the late Camden Professor of Ancient History at Oxford [E. Cardwell]*, London: Longman, Green, Longman and Roberts.

Liddell and Scott, 1997, *An Intermediate Greek Lexicon*, Oxford: Clarendon Press.

Lindgrén, S., and Neumann, J., 1985, 'Great Historical Events that were Significantly Affected by the Weather: 7. 'Protestant Wind' – 'Popish Wind': The Revolution of 1688 in England', *Bulletin of the American Meteorological Society*, 66, 6, 634-44.

McGrail, S., 1983, 'Cross-Channel Seamanship and Navigation in the Late First Millennium BC', *Oxford Journal of Archaeology*, 2(3), 299-337.

McGrail, S., 1987, *Ancient Boats in N. W. Europe: The Archaeology of Water Transport to AD 1500*, London and New York: Longman.

McGrail, S., 1995, 'Romano-Celtic Boats and Ships: Characteristic Features', *International Journal of Nautical Archaeology*, 24, 139-45.

McGrail, S., 2001A, *Boats of the World from the stone age to medieval times*, Oxford University Press.

McGrail, S., 2001B, 'The Barland's Farm Boat within the Romano-Celtic Tradition', *Archäologisches Korrespondenzblatt*, Vol. 1, 31, 117-32.

McGrail, S., and Roberts, O., 1999, 'A Romano-British Boat from the Shores of the Severn Estuary', *Mariner's Mirror*, 85, 133-46.

Manley, J., 2002, *AD 43: The Roman Invasion of Britain: a reassessment*, Stroud: Tempus.

Manley, J. and Rudkin, D., 2003, 'Fishbourne before the Conquest; royal capital of a client-kingdom', *Current Archaeology*, 187, 290-8.

Marsden, P., 1964, 'Warships on Roman coins', *Mariner's Mirror*, 50, 260.

Marsden, P., 1972, 'Ships of the Roman period and after in Britain', in Bass, G.F. (ed.), *A History of Seafaring based on Underwater Archaeology*, London: Thames and Hudson, 113-32.

Marsden, P., 1976, 'A boat of the Roman period found at Bruges, Belgium in 1899 and related finds', *International Journal of Nautical Archaeology*, 5.1, 23-55.

Marsden, P., 1993, 'A hydrostatic study of a reconstruction of Mainz Roman ship 9', *International Journal of Nautical Archaeology*, 22.2, 137-141.

Marsden, P., 1994, *Ships of The Port of London: First to Eleventh Centuries A.D.*, London: English Heritage.

Meaden, G.T., 1976, 'Late Summer Weather in Kent, 55 BC', *Weather*, 31, 8, 264-70.

Meaden, G.T., 1986, 'The storms of August 55 BC and July 54 BC and their consequences for Julius Caesar's invasions of Britain', *Journal of Meteorology*, 11, 108, 116-123.

Morrison, J.S., with contributions by Coates, J.F., 1996, *Greek and Roman Oared Warships,* Oxford: Oxbow Books.

Morrison, J.S., Coates, J.F., and Rankov, N.B., 2000, *The Athenian Trireme: the History and Reconstruction of an Ancient Greek Warship*, (2nd edition), Cambridge, New York and Oakleigh: Cambridge University Press.

Napoleon III, 1865-6, *History of Julius Caesar: The Wars in Gaul*, vol. II, London: Cassell, Petter and Galpin.

Nayling, N., Maynard, D., and McGrail, S., 1994, 'Barland's Farm, Magor, Gwent: a Romano-Celtic Boat', *Antiquity*, 68, 596-603.

Neumann, J., 1989, 'Hydrographic and Ship-Hydrodynamic Aspects of the Norman Invasion, AD 1066', *Anglo-Norman Studies*, XI, 221-43.

Nicolson, N., 2000, 'The Roman Invasion', *Current Archaeology*, 167, 442.

O'Neil, B.H.St., and O'Neil, H.E., 1952, 'The Roman Conquest of the Cotswolds',

Archaeological Journal, cix, 23-38.

Pearson, A., 2002, *The Roman shore forts: coastal defences of southern Britain*, Stroud, Tempus.

Peddie, J., 1997, *Conquest: The Roman Invasion of Britain*, Stroud: Sutton Publishing.

Philp, B., 1996, *The Roman Fort at Reculver*, Dover: Kent Archaeological Rescue Unit.

Philp, B., 2000, 'Dio Cassius', *Current Archaeology*, 167, 443.

Pirazzoli, P.A., 1991, *World Atlas of Holocene Sea-Level Changes*, Elsevier Oceanography Series, 58.

Richmond, I.A., 1962, *Hod Hill: Excavations Carried Out Between 1951 and 1958 for the Trustees of the British Museum*, London: Trustees of the British Museum.

Ridgeway, W., 1891, 'Caesar's Invasions of Britain', *Journal of Philology*, xix, 139-45; 200-10.

Riley, R.J.F., 1976A, *Stanford's Voyaging Companion*, London: Stanford Maritime.

Riley, R.J.F., 1976B, *Stanford's Sailing Companion*, London: Stanford Maritime.

Rule, M., and Monaghan, J., 1993, *A Gallo-Roman Trading Vessel from Guernsey: The Excavation and Recovery of a Third Century Shipwreck*, St Peter Port: Guernsey Museum Monograph No.5.

Salway, P., 1998, *Roman Britain*, Oxford: Oxford University Press.

Sauer, E.W., 2002, 'The Roman Invasion of Britain (AD 43) in Imperial Perspective: a Response to Frere and Fulford', *Oxford Journal of Archaeology*, 21(4), 333-63.

Seillier, C., 1996, 'Le camp de la flotte de Bretagne à Boulogne-sur-Mer (Gesoriacum)', in Reddé, M., *L'Armée en Gaule*, Paris: Éditions Errance, 212-19.

Severin, T., 1978, *The Brendan Voyage*, London: Hutchinson (republished by Arrow Books 1988).

Shewan, A., 1927 (republ. 1996), *The Great Days of Sail: Reminiscences of a Tea-clipper Captain*, London: Conway Maritime Press.

Smith, W., and Lockwood, J., 1976, *Chambers Murray Latin-English Dictionary*, London and Edinburgh: Chambers and John Murray.

Stevens, C.E., 1947, '55 B.C. and 54 B.C.', *Antiquity*, XXI, 3-9.

Stevens, C.E., 1952, 'The 'Bellum Gallicum' as a Work of Propaganda', *Latomus*, XI, 3-17, 165-79.

Taylor, E.G.R., 1956, *The Haven-Finding Art: A History of Navigation from Odysseus to Captain Cook*, London: Hollis and Carter.

Todd, M., 1997, *Roman Britain*, London: Fontana Press.

Tyers, I., 1994, 'Dendrochronology of Roman and Early Medieval Ships', in Marsden, P., *Ships of The Port of London: First to Eleventh Centuries A.D.*, London: English Heritage, 201-9.

Webster, G., 1999, *The Roman Invasion of Britain*, London and New York: Routledge.

Wells, C., 1992, *The Roman Empire (2nd edition)*, London: Fontana Press.

Wheeler, R.E.M., 1943, *Maiden Castle, Dorset*, London: Society of Antiquaries.

White, D.A., 1961, *Litus Saxonicum: the British Saxon Shore in Scholarship and History*, Madison, WI: University of Wisconsin.

INDEX

If you are interested in purchasing
other books published by Tempus, or in case you have
difficulty finding any Tempus books in your local bookshop, you can also place
orders directly through our website

www.tempus-publishing.com